# Mountain Bike
## AMERICA™

# INDIANA
### SECOND EDITION

# Contact

*Dear Readers:*

*Every effort was made to make this the most accurate, informative, and easy-to-use guide-book on the planet. Any comments, suggestions, and/or corrections regarding this guide are welcome and should be sent to:*

**Outside America™**
c/o Editorial Dept.
300 West Main St., Ste. A
Charlottesville, VA 22903
*editorial@outside-america.com*
**www.outside-america.com**

*We'd love to hear from you so we can make future editions and future guides even better.*

*Thanks and happy trails!*

# Mountain Bike

## INDIANA

SECOND EDITION

An Atlas of Indiana's Greatest
Off-Road Bicycle Rides

**by Layne Cameron**

Guilford, Connecticut

Published by
## The Globe Pequot Press
P.O. Box 480
Guilford, CT 06437
www.globe-pequot.com

Mountain Bike America is a trademark of Beachway Press
Publishing, Inc.

Produced by
**Beachway Press Publishing, Inc.**
300 West Main St., Ste A
Charlottesville, VA 22903
www.beachway.com

**Cover Design**   Beachway Press

**Photographer**   Layne Cameron

**Maps** designed and produced by Beachway Press

Find Outside America™ at **www.outside-america.com**

*Cover Photo: Cyclists cruising through the colors at Hickory
Ridge in Hoosier National Forest.*

**Library of Congress Cataloging-in-Publication Data**
is available

**ISBN 0-7627-0703-8**

Manufactured in the United States of America
**Second Edition/First Printing**

# Acknowledgments

**A** special thanks to Beachway Press for paying me to travel around seemingly every two-lane highway and ride every singletrack trail in the Hoosier state. What a great feeling it was to combine my writing profession with my cycling obsession.

Thanks to John Matthews at Bicycle Outfitters for providing mechanical support for the entire mountain bike tour. To everyone at the Hoosier National Forest Office for guiding me to the greatest trails in the state.

Special thanks to Connie Schmucker and the folks at the Indiana Bicycle Coalition. Thanks to all the guys who helped guide and accompany me through the singletrack: Les Wadzinski, Jeff DeCocq, Scott Rhoad, Norm Almodovar, Steve George, Tim McKenney, Ron Pendley, Curt Jones, Don Gary, Bob Brooks, Chris Arvin, Charlie McClary, Brent Mullen, and Steve Mullin.

Thanks to everyone at the Story Inn for a luxurious stay and some incredible food. Also to everyone at the Ohio River Cabins and the Cliff House for a great weekend and incredible views of the Ohio River.

Special thanks to my lovely wife Sandy Cameron for her helpful editing, understanding, and encouragement.

Thanks to my parents and friends for their support and willingness to allow me to wander off, weekend after weekend. And to my sons Alex and Kyle, who will someday ride these great trails with me.

Table Of

# Contents

# Preface

**M**ountain biking notwithstanding, what I enjoy most about loading up the truck and wandering out into the woods is the conversations around the campfire—in-depth, uninhibited, with time being measured not by a watch, but by a dying campfire. Huddled around glowing embers, topics of discussion cover relationships, religion, goals, observations, nostalgia, and, of course, mountain biking.

One particular night, as the cold began to overwhelm our circle, the conversations tapered off and sleep became imminent. I wandered off to bed and soon my body began to heat up in my sleeping bag. I began to relax. Lying on a cot under a sky that was riddled with stars and listening to a nearby owl's one-question lullaby, my mind began to review the time that was spent working on the book and becoming intimate with my home state.

Granted, Indiana's topography is somewhat limited. Thanks to the work of many glaciers, two-thirds of the state was cleared flat. Today, much of the land is used for farming, but those giant ice bulldozers did leave a few hilly moraines and kettle holes in the north. In most cases, the trail systems to the north make the most of these limited flaws on the topography. Trails circle shallow reservoirs, edge the sand dunes of Lake Michigan, or coil up and down a solitary hill before rolling into a surrounding field.

What these trails might lack in severity, they make up for with interesting histories. For example, following a portion of Indiana's northernmost trail, a man trundled across the state on a high-wheeler on his quest to ride around the world. Another loop serves as the model for all state-owned property, representing area cyclists' quest to gain access to more trails. And in Kokomo, a bike shop has been in business longer than most of us have been alive, yet one man has been at the helm for all but three years of the shop's existence.

Traveling down to the southern part of the state, one can see where the glaciers ended their trek and dumped their load. They upturned the soil and brought top-grade coal and limestone near the surface. Quarries and coalmines mark these easy-access extraction sites and interrupt the miles of rolling forest that sit atop this crumpled land. During the summer, the steam that settles between its ridges creates an Appalachian scene that inspires books and leads many to call this area the "Little Smokies."

Here, the trails lead past Native American ceremonial sites, historical markers documenting Civil War skirmishes, and towns with names like Story, Stonehead, Oolitic, Hindostan, and Gnaw Bone. Neighbors include deer, grouse, pileated and blackback woodpeckers, owls, wild turkeys, mink, skunks, and skinks. Limestone shelves serve as benches to offer a break from the granny-gear grinding climbs, as well as a place to think about the forthcoming fork-bending descents.

As I rolled over in my sleeping bag, I thought about the wear on my body and equipment—and the subsequent trips to the doctor and bike mechanic. I recalled the steroid shots for two major bouts of poison ivy, warming numb toes by the campfire, drinking gallons of water to drown out the heat exhaustion, barely controlling my arachnophobia as I picked spiders and webs off my face, charring the butts of ticks to entice them out of my skin, overhauling my bike four times, and replacing countless numbers of tubes.

In the zone between consciousness and dreaming, I remembered the people I've met while completing the mapping, research, writing, and riding. They include the rangers who patrol the forest and maintain the trails, the political leaders fighting for land access and rails-to-trails corridors, the equestrians I've shared campsites with, the concerned hunter who lent me a bright orange cap, the select few I've shared fire pizzas and ale with, the ranger who gave me a ride back to my truck after I flatted without a spare, the motherly innkeepers at the bed and breakfasts, and all the cyclists who shared their trails with me.

After reviewing the condition of the state's mountain biking, I drifted off with the understanding that I am merely a messenger. I have documented the work of the people who fought to keep land open, physically constructed the trails, and have made many sacrifices so that others can enjoy their work. When I wake, I will tread softly upon the trails they have created and enjoy another great day mountain biking in Indiana.

—Layne Cameron

## A note from the folks behind this endeavor...

*We at Outside America look at guidebook publishing a little differently. There's just no reason that a guidebook has to look like it was published out of your Uncle Ernie's woodshed. We feel that guidebooks need to be both easy to use and nice to look at, and that takes an innovative approach to design. You see, we want you to spend less time fumbling through your guidebook and more time enjoying the adventure at hand. At any rate, we hope you like what you see and enjoy the places we lead you. And most of all, we'd like to thank you for taking an adventure with us.*

*Happy Trails!*

**W**elcome to the new generation of bicycling! Indeed, the sport has evolved dramatically from the thin-tired, featherweight-frame days of old. The sleek geometry and lightweight frames of racing bicycles, still the heart and soul of bicycling worldwide, have lost much ground in recent years, unpaving the way for the mountain bike, which now accounts for the majority of all bicycle sales in the United States. And with this change comes a new breed of cyclist, less concerned with smooth roads and long rides, who thrives in places once inaccessible to the mortal road bike.

The mountain bike, with its knobby tread and reinforced frame, takes cyclists to places once unheard of—down rugged mountain trails, through streams of rushing water, across the frozen Alaskan tundra, and even to work in the city. There seem to be few limits on what this fat-tired beast can do and where it can take us. Few obstacles stand in its way, few boundaries slow its progress. Except for one—its own success. If trail closure means little to you now, read on and discover how a trail can be here today and gone tomorrow. With so many new off-road cyclists taking to the trails each year, it's no wonder trail access hinges precariously between universal acceptance and complete termination. But a little work on your part can go a long way to preserving trail access for future use. Nothing is more crucial to the survival of mountain biking itself than to read the examples set forth in the following pages and practice their message. Then turn to the maps, pick out your favorite ride, and hit the dirt!

## WHAT THIS BOOK IS ABOUT

Within these pages you will find everything you need to know about off-road bicycling in Indiana. This guidebook begins by exploring the fascinating history of the mountain bike itself, then goes on to discuss everything from the health benefits of off-road cycling to tips and techniques for bicycling over logs and up hills. Also included are the types of clothing to keep you comfortable and in style, essential equipment ideas to keep your rides smooth and trouble-free, and descriptions of off-road terrain to prepare you for the kinds of bumps and bounces you can expect to encounter. The major provisions of this book, though, are its unique perspectives on each ride, it detailed maps, and its relentless dedication to trail preservation.

Without open trails, the maps in this book are virtually useless. Cyclists must learn to be responsible for the trails they use and to share these trails with others. This guidebook addresses such issues as why trail use has become so controversial, what can be done to improve the image of mountain biking, how to have fun and ride responsibly, on-the-spot trail repair techniques, trail maintenance hotlines for each trail, and the worldwide-standard Rules of the Trail.

Each of the 31 rides is complete with maps, photos, trail descriptions and directions, local history, and a quick-reference ride information guide including such items as trail contact information, park schedules, fees/permits, local bike stores, dining, lodging, entertainment, alternative map resources and more. Also included at the end of each regional section is an "Honorable Mentions" list of alternative off-road rides (32 rides total).

It's important to note that mountain bike rides tend to take longer than road rides because the average speed is often much slower. Average speeds can vary from a climbing pace of three to four miles per hour to 12 to 13 miles per hour on flatter roads and trails. Keep this in mind when planning your trip.

## MOUNTAIN BIKE BEGINNINGS

It seems the mountain bike, originally designed for lunatic adventurists bored with straight lines, clean clothes, and smooth tires, has become globally popular in as short a time as it would take to race down a mountain trail.

Like many things of a revolutionary nature, the mountain bike was born on the west coast. But unlike Rollerblades, purple hair, and the peace sign, the concept of the off-road bike cannot be credited solely to the imaginative Californians—they were just the first to make waves.

The design of the first off-road specific bike was based on the geometry of the old Schwinn Excelsior, a one-speed, camel-back cruiser with balloon tires. Joe Breeze was the creator behind it, and in 1977 he built 10 of these "Breezers" for himself and his Marin County, California, friends at $750 apiece—a bargain.

Breeze was a serious competitor in bicycle racing, placing 13th in the 1977 U.S. Road Racing National Championships. After races, he and friends would scour local bike shops hoping to find old bikes they could then restore.

It was the 1941 Schwinn Excelsior, for which Breeze paid just five dollars, that began to shape and change bicycling history forever. After taking the bike home, removing the fenders, oiling the chain, and pumping up the tires, Breeze hit the dirt. He loved it.

His inspiration, while forerunning, was not altogether unique. On the opposite end of the country, nearly 2,500 miles from Marin County, east coast bike bums were also growing restless. More and more old, beat-up clunkers were being restored and modified. These behemoths often weighed as much as 80 pounds and were so reinforced they seemed virtually indestructible. But rides that take just 40 minutes on today's 25-pound featherweights took the steel-toed-boot- and-blue-jean-clad bikers of the late 1970s and early 1980s nearly four hours to complete.

Not until 1981 was it possible to purchase a production mountain bike, but local retailers found these ungainly bicycles difficult to sell and rarely kept them in stock. By 1983, however, mountain bikes were no longer such a fringe item, and large bike manufacturers quickly jumped into the action, producing their own versions of the off-road bike. By the 1990s, the mountain bike had firmly established its place with bicyclists of nearly all ages and abilities, and now command nearly 90 percent of the United States bike market.

There are many reasons for the mountain bike's success in becoming the hottest two-wheeled vehicle in the nation. They are much friendlier to the cyclist than traditional road bikes because of their comfortable upright position and shock-absorbing fat tires. And because of the health-conscious, environmentalist movement of the late 1980s and 1990s, people are more activity minded and seek nature on a closer front than paved roads can allow. The mountain bike gives you these things and takes you far away from the daily grind—even if you're only minutes from the city.

## MOUNTAIN BIKING INTO SHAPE

If your objective is to get in shape and lose weight, then you're on the right track, because mountain biking is one of the best ways to get started.

One way many of us have lost weight in this sport is the crash-and-burn-it-off method. Picture this: you're speeding uncontrollably down a vertical drop that you realize you shouldn't be on—only after it is too late. Your front wheel lodges into a rut and launches you through endless weeds, trees, and pointy rocks before coming to an abrupt halt in a puddle of thick mud. Surveying the damage, you discover, with the layers of skin, body parts, and lost confidence littering the trail above, that those unwanted pounds have been shed—*permanently*. Instant weight loss.

There is, of course, a more conventional (and quite a bit less painful) approach to losing weight and gaining fitness on a mountain bike. It's called the workout, and bicycles provide an ideal way to get physical. Take a look at some of the benefits associated with cycling.

Cycling helps you shed pounds without gimmicky diet fads or weight-loss programs. You can explore the countryside and burn nearly 10 to 16 calories per minute or close to 600 to 1,000 calories per hour. Moreover, it's a great way to spend an afternoon.

No less significant than the external and cosmetic changes of your body from riding are the internal changes taking place. Over time, cycling regularly will strengthen your heart as your body grows vast networks of new capillaries to carry blood to all those working muscles. This will, in turn, give your skin a healthier glow. The capacity of your lungs may increase up to 20 percent, and your resting heart rate will drop significantly. The Stanford University School of Medicine reports to the American Heart Association that people can reduce their risk of heart attack by nearly 64 percent if they can burn up to 2,000 calories per week. This is only two to three hours of bike riding!

Recommended for insomnia, hypertension, indigestion, anxiety, and even for recuperation from major heart attacks, bicycling can be an excellent cure-all as well as a great preventive. Cycling just a few hours per week can improve your figure and sleeping habits, give you greater resistance to illness, increase your energy levels, and provide feelings of accomplishment and heightened self-esteem.

## BE SAFE—KNOW THE LAW

Occasionally, even the hard-core off-road cyclists will find they have no choice but to ride the pavement. When you are forced to hit the road, it's important for you to know and understand the rules.

Outlined below are a few of the common laws found in Indiana's Vehicle Code book.

- **Bicycles are legally classified as vehicles in Indiana.** This means that as a bicyclist, you are responsible for obeying the same rules of the road as a driver of a motor vehicle.
- **Bicyclists must ride with the traffic—NOT AGAINST IT!** Because bicycles are considered vehicles, you must ride your bicycle just as you would drive a car—with traffic. Only pedestrians should travel against the flow of traffic.
- **You must obey all traffic signs.** This includes stop signs and stoplights.
- **Always signal your turns.** Most drivers aren't expecting bicyclists to be on the roads, and many drivers would prefer that cyclists stay off the roads altogether. It's important, therefore, to clearly signal your intentions to motorists both in front and behind you.
- **Bicyclists are entitled to the same roads as cars (except controlled-access highways).** Unfortunately, cyclists are rarely given this consideration.
- **Be a responsible cyclist.** Do not abuse your rights to ride on open roads. Follow the rules and set a good example for all of us as you roll along.

## THE MOUNTAIN BIKE CONTROVERSY

*Are Off-Road Bicyclists Environmental Outlaws? Do We have the Right to Use Public Trails?*

Mountain bikers have long endured the animosity of folks in the backcountry who complain about the consequences of off-road bicycling. Many people believe that the fat tires and knobby tread do unacceptable environmental damage and that our uncontrollable riding habits are a danger to animals and to other trail users. To the contrary, mountain bikes have no more environmental impact than hiking boots or horseshoes. This does not mean, however, that mountain bikes leave no imprint at all. Wherever man treads, there is an impact. By riding responsibly, though, it is possible to leave only a minimum impact—something we all must take care to achieve.

Unfortunately, it is often people of great influence who view the mountain bike as the environment's worst enemy. Consequently, we as mountain bike riders and environmentally concerned citizens must be educators, impressing upon others that we also deserve the right to use these trails. Our responsibilities as bicyclists are no more and no less than any other trail user. We must all take the soft-cycling approach and show that mountain bicyclists are not environmental outlaws.

## ETIQUETTE OF MOUNTAIN BIKING

When discussing mountain biking etiquette, we are in essence discussing the soft-cycling approach. This term, as mentioned previously, describes the art of minimum-impact bicycling and should apply to both the physical and social dimensions of the sport. But make no mistake—it is possible to ride fast and furiously while maintaining the balance of soft-cycling. Here first are a few ways to minimize the physical impact of mountain bike riding.

- *Stay on the trail.* Don't ride around fallen trees or mud holes that block your path. Stop and cross over them. When you come to a vista overlooking a deep valley, don't ride off the trail for a better vantage point. Instead, leave the bike and walk to see the view. Riding off the trail may seem inconsequential when done only once, but soon someone else will follow, then others, and the cumulative results can be catastrophic. Each time you wander from the trail you begin creating a new path, adding one more scar to the earth's surface.
- *Do not disturb the soil.* Follow a line within the trail that will not disturb or damage the soil.
- *Do not ride over soft or wet trails.* After a rain shower or during the thawing season, trails will often resemble muddy, oozing swampland. The best thing to do is stay off the trails altogether. Realistically, however, we're all going to come across some muddy trails we cannot anticipate. Instead of blasting through each section of mud, which may seem both easier and more fun, lift the bike and walk past. Each time a cyclist rides through a soft or muddy section of trail, that part of the trail is permanently damaged. Regardless of the trail's conditions, though, remember always to go over the obstacles across the path, not around them. Stay on the trail.
- *Avoid trails that, for all but God, are considered impassable and impossible.* Don't take a leap of faith down a kamikaze descent on which you will be forced to lock your brakes and skid to the bottom, ripping the ground apart as you go.

**Soft-cycling** should apply to the social dimensions of the sport as well, since mountain bikers are not the only folks who use the trails. Hikers, equestrians, cross-country skiers, and other outdoors people use many of the same trails and can be easily spooked by a marauding mountain biker tearing through the trees. Be friendly in the forest and give ample warning of your approach.

- *Take out what you bring in.* Don't leave broken bike pieces and banana peels scattered along the trail.
- *Be aware of your surroundings.* Don't use popular hiking trails for race training.

5

- *Slow down!* Rocketing around blind corners is a sure way to ruin an unsuspecting hiker's day. Consider this—If you fly down a quick singletrack descent at 20 mph, then hit the brakes and slow down to only six mph to pass someone, you're still moving twice as fast as they are!

Like the trails we ride on, the social dimension of mountain biking is very fragile and must be cared for responsibly. We should not want to destroy another person's enjoyment of the outdoors. By riding in the backcountry with caution, control, and responsibility, our presence should be felt positively by other trail users. By adhering to these rules, trail riding—a privilege that can quickly be taken away—will continue to be ours to share.

## TRAIL MAINTENANCE

Unfortunately, despite all of the preventive measures taken to avoid trail damage, we're still going to run into many trails requiring attention. Simply put, a lot of hikers, equestrians, and cyclists alike use the same trails—some wear and tear is unavoidable. But like your bike, if you want to use these trails for a long time to come, you must also maintain them.

Trail maintenance and restoration can be accomplished in a variety of ways. One way is for mountain bike clubs to combine efforts with other trail users (i.e. hikers and equestrians) and work closely with land managers to cut new trails or repair existing ones. This not only reinforces to others the commitment cyclists have in caring for and maintaining the land, but also breaks the ice that often separates cyclists from their fellow trailmates. Another good way to help out is to show up on a Saturday morning with a few riding buddies at your favorite off-road domain ready to work. With a good attitude, thick gloves, and the local land manager's supervision, trail repair is fun and very rewarding. It's important, of course, that you arrange a trail-repair outing with the local land manager before you start pounding shovels into the dirt. They can lead you to the most needy sections of trail and instruct you on what repairs should be done and how best to accomplish the task. Perhaps the most effective means of trail maintenance, though, can be done by yourself and while you're riding. Read on.

## ON–THE–SPOT QUICK FIX

Most of us, when we're riding, have at one time or another come upon muddy trails or fallen trees blocking our path. We notice that over time the mud gets deeper and the trail gets wider as people go through or around the obstacles. We worry that the problem will become so severe and repairs too difficult that the trail's access may be threatened. We also know that our ambition to do anything about it is greatest at that moment, not after a hot shower and a plate of spaghetti. Here are a few on-the-spot quick fixes you can do that will hopefully correct a problem before it gets out of hand and get you back on your bike within minutes.

**Muddy Trails.** What do you do when trails develop huge mud holes destined for the EPA's Superfund status? The technique is called corduroying, and it works much like building a pontoon over the mud to support bikes, horses, or hikers as they cross. Corduroy (not the pants) is the term for roads made of logs laid down crosswise. Use small-and medium-sized sticks and lay them side by side across the trail until they cover the length of the muddy section (break the sticks to fit the width of the trail). Press them into the mud with your feet, then lay more on top if needed. Keep adding sticks until the trail is firm. Not only will you stay clean as you cross, but the sticks may soak up some of the water and help the puddle dry. This quick fix may last as long as one month before needing to be redone. And as time goes on, with new layers added to the trail, the soil will grow stronger, thicker, and more resistant to erosion. This whole process may take fewer than five minutes, and you can be on your way, knowing the trail behind you is in good repair.

**Leaving the Trail.** What do you do to keep cyclists from cutting corners and leaving the designated trail? The solution is much simpler than you may think. (No, don't hire an off-road police force.) Notice where people are leaving the trail and throw a pile of thick branches or brush along the path, or place logs across the opening to block the way through. There are probably dozens of subtle tricks like these that will manipulate people into staying on the designated trail. If executed well, no one will even notice that the thick branches scattered along the ground in the woods weren't always there. And most folks would probably rather take a moment to hop a log in the trail than get tangled in a web of branches.

**Obstacle in the Way.** If there are large obstacles blocking the trail, try and remove them or push them aside. If you cannot do this by yourself, call the trail maintenance hotline to speak with the land manager of that particular trail and see what can be done.

We must be willing to sweat for our trails in order to sweat on them. Police yourself and point out to others the significance of trail maintenance. "Sweat Equity," the rewards of continued land use won with a fair share of sweat, pays off when the trail is "up for review" by the land manager and he or she remembers the efforts made by trail-conscious mountain bikers.

## RULES OF THE TRAIL

The International Mountain Bicycling Association (IMBA) has developed these guidelines to trail riding. These "Rules of the Trail" are accepted worldwide and will go a long way in keeping trails open. Please respect and follow these rules for everyone's sake.

**1. Ride only on open trails.** Respect trail and road closures (if you're not sure, ask a park or state official first), do not trespass on private property, and obtain permits or authorization if required. Federal and state wilderness areas are off-limits to cycling. Parks and state forests may also have certain trails closed to cycling.

**2. Leave no trace.** Be sensitive to the dirt beneath you. Even on open trails, you should not ride under conditions by which you will leave evidence of your passing, such as on certain soils or shortly after a rainfall. Be sure to observe the different types of soils and trails you're riding on, practicing minimum-impact cycling. Never ride off the trail, don't skid your tires, and be sure to bring out at least as much as you bring in.

**3. Control your bicycle!** Inattention for even one second can cause disaster for yourself or for others. Excessive speed frightens and can injure people, gives mountain biking a bad name, and can result in trail closures.

**4. Always yield.** Let others know you're coming well in advance (a friendly greeting is always good and often appreciated). Show your respect when passing others by slowing to walking speed or stopping altogether, especially in the presence of horses. Horses can be unpredictable, so be very careful. Anticipate that other trail users may be around corners or in blind spots.

**5. Never spook animals.** All animals are spooked by sudden movements, unannounced approaches, or loud noises. Give the animals extra room and time so they can adjust to you. Move slowly or dismount around animals. Running cattle and disturbing wild animals are serious offenses. Leave gates as you find them, or as marked.

**6. Plan ahead.** Know your equipment, your ability, and the area in which you are riding, and plan your trip accordingly. Be self-sufficient at all times, keep your bike in good repair, and carry necessary supplies for changes in weather or other conditions. You can help keep trails open by setting an example of responsible, courteous, and controlled mountain bike riding.

**7. Always wear a helmet when you ride.** For your own safety and protection, a helmet should be worn whenever you are riding your bike. You never know when a tree root or small rock will throw you the wrong way and send you tumbling.

Thousands of miles of dirt trails have been closed to mountain bicycling because of the irresponsible riding habits of just a few riders. Don't follow the example of these offending riders. Don't take away trail privileges from thousands of others who work hard each year to keep the backcountry avenues open to us all.

## THE NECESSITIES OF CYCLING

When discussing the most important items to have on a bike ride, cyclists generally agree on the following four items.

**Helmet.** The reasons to wear a helmet should be obvious. Helmets are discussed in more detail in the *Be Safe—Wear Your Armor* section.

**Water.** Without it, cyclists may face dehydration, which may result in dizziness and fatigue. On a warm day, cyclists should drink at least one full bottle during every hour of riding. Remember, it's always good to drink before you feel thirsty—otherwise, it may be too late.

**Cycling Shorts.** These are necessary if you plan to ride your bike more than 20 to 30 minutes. Padded cycling shorts may be the only thing preventing your derriere from serious saddle soreness by ride's end. There are two types of cycling shorts you can buy. Touring shorts are good for people who don't want to look like they're wearing anatomically correct cellophane. These look like regular athletic shorts with pockets, but have built-in padding in the crotch area for protection from chafing and saddle sores. The more popular, traditional cycling shorts are made of skin-tight material, also with a padded crotch. Whichever style you find most comfortable, cycling shorts are a necessity for long rides.

**Food.** This essential item will keep you rolling. Cycling burns up a lot of calories and is among the few sports in which no one is safe from the "Bonk." Bonking feels like it sounds. Without food in your system, your blood sugar level collapses, and there is no longer any energy in your body. This instantly results in total fatigue and light-headedness. So when you're filling your water bottle, remember to bring along some food. Fruit, energy bars, or some other forms of high-energy food are highly recommended. Candy bars are not, however, because they will deliver a sudden burst of high energy, then let you down soon after, causing you to feel worse than before. Energy bars are available at most bike stores and are similar to candy bars, but provide complex carbohydrate energy and high nutrition rather than fast-burning simple sugars.

## BE PREPARED OR DIE

Essential equipment that will keep you from dying alone in the woods:

- **Spare Tube**
- **Tire Irons**—See the Appendix for instructions on fixing flat tires.
- **Patch Kit**
- **Pump**
- **Money**—Spare change for emergency calls.
- **Spoke Wrench**
- **Spare Spokes**—To fit your wheel. Tape these to the chain stay.
- **Chain Tool**
- **Allen Keys**—Bring appropriate sizes to fit your bike.
- **Compass**
- **First-Aid Kit**
- **Rain Gear**—For quick changes in weather.
- **Matches**
- **Guidebook**—In case all else fails and you must start a fire to survive, this guidebook will serve as excellent fire starter!

To carry these items, you may need a bike bag. A bag mounted in front of the handlebars provides quick access to your belongings, whereas a saddle bag fitted underneath the saddle keeps things out of your way. If you're carrying lots of equipment, you may want to consider a set of panniers. These are much larger and mount on either side of each wheel on a rack. Many cyclists, though, prefer not to use a bag at all. They just slip all they need into their jersey pockets, and off they go.

## BE SAFE—WEAR YOUR ARMOR

While on the subject of jerseys, it's crucial to discuss the clothing you must wear to be safe, practical, and—if you prefer—stylish. The following is a list of items that will save you from disaster, outfit you comfortably, and most important, keep you looking cool.

**Helmet.** A helmet is an absolute necessity because it protects your head from complete annihilation. It is the only thing that will not disintegrate into a million pieces after a wicked crash on a descent you shouldn't have been on in the first place. A helmet with a solid exterior shell will also protect your head from sharp or protruding objects. Of course, with a hard-shelled helmet, you can paste several stickers of your favorite bicycle manufacturers all over the outer shell, giving companies even more free advertising for your dollar.

**Shorts.** Let's just say Lycra™ cycling shorts are considered a major safety item if you plan to ride for more than 20 or 30 minutes at a time. As mentioned in *The Necessities of Cycling* section, cycling shorts are well regarded as the leading cure-all for chafing and saddle sores. The most preventive cycling shorts have padded "chamois" (most chamois is synthetic nowadays) in the crotch area. Of course, if you choose to wear these traditional cycling shorts, it's imperative that they look as if someone spray painted them onto your body.

**Gloves.** You may find well-padded cycling gloves invaluable when traveling over rocky trails and gravelly roads for hours on end. Long-fingered gloves may also be useful, as branches, trees, assorted hard objects, and, occasionally, small animals will reach out and whack your knuckles.

**Glasses.** Not only do sunglasses give you an imposing presence and make you look cool (both are extremely important), they also protect your eyes from harmful ultraviolet rays, invisible branches, creepy bugs, dirt, and may prevent you from being caught sneaking glances at riders of the opposite sex also wearing skintight, revealing Lycra™.

**Shoes.** Mountain bike shoes should have stiff soles to help make pedaling easier and provide better traction when walking your bike up a trail becomes necessary. Virtually any kind of good outdoor hiking footwear will work, but specific mountain bike shoes (especially those with inset cleats) are best. It is vital that these shoes look as ugly as humanly possible. Those closest in style to bowling shoes are, of course, the most popular.

**Jersey or Shirt.** Bicycling jerseys are popular because of their snug fit and back pockets. When purchasing a jersey, look for ones that are loaded with bright, blinding, neon logos and manufacturers' names. These loudly decorated billboards are also good for drawing unnecessary attention to yourself just before taking a mean spill while trying to hop a curb. A cotton T-shirt is a good alternative in warm weather, but when the weather turns cold, cotton becomes a chilling substitute for the jersey. Cotton retains moisture and sweat against your body, which may cause you to get the chills and ills on those cold-weather rides.

## OH, THOSE COLD INDIANA DAYS

If the weather chooses not to cooperate on the day you've set aside for a bike ride, it's helpful to be prepared.

**Tights or leg warmers.** These are best in temperatures below 55 degrees. Knees are sensitive and can develop all kinds of problems if they get cold. Common problems include tendinitis, bursitis, and arthritis.

**Plenty of layers on your upper body.** When the air has a nip in it, layers of clothing will keep the chill away from your chest and help prevent the development of bronchitis. If the air is cool, a Polypropylene™ or Capilene™ long-sleeved shirt is best to wear against the skin beneath other layers of clothing. Polypropylene or Capilene, like wool, wicks away moisture from your skin to keep your body dry. Try to avoid wearing cotton or baggy clothing when the temperature falls. Cotton, as mentioned before, holds moisture like a sponge, and baggy clothing catches cold air and swirls it around your body. Good cold-weather clothing should fit snugly against your body, but not be restrictive.

**Wool socks.** Don't pack too many layers under those shoes, though. You may stand the chance of restricting circulation, and your feet will get real cold, real fast.

**Thinsulate or Gortex™ gloves.** We may all agree that there is nothing worse than frozen feet—unless your hands are frozen. A good pair of Thinsulate™ or Gortex™ gloves should keep your hands toasty and warm.

**Hat or helmet on cold days?** Sometimes, when the weather gets really cold and you still want to hit the trails, it's tough to stay warm. We all know that 80 percent of the body's heat escapes through the head (overactive brains, I imagine), so it's important to keep the cranium warm. Ventilated helmets are designed to keep heads cool in the summer heat, but they do little to help keep heads warm during rides in sub-zero temperatures. Cyclists should consider wearing a hat on extremely cold days. Polypropylene skullcaps are great head and ear warmers that snugly fit over your head beneath the helmet. Head protection is not lost. Another option is a helmet cover that covers those ventilating gaps and helps keep the body heat in. These do not, however, keep your ears warm. Some cyclists will opt for a simple knit cycling cap sans the helmet, but these have never been shown to be very good cranium protectors.

All of this clothing can be found at your local bike store, where the staff should be happy to help fit you into the seasons of the year.

## TO HAVE OR NOT TO HAVE... *(Other Very Useful Items)*

Though mountain biking is relatively new to the cycling scene, there is no shortage of items for you and your bike to make riding better, safer, and easier. We have rummaged through the unending lists and separated the gadgets from the good stuff, coming up with what we believe are items certain to make mountain bike riding easier and more enjoyable.

**Tires.** Buying yourself a good pair of knobby tires is the quickest way to enhance the off-road handling capabilities of your bike. There are many types of mountain bike tires on the market. Some are made exclusively for very rugged off-road terrain. These big-knobbed, soft rubber tires virtually stick to the ground with unforgiving traction, but tend to deteriorate quickly on pavement. There are other tires made exclusively for the road. These are called "slicks" and have no tread at all. For the average cyclist, though, a good tire somewhere in the middle of these two extremes should do the trick.

**Toe Clips or Clipless Pedals.** With these, you will ride with more power. Toe clips attach to your pedals and strap your feet firmly in place, allowing you to exert pressure on the pedals on both the downstroke and the upstroke. They will increase your pedaling efficiency by 30 percent to 50 percent. Clipless pedals, which liberate your feet from the traditional straps and clips, have made toe clips virtually obsolete. Like ski bindings, they attach your shoe directly to the pedal. They are, however, much more expensive than toe clips.

**Bar Ends.** These great clamp-on additions to your original straight bar will provide more leverage, an excellent grip for climbing, and a more natural position for your hands. Be aware, however, of the bar end's propensity for hooking trees on fast descents, sending you, the cyclist, airborne.

**Fanny Pack.** These bags are ideal for carrying keys, extra food, guidebooks, tools, spare tubes, and a cellular phone, in case you need to call for help.

**Suspension Forks.** For the more serious off-roaders who want nothing to impede their speed on the trails, investing in a pair of suspension forks is a good idea. Like tires, there are plenty of brands to choose from, and they all do the same thing—absorb the brutal beatings of a rough trail. The cost of these forks, however, is sometimes more brutal than the trail itself.

**Bike Computers.** These are fun gadgets to own and are much less expensive than in years past. They have such features as trip distance, speedometer, odometer, time of day, altitude, alarm, average speed, maximum speed, heart rate, global satellite positioning, etc. Bike computers will come in handy when following these maps or to know just how far you've ridden in the wrong direction.

**Water Pack.** This is quickly beccoming an essential item for cyclists pedaling for more than a few hours, especially in hot, dry conditions. The most popular brand is, of course, the Camelback™, and these water packs can carry in their bladder bags as much as 100 ounces of water. These packs strap onto your back with a handy hose running over your shoulder so you can be drinking water while still holding onto the bars on a rocky descent with both hands. These packs are a great way to carry a lot of extra liquid on hot rides in the middle of nowhere.

## TYPES OF OFF-ROAD TERRAIN

Before roughing it off road, we may first have to ride the pavement to get to our destination. Please, don't be dismayed. Some of the country's best rides are on the road. Once we get past these smooth-surfaced pathways, though, adventures in dirt await us.

**Rails-to-Trails.** Abandoned rail lines are converted into usable public resources for exercising, commuting, or just enjoying nature. Old rails and ties are torn up and a trail, paved or unpaved, is laid along the existing corridor. This completes the cycle from ancient Indian trading routes to railroad corridors and back again to hiking and cycling trails.

**Unpaved Roads** are typically found in rural areas and are most often public roads. Be careful when exploring, though, not to ride on someone's unpaved private drive.

**Forest Roads.** These dirt and gravel roads are used primarily as access to forest land and are generally kept in good condition. They are almost always open to public use.

**Singletrack** can be the most fun on a mountain bike. These trails, with only one track to follow, are often narrow, challenging pathways through the woods. Remember to make sure these trails are open before zipping into the woods. (At the time of this printing, all trails and roads in this guidebook were open to mountain bikes.)

**Open Land.** Unless there is a marked trail through a field or open space, you should not plan to ride here. Once one person cuts his or her wheels through a field or meadow, many more are sure to follow, causing irreparable damage to the landscape.

## TECHNIQUES TO SHARPEN YOUR SKILLS

Many of us see ourselves as pure athletes—blessed with power, strength, and endless endurance. However, it may be those with finesse, balance, agility, and grace that get around most quickly on a mountain bike. Although power, strength, and endurance do have their places in mountain biking, these elements don't necessarily form the framework for a champion mountain biker.

The bike should become an extension of your body. Slight shifts in your hips or knees can have remarkable results. Experienced bike handlers seem to flash down technical descents, dashing over obstacles in a smooth and graceful effort as if pirouetting in Swan Lake. Here are some tips and techniques to help you connect with your bike and float gracefully over the dirt.

### Braking

Using your brakes requires using your head, especially when descending. This doesn't mean using your head as a stopping block, but rather to think intelligently. Use your best judgment in terms of how much or how little to squeeze those brake levers.

The more weight a tire is carrying, the more braking power it has. When you're going downhill, your front wheel carries more weight than the rear. Braking with the front brake will help keep you in control without going into a skid. Be careful, though, not to overdo it with the front brakes and accidentally toss yourself over the handlebars. And don't neglect your rear brake! When descending, shift your weight back over the rear wheel, thus increasing your rear braking power as well. This will balance the power of both brakes and give you maximum control.

Good riders learn just how much of their weight to shift over each wheel and how to apply just enough braking power to each brake, so not to "endo" over the handlebars or skid down a trail.

## GOING UPHILL—*Climbing Those Treacherous Hills*

**Shift into a low gear** (push the shifter away from you). Before shifting, be sure to ease up on your pedaling so there is not too much pressure on the chain. Find the gear best for you that matches the terrain and steepness of each climb.

**Stay seated.** Standing out of the saddle is often helpful when climbing steep hills with a road bike, but you may find that on dirt, standing may cause your rear tire to lose its grip and spin out. Climbing requires traction. Stay seated as long as you can, and keep the rear tire digging into the ground. Ascending skyward may prove to be much easier in the saddle.

**Lean forward.** On very steep hills, the front end may feel unweighted and suddenly pop up. Slide forward on the saddle and lean over the handlebars. This will add more weight to the front wheel and should keep you grounded.

**Keep pedaling.** On rocky climbs, be sure to keep the pressure on, and don't let up on those pedals! The slower you go through rough trail sections, the harder you will work.

## GOING DOWNHILL—*The Real Reason We Get Up in the Morning*

**Shifting into the big chainring** before a bumpy descent will help keep the chain from bouncing off. And should you crash or disengage your leg from the pedal, the chain will cover the teeth of the big ring so they don't bite into your leg.

**Relax.** Stay loose on the bike, and don't lock your elbows or clench your grip. Your elbows need to bend with the bumps and absorb the shock, while your hands should have a firm but controlled grip on the bars to keep things steady. Steer with your body, allowing your shoulders to guide you through each turn and around each obstacle.

**Don't oversteer or lose control.** Mountain biking is much like downhill skiing, since you must shift your weight from side to side down narrow, bumpy descents. Your bike will have the tendency to track in the direction you look and follow the slight shifts and leans of your body. You should not think so much about steering, but rather in what direction you wish to go.

**Rise above the saddle.** When racing down bumpy, technical descents, you should not be sitting on the saddle, but standing on the pedals, allowing your legs and knees to absorb the rocky trail instead of your rear.

**Drop your saddle.** For steep, technical descents, you may want to drop your saddle three or four inches. This lowers your center of gravity, giving you much more room to bounce around.

**Keep your pedals parallel to the ground.** The front pedal should be slightly higher so that it doesn't catch on small rocks or logs.

**Stay focused.** Many descents require your utmost concentration and focus just to reach the bottom. You must notice every groove, every root, every rock, every hole, every bump. You, the bike, and the trail should all become one as you seek singletrack nirvana on your way down the mountain. But if your thoughts wander, however, then so may your bike, and you may instead become one with the trees!

## WATCH OUT!
### Back-road Obstacles

**Logs.** When you want to hop a log, throw your body back, yank up on the handlebars, and pedal forward in one swift motion. This clears the front end of the bike. Then quickly scoot forward and pedal the rear wheel up and over. Keep the forward momentum until you've cleared the log, and by all means, don't hit the brakes, or you may do some interesting acrobatic maneuvers!

**Rocks and Roots.** Worse than highway potholes! Stay relaxed, let your elbows and knees absorb the shock, and always continue applying power to your pedals. Staying seated will keep the rear wheel weighted to prevent slipping, and a light front end will help you to respond quickly to each new obstacle. The slower you go, the more time your tires will have to get caught between the grooves.

**Water.** Before crossing a stream or puddle, be sure to first check the depth and bottom surface. There may be an unseen hole or large rock hidden under the water that could wash you up if you're not careful. After you're sure all is safe, hit the water at a good speed, pedal steadily, and allow the bike to steer you through. Once you're across, tap the breaks to squeegee the water off the rims.

**Leaves.** Be careful of wet leaves. These may look pretty, but a trail covered with leaves may cause your wheels to slip out from under you. Leaves are not nearly as unpredictable and dangerous as ice, but they do warrant your attention on a rainy day.

**Mud.** If you must ride through mud, hit it head on and keep pedaling. You want to part the ooze with your front wheel and get across before it swallows you up. Above all, don't leave the trail to go around the mud. This just widens the path even more and leads to increased trail erosion.

## Urban Obstacles

**Curbs** are fun to jump, but like with logs, be careful.

**Curbside Drains** are typically not a problem for bikes. Just be careful not to get a wheel caught in the grate.

**Dogs** make great pets, but seem to have it in for bicyclists. If you think you can't outrun a dog that's chasing you, stop and walk your bike out of its territory. A loud yell to *Get!* or *Go home!* often works, as does a sharp squirt from your water bottle.

**Cars** are tremendously convenient when we're in them, but dodging irate motorists in big automobiles becomes a real hazard when riding a bike. As a cyclist, you must realize most drivers aren't expecting you to be there and often wish you weren't. Stay alert and ride carefully, clearly signaling all of your intentions.

**Potholes**, like grates and back-road canyons, should be avoided. Just because you're on an all-terrain bicycle doesn't mean you're indestructible. Potholes regularly damage rims, pop tires, and sometimes lift unsuspecting cyclists into a spectacular swan dive over the handlebars.

## LAST-MINUTE CHECKOVER

Before a ride, it's a good idea to give your bike a once-over to make sure everything is in working order. Begin by checking the air pressure in your tires before each ride to make sure they are properly inflated. Mountain bikes require about 45 to 55 pounds per square inch of air pressure. If your tires are underinflated, there is greater likelihood that the tubes may get pinched on a bump or rock, causing the tire to flat.

Looking over your bike to make sure everything is secure and in its place is the next step. Go through the following checklist before each ride.

- *Pinch the tires to feel for proper inflation.* They should give just a little on the sides, but feel very hard on the treads. If you have a pressure gauge, use that.
- *Check your brakes.* Squeeze the rear brake and roll your bike forward. The rear tire should skid. Next, squeeze the front brake and roll your bike forward. The rear wheel should lift into the air. If this doesn't happen, then your brakes are too loose. Make sure the brake levers don't touch the handlebars when squeezed with full force.
- *Check all quick releases on your bike.* Make sure they are all securely tightened.
- *Lube up.* If your chain squeaks, apply some lubricant.
- *Check your nuts and bolts.* Check the handlebars, saddle, cranks, and pedals to make sure that each is tight and securely fastened to your bike.
- *Check your wheels.* Spin each wheel to see that they spin through the frame and between brake pads freely.
- *Have you got everything?* Make sure you have your spare tube, tire irons patch kit, frame pump, tools, food, water, and guidebook.

## Liability Disclaimer

Neither the producers nor the publishers of this guide assumes any liability for cyclists traveling along any of the suggested routes in this book. At the time of publication, all routes shown on the following maps were open to bicycles. They were chosen for their safety, aesthetics, and pleasure, and are deemed acceptable and accommodating to bicyclists. Safety upon these routes, however, cannot be guaranteed. Cyclists must assume their own responsibility when riding these routes and understand that with an activity such as mountain bike riding, there may be unforeseen risks and dangers.

# HOW TO USE THESE MAPS   Map Descriptions

**1 Area Locator Map**

This thumbnail relief map at the beginning of each ride shows you where the ride is within the state. The ride area is indicated with a star.

**2 Regional Location Map**

This map helps you find your way to the start of each ride from the nearest sizeable town or city. Coupled with the detailed directions at the beginning of the cue, this map should visually lead you to where you need to be for each ride.

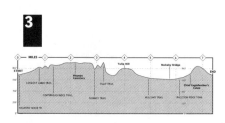

**3 Profile Map**

This helpful profile gives you a cross-sectional look at the ride's ups and downs. Elevation is labeled on the left, mileage is indicated on the top. Road and trail names are shown along the route with towns and points of interest labeled in bold.

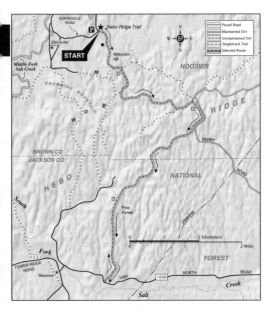

## 4 Route Map

This is your primary guide to each ride. It shows all of the accessible roads and trails, points of interest, water, towns, landmarks, and geographical features. It also distinguishes trails from roads, and paved roads from unpaved roads. The selected route is highlighted, and directional arrows point the way. Shaded topographic relief in the background gives you an accurate representation of the terrain and landscape in the ride area.

## Ride Information *(Included in each ride section)*

**📞 Trail Contacts:**

This is the direct number for the local land managers in charge of all the trails within the selected ride. Use this hotline to call ahead for trail access information, or after your visit if you see problems with trail erosion, damage, or misuse.

**🕐 Schedule:**

This tells you at what times trails open and close, if on private or park land.

**💲 Fees/Permits:**

What money, if any, you may need to carry with you for park entrance fees or tolls.

**Ⓝ Maps:**

This is a list of other maps to supplement the maps in this book. They are listed in order from most detailed to most general.

Any other important or useful information will also be listed here such as local attractions, bike shops, nearby accommodations, etc.

# THE MAPS — Map Legend

We don't want anyone, by any means, to feel restricted to just the roads and trails that are mapped here. We hope you will have an adventurous spirit and use this guide as a platform to dive into Indiana's backcountry and discover new routes for yourself. One of the simplest ways to begin this is to just turn the map upside down and ride the course in reverse. The change in perspective is fantastic, and the ride should feel quite different. With this in mind, it will be like getting two distinctly different rides on each map.

For your own purposes, you may wish to copy the directions for the course onto a small sheet to help you while riding, or photocopy the map and cue sheet to take with you. These pages can be folded into a bike bag, stuffed into a jersey pocket, or better still, used with the **BarMap** or **BarMapOTG** (see www.cycoactive.com for more info). Just remember to slow or even stop when you want to read the map.

| Symbol | Description |
|---|---|
| 5 | Interstate Highway |
| 8 | U.S. Highway |
| 3 | State Road |
| CR 23 | County Road |
| T 145 | Township Road |
| FS 45 | Forest Road |
|  | Paved Road |
|  | Paved Bike Lane |
|  | Maintained Dirt Road |
|  | Unmaintained Jeep Trail |
|  | Singletrack Trail |
|  | Highlighted Route |
|  | Ntl Forest/County Boundaries |
|  | State Boundaries |
|  | Railroad Tracks |
|  | Power Lines |
|  | Special Trail |
|  | Rivers or Streams |
|  | Water and Lakes |
|  | Marsh |

| Symbol | Description | Symbol | Description |
|---|---|---|---|
| ✝ | Airfield | ⛳ | Golf Course |
| ✈ | Airport | 🚶 | Hiking Trail |
| 🚲 | Bike Trail | ⛏ | Mine |
| 🚫 | No Bikes | ✕ | Overlook |
| ⛴ | Boat Launch | ⛩ | Picnic |
| )( | Bridge | P | Parking |
| 🚌 | Bus Stop | ✕ | Quarry |
| A | Campground | ((A)) | Radio Tower |
| ♣ | Campsite | 🧗 | Rock Climbing |
| ⚓ | Canoe Access | ⛏ | School |
| 目 | Cattle Guard | ▲ | Shelter |
| † | Cemetery | ρ | Spring |
| ⛪ | Church | ☊ | Swimming |
| ⛺ | Covered Bridge | ♟ | Train Station |
| ➤ | Direction Arrows | ⟁ | Wildlife Refuge |
| ⛷ | Downhill Skiing | 🍇 | Vineyard |
| 🏛 | Fire Tower | ♦♦ | Most Difficult |
| ♦ | Forest HQ | ♦ | Difficult |
| 🚙 | 4WD Trail | ☐ | Moderate |
| I | Gate | ● | Easy |

# MOUNTAIN BIKE INDIANA

## The Rides

1. Calumet Bike Trail
2. Rum Village Pathway
3. Wellington Farm Mountain Bike Trail
4. J.B. Franke Park
5. Kekionga Mountain Bike Trail
6. France Park
7. Oakbrook Valley
8. Prairie Creek Reservoir
9. Town Run Trail Park
10. River's Edge Trail
11. Central Canal Towpath
12. Whitewater Canal Trail
13. Linton Conservation Club
14. Wapehani Mountain Bike Park
15. Clear Creek Rail Trail
16. Madison's County Roads
17. Lynnville Park
18. Yellow Banks Recreaton Area
19. Gnaw Bone Camp
20. Nebo Ridge
21. Hardin Ridge
22. Hickory RIdge Recreation Area
23. Ogala Mountain Bike Trail
24. Shirley Creek Trail
25. Youngs Creek Trail
26. Lick Creek
27. Birdseye Trail
28. Oriole Trail
29. Tipsaw Lake
30. Mogan Ridge Mountain Bike Trails
31. German Ridge Recreation Area

## Honorable Mentions

A. Roger Shaw Memorial Park

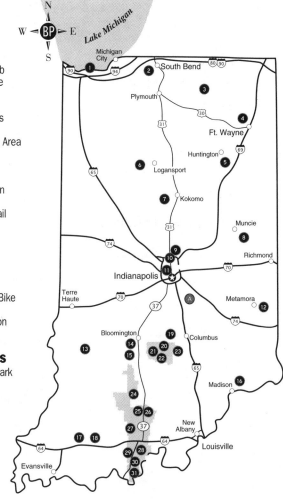

21

# COURSES AT A GLANCE

## Ride Profiles

### 1. Calumet Bike Trail

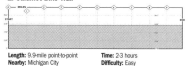

**Length:** 9.9-mile point-to-point   **Time:** 2-3 hours
**Nearby:** Michigan City   **Difficulty:** Easy

### 2. Rum Village Pathway

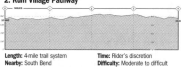

**Length:** 4-mile trail system   **Time:** Rider's discretion
**Nearby:** South Bend   **Difficulty:** Moderate to difficult

### 3. Wellington Farm Mountain Bike Trail

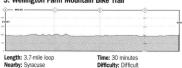

**Length:** 3.7-mile loop   **Time:** 30 minutes
**Nearby:** Syracuse   **Difficulty:** Difficult

### 4. J.B. Franke Park

## Multiple Route Options

**Length:** 10-mile trail system   **Time:** Rider's discretion
**Nearby:** Fort Wayne   **Difficulty:** Moderate

### 5. Kekionga Mountain Bike Trail

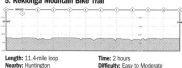

**Length:** 11.4-mile loop   **Time:** 2 hours
**Nearby:** Huntington   **Difficulty:** Easy to Moderate

### 6. France Park

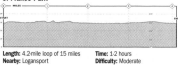

**Length:** 4.2-mile loop of 15 miles   **Time:** 1-2 hours
**Nearby:** Logansport   **Difficulty:** Moderate

### 7. Oakbrook Valley

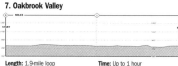

**Length:** 1.9-mile loop   **Time:** Up to 1 hour
**Nearby:** Kokomo   **Difficulty:** Moderate

### 8. Prairie Creek Reservoir

## Multiple Route Options

**Length:** 5-mile trail system   **Time:** Rider's discretion
**Nearby:** Muncie   **Difficulty:** Moderate

### 9. Town Run Trail Park

## Multiple Route Options

**Length:** 8-mile loop   **Time:** Rider's discretion
**Nearby:** Indianapolis   **Difficulty:** Moderate

### 10. River's Edge Trail

**Length:** 8-mile system   **Time:** Rider's discretion
**Nearby:** Indianapolis   **Difficulty:** Easy to Moderate

### 11. Central Canal Towpath

**Length:** 5.6-mile point-o-point   **Time:** 1-2 hours
**Nearby:** Indianapolis   **Difficulty:** Easy

### 12. Whitewater Canal Trail

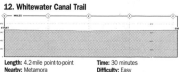

**Length:** 4.2-mile point-to-point   **Time:** 30 minutes
**Nearby:** Metamora   **Difficulty:** Easy

### 13. Linton Conservation Club

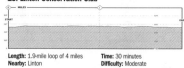

**Length:** 1.9-mile loop of 4 miles   **Time:** 30 minutes
**Nearby:** Linton   **Difficulty:** Moderate

### 14. Wapehani Mountain Bike Park

## Multiple Route Options

**Length:** 7-mile trail system   **Time:** Rider's discretion
**Nearby:** Bloomington   **Difficulty:** Moderate

### 15. Clear Creek Rail Trail

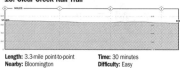

**Length:** 3.3-mile point-to-point   **Time:** 30 minutes
**Nearby:** Bloomington   **Difficulty:** Easy

### 16. Madison's County Roads

**Length:** 16.8-mile loop   **Time:** 2 hours
**Nearby:** Madison   **Difficulty:** Moderate

### 17. Lynnville Park

**Length:** 2.6-mile loop
**Nearby:** Lynnville
**Time:** 45 minutes
**Difficulty:** Difficult

### 18. Yellow Banks Recreation Area

**Length:** 4.4-mile loop of 10 miles
**Nearby:** Dale
**Time:** 45 minutes
**Difficulty:** Moderate

### 19. Gnaw Bone Camp

**Length:** 7.1-mile loop of 25 miles
**Nearby:** Gnaw Bone
**Time:** 45 minutes-2 hours
**Difficulty:** Moderate

### 20. Nebo Ridge Trail

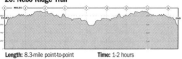

**Length:** 8.3-mile point-to-point
**Nearby:** Story
**Time:** 1-2 hours
**Difficulty:** Moderate

### 21. Hardin Ridge

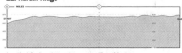

**Length:** 1.9-mile point-to-point
**Nearby:** Bloomington
**Time:** 30 minutes
**Difficulty:** Easy

### 22. Hickory Ridge Recreation Area

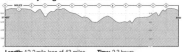

**Length:** 12.2-mile loop of 43 miles
**Nearby:** Norman Station
**Time:** 2-3 hours
**Difficulty:** Moderate

### 23. Ogala Mountain Bike Trail

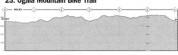

**Length:** 6.3-mile loop of 7 miles
**Nearby:** Freetown
**Time:** 1-2 hours
**Difficulty:** Moderate

### 24. Shirley Creek Trail

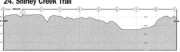

**Length:** 8.75-mile loop of 11.3 miles
**Nearby:** French Lick
**Time:** 2 hours
**Difficulty:** Moderate to Dificult

### 25. Youngs Creek Trail

**Length:** 10.8-mile loop
**Nearby:** Paoli
**Time:** 2-3 hours
**Difficulty:** Difficult

### 26. Lick Creek

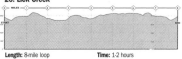

**Length:** 8-mile loop
**Nearby:** Paoli
**Time:** 1-2 hours
**Difficulty:** Moderate

### 27. Birdseye Trail

**Length:** 6-mile loop of 10 miles
**Nearby:** Birdseye
**Time:** 1-2 hours
**Difficulty:** Easy to Moderate

### 28. Oriole Trail

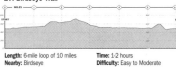

**Length:** 6.2-mile loop of 10 miles
**Nearby:** Sulphur
**Time:** 1-2 hours
**Difficulty:** Easy to Moderate

### 29. Tipsaw Lake

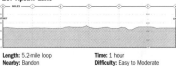

**Length:** 5.2-mile loop
**Nearby:** Bandon
**Time:** 1 hour
**Difficulty:** Easy to Moderate

### 30. Mogan Ridge Mountain Bike Trails

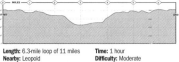

**Length:** 6.3-mile loop of 11 miles
**Nearby:** Leopold
**Time:** 1 hour
**Difficulty:** Moderate

### 31. German Ridge Recreation Area

**Length:** 12.3-mile loop of 23 miles
**Nearby:** Rome
**Time:** 2-3 hours
**Difficulty:** Moderate to Difficult

Northern

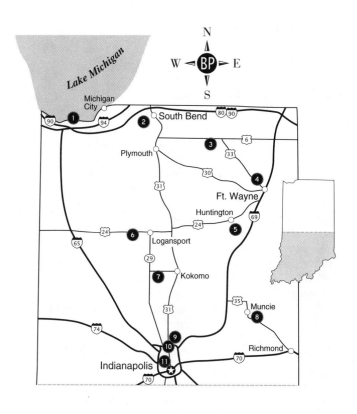

Lake Michigan

N
W BP E
S

Michigan
City

90
94

2
South Bend

80 90

1

Plymouth

3

6

33

31

30

4
Ft. Wayne

Huntington

69

24
24

5

65
24

6

Logansport

29

7
Kokomo

31

35

Muncie

8

74

9

10

Richmond

Indianapolis

11

70

70

Indiana

# Northern Indiana

Most people describe northern Indiana one of three ways: flat, flatter, or flattest. Thanks to the work of glaciers—the great ecological erasers—the northern two-thirds of the state are mostly slate-flat and better suited for tractor tires than knobby tread. Perhaps out of sympathy for mountain bikers though, the ice that leveled the land 10,000 years ago left a few wrinkles, mounds, and run-off carved ravines.

Fat-tire enthusiasts, being a tenacious bunch, took what was given to them and began cutting trails. Some trails such as Calumet and Central Canal embrace their level surroundings and afford cyclists leisurely rides to amble away afternoons. Other trail systems like Wellington Farm exploit a single topographic enigma. The trail builders created a challenging ride by weaving a single-strand maze over a solitary hill.

Some cyclists took to the political arena to adopt abandoned parcels of land and open them to mountain biking. Rum Village Pathway, once a haven for riff-raff, has been cleaned up and transformed into a mountain bike park. The hordes of responsible trail users filling the parking area stand as a testimonial to the positive impact mountain bikers can have on their communities.

While some activists have been successful on the local level, others have scored victories at the state level. Huntington's Kekionga Trail holds the fate of mountain biking on state-owned property. The trail was opened as a pilot program and will serve as the Department of Natural Resource's model for other state parks. Kekionga's property manager has supported the program since its inception, and the 11-miles of singletrack and doubletrack have held up well to the increased traffic.

France Park also sees its fair share of mountain bike traffic. For those who wish to challenge themselves, this Logansport-area park holds a surprising number of moderate-to-difficult descents, climbs, and challenging sections. Before writing off mountain biking in this area due to its lack of geographical severity, just remember one thing: If Jamaicans can sponsor a bobsled team, fat-tire cycling can flourish in the northern Hoosier state.

# Calumet Trail

## Ride Summary

The demise of the paved Calumet Trail was a sad day for road cyclists. Mountain bikers, however, rejoiced in having the trail fall into their Lycra-clad laps. The trail is wide, flat, and perfect for a family ride to the beach. Campsites and excellent hiking trails through bogs and over sand dunes offer an alternative to cruising the pedal-power byway.

## Ride Specs

**Start:** Dune Acres Road parking area
**Length:** 9.9 mile-point-to-point
**Approximate Riding Time:** 2½ hours
**Technical Difficulty Rating:** Easy
**Physical Difficulty Rating:** Moderate due to length
**Trail Surface:** Flat, sand, and gravel rail trail
**Lay of the Land:** High-speed spinning or leisurely pedaling awaits on this flat, straight trail
**Land Status:** Indiana Dunes State Park, Indiana National Lakeshore
**Nearest Town:** Michigan City
**Other Trail Users:** Hikers and joggers

## Getting There

**From Michigan City:** Take U.S. 12 west approximately 12 miles to Dune Acres Road. Take a right on Dune Acres Road and travel 0.2 miles to the parking area on the left. *DeLorme: Indiana Atlas & Gazetteer:* Page 19, B-9

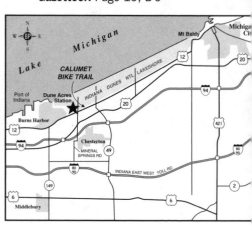

Over 100 years ago, adventure journalist Thomas B. Stephens pedaled along the northern edge of the state on his high-wheeler bicycle during his successful quest to ride around the world. On a portion of his 2,500-mile jaunt, Stephens rode from Chicago to South Bend, at one point actually riding along the shore of Lake Michigan on the Calumet Trail.

While riding along that same trail, one can't help but wonder how the sights have changed since Stephens' trek. And on summer days in the sweltering heat, one can't help feel the same discomforts as Stephens might have felt.

After 18 miles of good riding and tough trundling through deep sand, Stephens pedaled over the Indiana state line. For the first 35 miles, however, he rode around the edge of Lake Michigan. Finding the wagon roads next to impossible, he pedaled around the hard, wet sand near the water's edge.

From Stevens' book, *Around the World on a Bicycle,* he recalls the Hoosier state: "This place is enough to give one the yellow-edged blues: nothing but swamps, sand, sad-eyed turtles, and ruthless, relentless mosquitoes. At Chesterton the roads improve, but still enough sand remains to break the force of headers, which, notwithstanding my long experience on the road, I still manage to execute with undesirable frequency."

Today the trail is in a dilapidated state and possibly resembles what Stephens crossed during his journey. The route's neglected state is probably what led many officials to redirect my calls before admitting the trail was officially open. And with good reason. At one point, underneath the gravel, sand, and grassy remains, the path appears to have once been paved and maintained. In its present state it looks as if a crew simply bushhogs the weeds to clear a path.

As road cyclists witness the demise of Calumet Trail, though, mountain bikers rejoice and claim the route as their own. Less maintenance means less traffic, which offers the possibility of riding the entire straight and flat corridor without passing a single cyclist.

In the height of summer, the trail is surrounded by shoulder-high wildflowers. Bordering the wildflowers to the north is a thick hardwood forest that acts as a breaker from the lake's winds.

## Mt. Baldy

*One of the largest dunes on the southern shore of Lake Michigan, it is 123 feet tall and is advancing inland at a rate of four to five feet per year. Northwest winds move Mt. Baldy inland, slowly burying the forest just south of the dune. Winds pick up the sand grains from the beach and blow them inland. The sand grains roll and bounce along in a process referred to as "saltation." As the wind speed increases, the sand is picked up and carried. Viewed from a distance, the sand blowing off the top of Mt. Baldy appears as wisps of smoke, thus the term "smoking dune." —Department of Natural Resources, Indiana Dunes National Lakeshore.*

# Ride Information

## Trail Contact:
**Indiana Dunes National Lakeshore** (219) 926-7561 • **Indiana Dunes State Park** (219) 926-1952 • **Emergencies**—Bailly Ranger Station; 1-800-727-5847

## Schedule:
Open daily, year-round

## Fees/Permits:
None

## Local Information:
**Duneland Chamber of Commerce,** Chesterton, IN (219) 926-5513

## Local Events/Attractions:
Visitors Center is open daily except Thanksgiving, Christmas, and New Year's Day

## Accommodations:
**Indiana Dunes State Park Campground** (219) 926-1952 • **Dunes Shore Inn B&B**, Beverly Shores, IN (219) 879-9029

## Restaurants:
**Benny's Pizza,** Michigan City, IN (219) 874-3663 • **China Garden,** Michigan City, IN (219) 873-9688

## Other Resources:
*Around the World on a Bicycle,* Thomas B. Stevens • *'Round and About the Dunes,* Norma Schaeffer

## Local Bike Shop:
**Bike Stop,** Michigan City, IN (219) 872-9228

## Maps:
**USGS maps:** Dune Acres, IN; Michigan City West, IN • **Indiana Dunes Official Map and Guide**

A completely different landscape rewards cyclists at the ride's completion. Shoulder your bike and climb Mt. Baldy. The unobstructed view from atop this mountain dune is surreal and takes your imagination from Midwestern farmland to the ocean coast of your choice.

A constant breeze whispers through the dune grass as waves roll against the shore. This breeze keeps Mt. Baldy and the other dunes alive. The stiff lake wind lifts sand particles and deposits them on the ever-moving dunes, while on the backside of the dunes, the sand blowing over the top looks as if the dune is smoking.

The Indiana Dunes is also noted for having one of the few singing beaches in the world. Of course, the dunes don't just sing for anyone; they must be prompted. To start the chorus, walk near the water's edge with your bare feet. The compression of the quartz crystals, moisture, and friction from your feet creates a clear ringing sound.

The work of the Ice Age can also be spotted on the dunes. But instead of crumpling the landscape like the glaciers did to the southern third of the state, the remnants are a multitude of plants from many different environments. Arctic bearberry bushes can be found next to desert-like prickly pear cactus, and dogwoods from southern latitudes can be found growing in proximity to northern jack pines.

Walking along the shore, looking north, Lake Michigan appears endless. To the west lies a reminder of the dunes proximity to Chicago. On clear days, the tops of the City of Broad Shoulder's skyscrapers can be seen over the lake's western horizon.

Take in the sites along the shore, then move inward to the bogs. Your options include hiking along Cowles Bog Trail, bird watching on the Island Marsh Trail, searching for the sad-eyed turtles Thomas Stephens wrote about, or visiting the nature center near Mt. Tom.

After a full day of riding, beach combing, bird watching, and ecological study, mosey on over to the Dunewood Campground and pitch your tent for the night. The dunes hold something for everyone.

## **Miles**Directions

**0.0 START** at Dune Acres Road parking area. Find the trailhead east of the parking area, just across the street.

**0.5** Calumet Trail crosses a gravel driveway.

**1.1** Calumet Trail crosses Waverly Road.

**1.5** Arrive at a trail intersection. Continue straight on the Calumet Trail, passing the Dune Park Railroad Station on the right.

**2.1** Calumet Trail crosses a gravel driveway.

**2.2** Calumet Trail crosses Tremont Road.

**4.5** Calumet Trail crosses East State Park Road.

**4.6** Pass a trail heading off to the left. Continue straight on Calumet Trail.

**5.9** Calumet Trail intersects with Broadway. Turn left on Broadway, then take a quick right into a gravel parking lot to the trailhead.

**7.5** Pass a trail on the right. Continue straight on Calumet Trail.

**7.6** Turn right on the singletrack trail. Follow the trail along railroad tracks. Cyclists cannot go straight along Calumet Trail proper. Calumet Trail is washed out and cyclists must go around to the tracks and back down to the trail.

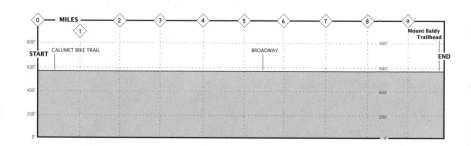

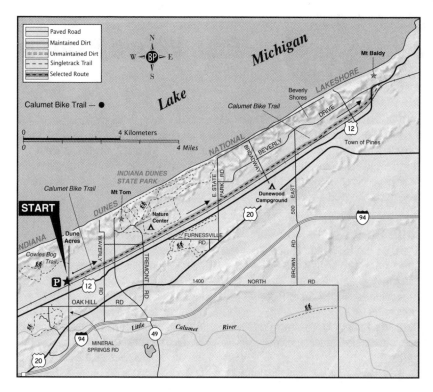

**7.7** Take the singletrack trail off the tracks and back to Calumet Trail.

**8.1** Calumet Trail crosses an unmarked gravel road.

**8.7** Calumet Trail crosses Central Avenue.

**8.8** Calumet Trail crosses an unmarked dirt road.

**9.1** Calumet Trail crosses an unmarked paved road. An electrical cooling tower that looks like a nuclear power plant is now in view. We can only hope that Homer Simpson is not at the controls!

**9.3** Calumet Trail ends at U.S. 12. Turn left on U.S. 12.

**9.7** Turn left on Rice Street. The road is marked by the "Indiana Dunes National Lakeshore/Mt. Baldy" sign

**9.9** Rice Street ends at the Mt. Baldy parking area and trailhead. Restrooms are also available here.

# Rum Village Pathway

## Ride Summary

Who knew so much trail could be packed into such a small area? Instead of criss-crossing many trails like other Hoosier micro-trail systems, volunteers from the Northern Indiana Mountain Bike Association carved a single winding trail that uses nearly every inch of the park. This singletrack playground has sections that will challenge even hard-core cyclists.

## Ride Specs

**Start:** At the trailhead sign across the street from the parking area
**Length:** 4-mile trail system
**Approximate Riding Time:** Rider's discretion
**Difficulty Rating:** Moderate to difficult due to tight singletrack and challenging terrain
**Trail Surface:** Winding, tight singletrack laces through mostly flat woods
**Lay of the Land:** Singletrack winds through woodlands
**Land Status:** City Park
**Nearest Town:** South Bend
**Other Trail Users:** Joggers and hikers

## Getting There

**From Downtown South Bend:** At the intersection of Main Street and Ewing Avenue follow Ewing Avenue west. Pass the entrance to Rum Village Park and continue 1.1 miles to Gertrude Road. Turn left onto Gertrude Road and continue for a half-mile to the parking area on the left and trailhead on the right. Park in the parking area on the left. *DeLorme: Indiana Atlas & Gazetteer:* Page 20, B-6

### Rum Village Pathway Trail Rules

- *Motorized vehicles prohibited*
- *Be courteous, and yield to pedestrians*
- *Don't ride when trails are muddy*
- *Stay on trails and do not cut corners*
- *Do not litter—pack it out*
- *Leave trail as you found it*
- *Do not cut trees, brush, or foliage (As an alternative, bang trees repeatedly with shoulders, knees, and elbows until tree falls over)*

Welcome to the heart of Michiana. South Bend, one of the area's largest cities, grew as fur traders and explorers canoed down Lake Michigan, followed the St. Joseph River, and portaged to the Kankakee River. By and by a trader decided to put down some roots and build an outpost; from this outpost a town formed and began to sprawl. From these early entrepreneurial beginnings, South Bend became a hotbed of industry and its businesses and schools developed a chameleon-like personality in regard to their ability to transform themselves.

Many people define the city by its Catholic school of higher learning. Passersby spot Notre Dame easily enough by its sparkling golden dome.

Beautiful murals on the walls of the university's buildings are intended to serve as religious icons. The Fighting Irish, however, are known for their football prowess, and these murals are better known today by nicknames such as "Touchdown Jesus" and "Fair Catch Moses."

But, before the likes of Knute Rockne, Ara Parseghian, and Lou Holtz came along, Notre Dame was an infant institution known more for fumbling than strong finishes. Father Edward Sorin, with the help of some dedicated brethren, carved the small campus from the woods along the shore of St. Mary's Lake. Father Sorin must have felt kindred spirits with Job as he shepherded the school through years of underfunding and a devastating fire, which burnt down the main building. In 1924, the Four Horsemen—the legendary backfield coached by Knute Rockne—led the Irish to an undefeated season, a Rose Bowl title, and national acclaim as a football powerhouse. The team has gone on to win many national titles and produced players the likes of Joe Montana and Tim Brown. (Oh yeah, Notre Dame has many heralded academic programs as well.)

Away from the co-ed clamor of Notre Dame, one car manufacturer wasn't blessed with the luck of the Irish. This company's transformation is synonymous with automobile failure—Studebaker. In the 1870s, Studebaker claimed to be the world's largest wagon works. By 1916, Studebaker crossed over to motorized carriages, and business grew largely

because of the production demands of World War I. By the mid-1920s car sales had reached their peak. The company did manage to sputter through the Depression, and was reinvigorated by the economic boom created by World War II. A day after the Japanese surrendered, however, Studebaker began laying off workers. As the Big Three became America's carmakers and left little room for small upstarts, Studebaker finally closed its doors in 1963.

One industry's demise can be another's gain. Along the St. Joseph River, between Madison Street and Jefferson Street, is the East Race Whitewater Rapids. The purpose of the East Race Whitewater Rapids was to provide hydraulic power to factories. However, the decline of industrial production resulted in the abandonment of the waterway. South Bend spent $4.5 million to turn the area into a recreational waterway, and in June of 1984 the East Race was opened as a world-class whitewater course.

The Rum Village Pathway has also enjoyed its own renaissance. Ten years ago this annex of the main park was a vestige for vagrants. The Northern Indiana Mountain Bike Association saw a potential off-road diamond in the rough, and petitioned the city to rejuvenate the land. NIMBA proposed that they come in, clean up the area, cut some trails, and claim the area as a city-sponsored mountain bike park. The results have been promising and prosperous.

On most weekends, area cyclists and families can be spotted in droves cranking through the tight singletrack. Upon entering the four-mile pathway, cyclists come to a signpost marked with "Bike" and "Hike" signs. The level of difficulty varies depending upon which trailhead cyclists choose. The trail to the far right leads to the easy-to-moderate section. The middle prong leads directly to the moderate-to-difficult section. The prong splitting from the middle trail marked "Hike," however, is actually the exit of the one-way, moderate-to-difficult section. Do not enter here! To reduce collisions, trail builders made the system one-way. Blue arrows are displayed around the course as reminders.

There are enough tree roots, switchbacks, hairpins, and off-camber sections to satisfy even the most hard-core cyclists. Beware of the cull trees that act as slalom gates, and are much less forgiving. Bruised elbows, shoulders, and knees are common injuries.

The trail is predominantly flat, but subtle changes in the topography keep cyclists shifting constantly throughout the course to maximize rpms. There are even some surprise uphill and downhill pitches to keep everyone on their toes.

Since Jesus and Moses have already been honored, how about a "Gnarly Noah" grabbing some big air or a "Moab Mary" speeding through some particularly tricky singletrack?

## Ride Information

🞂 **Trail Contacts:**
**South Bend Park & Recreation**, South Bend, IN (219) 272-4864

🕐 **Schedule:**
Open daily, year-round

❓ **Local Information:**
**South Bend Visitors Guide** at *www.livethelegends.com*

📍 **Local Events/Attractions:**
**Notre Dame University**, South Bend, IN • **East Race Waterway**, South Bend, IN (219) 235-9328 • **Studebaker National Museum**, South Bend, IN (219) 235-9479 • **College Football Hall of Fame**, South Bend, IN (219) 235-9999

🛏 **Accommodations:**
**Book Inn Bed and Breakfast**, South Bend, IN (219) 288-1990

🍴 **Restaurants:**
**East Bank Emporium**, South Bend, IN (219) 234-9000 • **Bruno's Pizza**, South Bend, IN (219) 234-9000

🚴 **Group Rides:**
**Pro Form Bike, Run, Swim Shop**, South Bend, IN (219) 272-0129—*rides start 9 A.M. Saturdays at the Pathway*

👥 **Organizations:**
**NIMBA (Northern Indiana Mountain Bike Association)** P. O. Box 6383, South Bend, IN 46628 or *www.nd.edu/~ktrembat/www-bike/NIMBA/NIMBAidx.html*

🚲 **Local Bike Shops:**
**Pro Form Bike, Run, Swim Shop**, South Bend, IN (219) 272-0129

🅝 **Maps:**
**USGS maps:** South Bend, IN

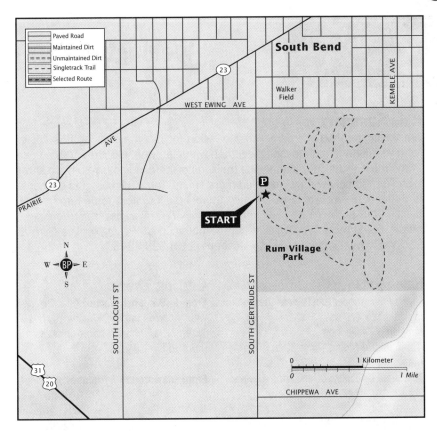

## **Miles**Directions

Because of the nature of the trails in Rum Village Park, specific directions aren't needed. Getting lost is not a problem, though, as all the trails loop back to the start. The trailhead can easily be reached from the parking area. Just ride wherever your bike takes you and enjoy. *The map indicates general location of the Rum Village Park trails only.*

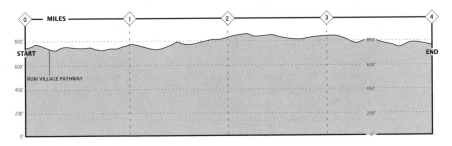

# Wellington Farm

## Ride Summary

Jim Wellington had a dream and a passion for mountain biking. His uncle, John Wellington, had the land. Together, with plenty of help, they created one of the most technically demanding trails in northern Indiana. Yes, it's a short loop. Yet, somehow they crammed more twists, turns, climbs, and descents into this little patch of land, creating the only trail system to be rated as difficult in the northern Hoosier hinterlands. [**NOTE:** A waiver must be signed before riding the trails. Waivers can be obtained at Wellington Eye Care at 116 West Washington in nearby Goshen; (219) 533-7345.]

## Ride Specs

**Start:** Four wooden posts near the parking area
**Length:** 3.7-mile loop
**Approximate Riding Time:** 30 to 45 minutes
**Technical Difficulty:** Difficult due to winding singletrack and a multitude of short, steep climbs
**Physical Difficulty:** Moderate as neither climbs nor length are overbearing
**Trail Surface:** Singletrack
**Lay of the Land:** Singletrack serpentines through a solitary, wooded hill and pasture
**Land Status:** Private Property
**Nearest Town:** Syracuse
**Other Trail Users:** None

## Getting There

**From I-69 in Fort Wayne:** Take U.S. 30 west approximately 28 miles to IN 13. Take IN 13 north approximately 17 miles to Syracuse.

**From downtown Syracuse,** continue north on IN 13 approximately one mile. Take the first left (it's a dirt driveway that is actually a two-rut dirt path) past County Line Road South and the guardrail. If you drive past Commodore Homes or U.S. 6, you have driven too far. Follow the driveway past the house and barn. Park in the open area near the treeline. *DeLorme: Indiana Atlas & Gazetteer: Page* 21, F-12

Over 10,000 years ago, glaciers cleared the topographic slate clean and left little landscape in what is now northern Indiana for mountain bikers to enjoy. Today the majority of this area is farmland. Thus, pursuit of challenging legal trails is a never-ending battle.

However, the glaciers did leave behind a few hilly moraines and kettle holes for mountain bikers to work with in this area of northeastern Indiana. These holes filled with water long ago and formed a condensed cluster of lakes, the largest being Lake Wawasee.

Spanning 2,618 acres, Lake Wawasee is Indiana's largest natural lake. Years ago the body of water was named Turkey Lake, but was later renamed after Miami Chief Wau-wa-aus-see. Lake Wawasee is now surrounded by hotels, camps, cottages, boat liveries, riding stables, golf courses, and a repertory theater.

Traditionally, the lake has been a summer playground. But with the addition of many winter sports to the area, there is year-round activity in town. With the addition of a mountain bike loop at Wellington Farm, mountain biking can also be added to the list of recreational activities, summer or winter.

Granted, this area is topographically challenged, but there are just enough features on the 96-acre Wellington Farm for a solid trail system. And Jim Wellington and his uncle John Wellington did the most with what they had. John owned the acreage north of Syracuse, and Jim had the gumption to cut the trails.

Yeeha!

# Ride Information

**Trail Contacts:**
**Wellington Eye Care,** 116 W. Washington, in nearby Goshen (219) 533-7345

**Schedule:**
Open dawn to dusk, year-round

**Fees/Permits:**
None

**Local Information:**
*www.indico.net/counties/elkhart*

**Local Events/Attractions:**
Lake Syracuse

**Accommodations:**
Anchor Inn B&B (219) 457-4714

**Restaurants:**
**Gropp's Famous Fish of Stroh,** Syracuse, IN (219) 457-4353

**Maps:**
**USGS Maps:** Milford, IN; Lake Wawasee, IN

While most trail construction projects occur during the winter when thickets and thorns are most vulnerable, Jim decided to complete the work during summertime. In the sweltering heat and humidity, the thorny briars' tentacles sprawl across the ground. Undaunted, Jim and a few friends tackled the project with chainsaws and axes. Jim crawled under the briar bushes and cut through their center. The bush would fall on top of him, he'd climb out, then move on to the next bush.

The biggest physical challenges were the briars, thickets, and grapevines that flourished on the property. An even larger obstacle, though, was the fact that there was only one major hill on the whole property. Jim capitalized on this one hill, as the trail climbs and descends it six times.

After six months, a four-mile course was laid out. One year later, the Wellingtons pulled off a successful mountain bike race, earning the accolades of cyclists across the state. To the trail's benefit, cyclists packed down the muddy trail and cleared out the freshly cut grass during the race, which helped form the course.

The trails of Wellington Farm are well laid out and seem to have little environmental impact. This short-course system winds through oak, hickory, redbud, and dogwood trees, enhancing the area as opposed to disrupting it. Wildlife have taken to the area's newest arrival as well, and appear to co-exist quite nicely. Barn owls, deer, wild turkey, and waterfowl can all be spotted on the property.

This single-loop trail squeezes in twists and turns, climbs and descents, and high-speed field crossings through some very challenging singletrack without damaging the field and wooded areas.

This course is not beginner friendly by any means. In the condensed sections, there are more switchbacks than the Alpe d'Huez stage of the Tour de France. From each winding section there is a short, straight sec-

Through the wildflowers...

tion that barely allows cyclists to catch their breath. And the climbs, though limited to one hill, require strong legs to summit.

Before hitting the trail, cyclists need to stop by Wellington Eye Care to sign a waiver. Also, the owner, requests that all cyclists stay on the Wellington property—*the house and barn are not Wellington property*. As of yet, folks residing in the house don't seem to mind the cyclists. The main drive at this house leads back to the parking area, but John prefers cyclists use the field entrance just past County Line Road South and the guardrail.

## **Miles**Directions

**0.0 START** at the four posts and follow the trail toward the treeline, away from IN. 13.

**0.1** The trail leaves the field and bends into the trees. This is the first switchback section.

**0.4** A trail goes off to left. Continue straight on the main trail. The trail on the left leads back to the parking area.

**0.5** The trail splits. Follow the singletrack split to the right and follow the perimeter of the field.

**0.55** The trail leads back into the woods.

**0.7** A trail goes off to the left. Follow the main trail and bend to the right. There are many climbs, descents, and switchbacks in this section.

**1.3** The trail follows the low point on the topo before turning and climbing back into the woods.

**1.7** Pass a swamp on the left.

**2.1** The trail splits. Take the left split.

**2.2** The singletrack dumps out into the field. It follows the perimeter of the field and is across from the parking area.

**2.4** Pass between two ponds. Now near IN **13.** A few switchbacks are in this section.

**2.6** The trail dumps out into the field.

**2.9** The trail crosses a fenceline and winds through some shrubs.

**3.2** The trail dumps back out to the field and bends to the right.

**3.3** The trail splits. Take the left split and cross the field.

**3.4** The trail bends to the right and runs parallel to IN 13.

**3.7** Pass the four poles sticking out of the ground to complete the loop.

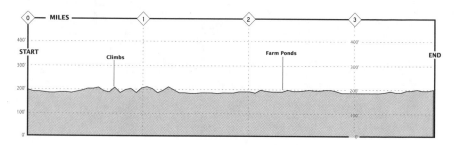

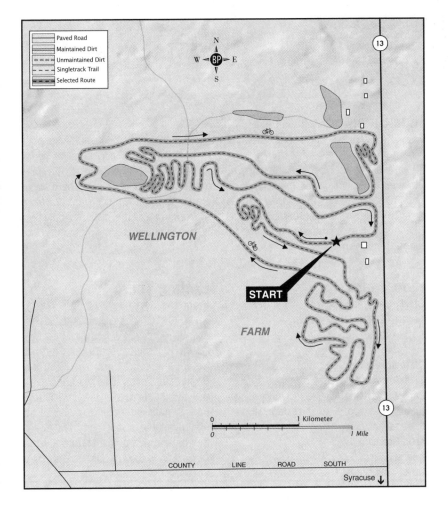

START

# J.B. Franke Park

## Ride Summary

Franke Park has really served mountain bikers well as a model multi-use park. Mountain biking has peacefully co-existed with many other activities for years. The trails themselves are not a travel destination for out-of-towners. They are, however, a great ride for locals who wish to exercise after work or prepare for an upcoming race. For those looking for an adrenaline rush, a quick drop down the soapbox derby hill trail has raised a few heart rates in its time. Johnny Appleseed himself was even rumored to have taken the downhill plunge—planting seeds along the way, mind you.

## Ride Specs

**Start:** Trailheads north of Schoaff Lake
**Length:** 10-mile trail system
**Approximate Riding Time:** Rider's discretion
**Difficulty Rating:** Moderate
**Trail Surface:** Singletrack
**Lay of the Land:** Singletrack threading through the woods, exciting downhill off the soapbox derby hill
**Land Status:** City Park
**Nearest Town:** Fort Wayne
**Other Trail Users:** Hikers and joggers

## Getting There

**From the north side of Fort Wayne:** Take I-69 to Exit 109A and Goshen Avenue (Exit 109A actually becomes Goshen Avenue) south to Sherman Boulevard. Turn left on Sherman Boulevard. Follow Sherman Boulevard 0.4 miles, then turn left into Franke Park's main entrance. Turn left at the first available opportunity and follow the park road to the Nature Center. ***DeLorme: Indiana Atlas & Gazetteer:*** Page 29, C-8

As Indiana's second largest city, Fort Wayne's roots can be traced to when it was once a prime military outpost. This garrison served as a trading and military center to the Miami, Iroquois, French, English, and finally the Americans. This strategic post placement sits at the convergence of three rivers: the St. Joseph, the St. Marys, and the Maumee, each of which is connected to the Great Lakes and the Mississippi River.

So it came as no surprise then, as riverboat commerce and canal popularity increased that Fort Wayne grew to become, at the time, Indiana's fifth largest city. When river travel was replaced by the railroad, Fort Wayne smartly replaced its canals with rails and continued to grow.

This prosperous city attracted many famous early Americans. Thomas Edison arrived in town and worked the railroad for nearly six months. Not to be outdone, his-soon-to-be-competitor, George Westinghouse, came to

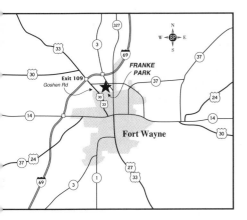

Fort Wayne to test his first air brake.

John Chapman, another early American icon, is buried within the city limits. Chapman, better known as "Johnny Appleseed," traveled the country wearing his trademark hat, bare feet, and flour sack full of seeds, planting apple trees and other fruits and vegetables along the way. Chapman has since risen to legendary lore rivaling John Henry and Paul Bunyan.

John B. Franke may not have planted apple trees, but he was owner of the Perfection Biscuit Company, and he too has left his mark on the city. Franke Park, named after John Franke, holds an estimated 10 miles of trails, a 13-acre pond, nature center, BMX course, playgrounds, picnic shelters, baseball diamonds, football field, soap box derby track, the Foellinger Theatre, and the Fort Wayne Children's Zoo.

The Zoo, open from late April to late October, has over 1,000 animals in its 40-acre park. A visit to the zoo is a great reward for completing this challenging singletrack ride. You could also enjoy a picnic lunch or just rest beneath one of the plentiful shade trees.

The trails of this 280-acre park are intertwining, challenging, twisting, and predominantly singletrack. This system offers an inner-city getaway for urban cyclists without the long drive to make such an escape. While these trails were a challenge to map, an even bigger challenge would be to ride the same loop twice. The benefit of having such a condensed trail system as this is that it's possible to get a great workout without fear of getting lost.

A couple of trail highlights include the two racecourses at the back of the park. Take a lap around the BMX track and test your skills on the camelback hills and the banked, hairpin turns. Climb the hill to the top of the soap box derby track, which is also used as a toboggan run in the winter, and take in the view of the park and surrounding subdivision.

For advanced cyclists, the exhilarating downhill run off the backside of the soap box derby track definitely gets the blood pumping. A clear stretch after the hill allows cyclists to enjoy the speed before the trail twists back into the woods, causing cyclists to brake for those pesky speed barriers otherwise known as trees.

Also for advanced cyclists, the most challenging portion of the trail is just west of the soap box derby track. Behind the tree line are some challenging climbs and descents as the trail threads up and down the hills along the creek.

Cyclists looking to improve their technical skills could create a short loop in this section. But make sure you don't wear yourself out. With so much fun condensed into such a small park, it would be a shame not to take advantage of it all.

Advanced technology at Franke Park.

## Johnny Appleseed

John Chapman was born on September 26, 1774, in Leominster, Massachusetts. In the fall of 1797, Chapman decided to head west, hiking to Pennsylvania's Allegheny Mountains. Blue-eyed and shoeless, Chapman carried a rifle, hatchet, and a knapsack of food and apple seeds he had gathered from the cider mills of eastern Pennsylvania.

Fighting an early squall, John wrapped his feet with cloth and descended to the town of Warren, Pennsylvania. It was here that he cleared a plot and planted his first orchard. He knew he could make a business of raising apple trees and selling the fruit to frontiersmen. This particular fruit was extremely practical, as it was used for pies, butter, cider, fermented hard cider, or eaten raw.

So every fall, Chapman traveled east to collect free bushels of apple seeds from the cider mills. Carrying his precious cargo by horseback or canoe, Chapman scouted for new sites farther west. Once found, the land was cleared, a fence was built, and the seeds were planted.

Chapman spent his summers tending to his nurseries. By the time he was 40, Chapman had orchards in Pennsylvania, Ohio, and Indiana. Before his death on March 18, 1845, Chapman's estate had grown to 15,000 trees, 2,000 seedlings, and approximately 800 acres of land. Active to his last day, Chapman traveled barefoot and unarmed through the hostile wilderness, giving apple seeds and fruit to pioneer children and the poor, helping to perpetuate the legend of Johnny Appleseed.

Throughout his living days, no one actually called Chapman "Johnny Appleseed," but Chapman did sign some forms as John Appleseed. Chapman never wore a tin-pan for a hat. He wore coonskin or cloth hats and an army officer's hat, but never a tin mush pot. Constant foot travel led Chapman only to wear his shoes when he needed to keep his feet warm. One pioneer described his bare feet as "dark, hard, and horny."

Chapman walked long distances till the day he died. If he wasn't walking, he was canoeing or riding a horse to tend to his trees. One tale even recalls Chapman riding a Cannondale dual-suspension frame down the backside of the soap box derby hill at Franke Park. Wearing a mush-pot shaped helmet, Johnny raced at high speeds pedaling with bare feet, spreading apple seeds as he went, while still leading a field of professional mountain bike racers.

Sometimes it's so difficult to separate myth from fact.

## Ride Information

**Trail Contact:**
Fort Wayne Parks Department
(219) 427-6000

**Schedule:**
Park hours are 5 A.M. to 11 P.M.

**Fees/Permits:**
None

**Local Information:**
Fort Wayne/Allen County Convention
& Visitors Bureau, Fort Wayne, IN
1-800-767-7752, (219) 424-3700

**Local Events/Attractions:**
Children's Zoo, Open late April to late
October, Monday-Saturday, 9 A.M.-5
P.M., Sunday; Holidays from 9 A.M.-6
P.M. (219) 427-6800 • Drive-In
Theatre 1-800-727-5847

**Accommodations:**
Red Roof Inn, Fort Wayne, IN
(219) 484-8641

**Restaurants:**
Azar's Big Boy, Fort Wayne, IN
(219) 483-7442

**Local Bike Shops:**
Cycle Path, Fort Wayne, IN (219) 436-
4760 • Summit City Bicycles, Fort
Wayne, IN (219) 484-0182

**Maps:**
USGS map: Fort Wayne West, IN

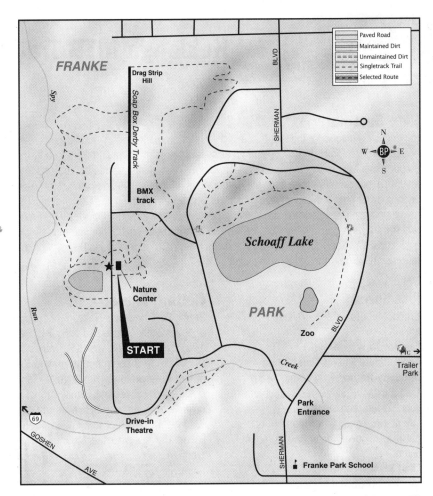

## **Miles**Directions

[**Note:** Because Franke Park has so many individual trails suitable for cycling, it would be unreasonable to create a single loop. Instead, cyclists are encouraged to use the map provided and select your own routes through the park, cycling from the Nature Center to Drag Strip Hill, past Schoaff Lake toward the zoo, and everywhere in-between. For this reason, there is no profile map available.]

# Kekionga MTB Trail

## Ride Summary

Huntington is unique for the fact that it is the first state park property to allow mountain biking. The pilot program has been a great success in that mountain bikers love it, the property manager supports it, and there have been no major instances of problems with mountain bikers. Why then has the Department of Natural Resources not officially endorsed the program and applied it to other properties? Therein lies the mystery. The predominately singletrack trail circumnavigates the reservoir, and although there are no real climbs, provides a great ride for novices and grizzled, knobby-tire veterans. If you enjoy the trail, voice your opinion to the Indiana Bicycle Coalition, Indiana DNR, your state representative, and the property manager.

## Ride Specs

**Start:** Mountain Bike Trailhead parking area
**Length:** 11.4 mile-loop
**Approximate Riding Time:** 2 hours
**Difficulty Rating:** Easy to moderate
**Trail Surface:** Singletrack, doubletrack, county road, and state highway
**Lay of the Land:** Singletrack introduces, but doesn't overwhelm novice mountain bikers
**Land Status:** State Park
**Nearest Town:** Huntington
**Other Trail Users:** Hikers and joggers

## Getting There

**From Fort Wayne:** Take I-69 south approximately 7 miles to U.S. 24 (Exit 102). Take U.S. 24 west 18.8 miles to IN 5. Take IN 5 south approximately 1.9 miles to downtown Huntington. Take U.S. 224/IN 5 south 1.7 miles to IN 5 split. Take IN 5 south 2.1 miles to Little Turtle S.R.A (State Recreation Area). Follow the signs to the Mountain Bike Trailhead. *DeLorme: Indiana Atlas & Gazetteer:* Page 28, G-4

Dan Quayle was the fifth Hoosier to be elected vice president and the ninth to be nominated. This distinction has earned Indiana the nickname the "Mother of Vice Presidents."

I spell it potatoe, you spell it potato. Potatoe. Potato. What's going on here? Why open the Kekionga Trail ride with song, you ask? And misspell potato no less? That's because the Huntington Reservoir, around which the Kekionga Trail travels, not only supplies water to the city of Huntington, but, more importantly, to the Dan Quayle Center and Museum. Built in 1992, this building houses many exhibits highlighting our 44th vice president's career. For more information, call or write the Dan Quayle Center and Museum *(see the Ride Information box)*.

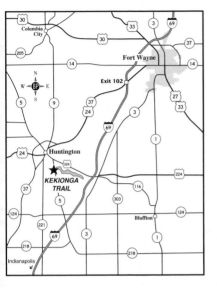

Vice-presidential satire aside, the Kekionga Trail stands out in Hoosier history not for being the closest trail to the museum, but as the first legal trail opened on state-owned property. As many cyclists know, many of the state's best trails are found in Indiana state parks. As of yet, all of these state parks, with the exception of Kekionga, are closed to mountain biking. But if all continues to goes well along the Kekionga, much of that may change.

In the state's defense, it should be noted that mountain biking has always been permitted on state property, but only in designated areas. The irony here is that there were never any designated areas established. So after years of debate, the Indiana Bicycle Coalition (IBC), in conjunction with the Department of Natural Resources, have developed the pilot trail program at Huntington. The Little Turtle SRA Property Manager claims to see 40 to 50 cyclists using these trails on any given weekend.

Both agencies will monitor trail usage, as well as the impact cyclists have on the trail. From their reports, the agencies will write the standards and policies that will govern mountain bike trail areas around the state. The IBC has taken the first step here at Huntington in helping to open the many great trails within Indiana's state parks.

For cyclists in northern Indiana, the Kekionga Trail is one of these great places to ride. This 11-mile loop is evenly divided between singletrack and easy-rolling grassy trails. It is a predominantly easy loop, but listed as slightly moderate for its distance and somewhat challenging singletrack on the north side of the reservoir.

One treat the trail offers is found at the reservoir's east end. County Road 200 East causeway acts as an aviary watchtower, affording an incredible view of the lake and its raptor inhabitants, without disturbing the birds' daily routines. On a typical day turkey vultures circle on rising air currents or rest on the dead, gray branches of shoreline trees. Great blue herons are also seen wading through shallow water in flocks, hunting for their next meal.

Continuing along the trail, cyclists come upon a series of fitness stations. If for some reason you feel that the ride is not enough of a workout, you have the option of dismounting and performing the suggested exercises.

Near the end of the loop along IN 5, cyclists will approach the Observation Mound. Artifacts, skeletons, and other mounds have been discovered in this area. The Observation Mound stands as a preserved natural monument to the ancient Native American Adena Culture.

At the end of the trail, campsites are found near the gate of the Little Turtle State Recreation Area. There are no showers at this campground, but clean restrooms are found near the beach area. Additional campsites are available on the other side of the reservoir.

Other post-ride activities Huntington has to offer include flying airplanes at the model airplane area, fishing, boating, and, of course, a trip to the Dan Quayle Center and Museum. Just don't make any "potatoe" cracks while you're there. The curators just don't seem to see the humor.

## Ride Information

**Trail Contact:**
Huntington Lake, Huntington, IN
(219) 468-2165

**Schedule:**
Open dawn to dusk, year-round

**Fees/Permits:**
$2

**Local Information:**
Huntington County Chamber of Commerce, Huntington, IN
(219) 356-5300, www.huntington.in.us

**Local Events/Attractions:**
Dan Quayle Center and Museum, 815 Warren Street, Huntington, IN 46750
(219) 356-6356

**Accommodations:**
Huntington Lake Campgrounds, Huntington, IN (219) 468-2165 •
Marriott, Huntington, IN
(219) 359-1438

**Restaurants:**
Pizza Junction, Huntington, IN
(219) 356-4700

**Organizations:**
Indiana Bicycle Coalition, Indianapolis, IN 1-800-Bike-110,
(317) 327-8356

**Local Bike Shops:**
Cycle Path, Fort Wayne, IN (219) 436-4760 • Summit City Bicycles, Fort Wayne, IN (219) 484-0182

**Maps:**
USGS maps: Majenica, IN • Kekionga Trail Map available at the gatehouse

## **Miles**Directions

**0.0 START** at the entrance of the Mountain Bike Trailhead. Take a right on the Main Entrance Road.

**0.2** Veer off the Main Entrance Road at the entrance to the campground. Ride along fence and treeline. Believe it or not, this is the trail. The trail eventually leads to a doubletrack path.

**1.3** The trail crosses a gravel road and the parking area for the Model Plane Airstrip.

**1.5** Follow sign and trail to the right. The trail then turns left as it leads across a flat field.

**1.65** The singletrack trail comes to a "T." Take the right trail.

**1.8** The trail crosses a paved road. Continue straight on the trail. You should now be on grassy doubletrack, which soon changes to singletrack.

**2.2** The trail crosses a creek.

**3.9** The trail comes to a "T." Take the left trail and roll past the gate. The trail then crosses a gravel road.

**4.4** Come to an open area with a pond on the right. Follow signs across an open area to a gravel road. Take a right on the gravel road that follows the perimeter of the pond.

**4.7** Arrive at CR 200 East. Turn left and cross the causeway.

**5.35** Turn left off CR 200 East onto a grassy trail. For cyclists seeking solitude, there is a small parking area here.

**6.5** The trail crosses a wooden bridge and comes to a trail intersection. Follow the bike trail to the right. Turning left leads to Kilsoquah campground.

**6.75** Arrive at a trail intersection. Continue straight on the singletrack.

**6.85** The trail crosses a wooden bridge.

**7.7** The trail passes a grassy trail on the left. Continue straight.

**7.75** The trail intersects with a paved road that leads to the Kilsoquah campground. Take a right on the paved road.

**7.85** Turn left onto singletrack at the trail-head.

**8.9** The trail intersects with Meridian Road, which leads to the Kilsoquah boat ramp. Continue straight on the trail.

**9.8** The trail ends at the Observation Mound Road. Turn right on this road.

**9.95** Turn left on IN 5. Cross the Huntington Reservoir Dam.

**11.1** Pass the Huntington Reservoir head-quarters on the left. Cut diagonally across the grassy field toward the gatehouse. Turn left on Main Entrance Road.

**11.4** Turn right at the Mountain Bike Trailhead sign. Your ride is complete. Unless you're up for another lap!

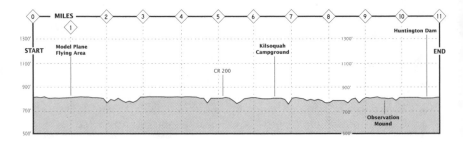

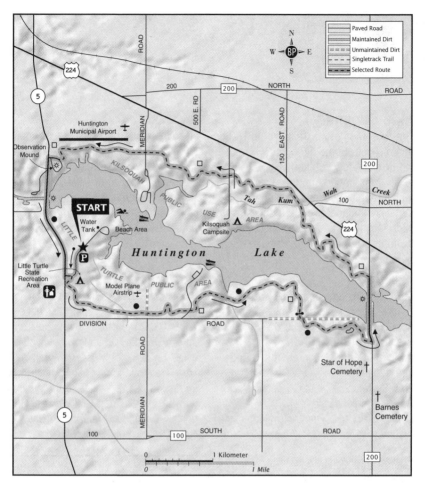

# 6

# France Park

## Ride Summary

The fifteen miles of trails within France Park range from flat and easy to gnarly and difficult. Some descents will cause cyclists to take pause and consider walking down. A few cobbled climbs will have most cyclists dismounting and doing a cyclo-cross impersonation. There are plenty of flat sections, however, that offer a nice respite between challenges. The price of admission is a bit much, and helmets are mandatory. The good news, though, is that some of that money goes back into the trails. Maps at many of the park's trail intersections are just one example.

## Ride Specs

**Start:** Parking area above the waterfalls
**Length:** 4.2 miles of a 15-mile system
**Approximate Riding Time:** 45 minutes to 2 hours
**Difficulty Rating:** Moderate due to rock-strewn climbs
**Trail Surface:** Singletrack, doubletrack, gravel, and asphalt
**Lay of the Land:** Flat trails leading to technically challenging climbs and descents
**Land Status:** County park
**Nearest Town**: Logansport
**Other Trail Users:** Hikers, joggers, and horseback riders

## Getting There

**From Lafayette:** Take IN 25 north approximately 38 miles to Logansport. Take U.S. 35 north approximately one mile to U.S. 24. Go approximately three miles on U.S. 24 west, then turn left into France Park. Follow the Park Entrance Road 0.5 miles to the parking area at the "Frisbee Golf" sign on the right. *DeLorme: Indiana Atlas & Gazetteer:* Page 32, A-4

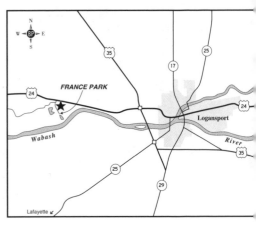

L ogansport, nicknamed "The Bridge City" for its numerous structures straddling the Eel and Wabash rivers, hosts one of Northern Indiana's larger mountain bike trail systems.

The primarily singletrack trails of France Park wind through land once occupied by the Miami and Potawatomi people. The Erie Canal also edges

one of the trails—a faint reminder of the historical importance placed on water travel.

Local mountain biker Brent Mullen introduced me to the trails, leading me through the different loops that wind around quarries, through woods, and past patches of stinging nettles. He even managed to shed some positive light on the abundance of this prickly vegetation, explaining how to boil their leaves to make a delicious tea (see Nettle Tea Sidebar).

France Park was established in 1967. In addition to mountain biking, the park provides many family activities, including numerous campsites, a scenic picnic area at the base of the falls, a well-groomed beachfront, and even a putt-putt golf course.

While riding on the trail, stop to savor the view atop the ridge of the swimming quarry. Look into the pearly green water and try to spot one of the many spoonbilled paddlefish snaking around just below the surface. These algae eaters were imported from Missouri and stocked at a cost of $500. Locals claim some grow as long as seven feet! You may also spot moving fountains of air bubbles dotting the water's surface. These are schools of scuba divers viewing the remains of a bus, truck, and train wheels that have been laid to rest at the bottom of the pit.

Farther along, the trail crosses the handicap-accessible path that leads to the back half of the fishing quarry. The path begins from reserved handicap

## Ride Information

**☏ Trail Contact:**
**Cass County Parks and Recreation Board,** Logansport, IN (219) 753-2928

**🕐 Schedule:**
Open dawn to dusk, year-round

**$ Fees/Permits:**
$5

**❓ Local Information:**
**Official France Park website;** *www.francepark.com* • **Logansport, Indiana website;** *www.onlinecities .net/usa/in/logansport*

**🛏 Accommodations:**
**France Park Campground,** Logansport, IN (219) 753-2928

**⬤ Other Resources:**
For more information on diving call or write **Diving Den Inc.,** Kokomo, IN (317) 452-1034

**🚲 Local Bike Shop:**
**Mark's Bicycle World,** Logansport, IN (219) 753-9630

**🛏 Maps:**
**USGS maps:** Clymers, IN; Lucerne, IN • **France Park Trail Map** available at gatehouse

spaces off the main road and ends at a ramped viewing area for individuals to view the wild birds roosting in trees sprouting from the quarry. From this perch, great blue herons can be seen patiently waiting to catch their day's meal. (More information on the area's plants and wildlife can be found at the wildlife observation building.)

The trails of France Park provide cyclists with a variety of terrain and trail surfaces. Rolling across the dry quarry is like riding on a rough gravel road. Once the trail climbs out of the quarry, a smooth pea gravel path eases toward the swimming area and acts as a nice transition to the singletrack.

As the singletrack edges the swimming quarry, the trail harbors several challenging climbs and one particularly challenging descent. After the descent the trail begins to resemble a mountain biker's version of the spring road racing classic, Paris Roubaix—*The Hell of the North*. Cobblestones are replaced with limestone nubs, making an interesting view as well as a challenge to negotiate.

## Nettle Tea

*How to make Nettle Tea:*
*1. Mix two cups of water with a handful of nettle leaves. The amount of leaves will vary the strength of the tea.*
*2. Bring the water to a boil.*
*3. Let simmer for ten minutes.*
*4. Strain the leaves when pouring. Enjoy.*

Once through this technical section, the trail mellows, descends to the perimeter of a field, then eases down to the Wabash River. A non-threatening uphill along a gravel road leads away from the river and back to the singletrack.

The trail crosses a wooden bridge and changes surface again. Resembling a hamster cage, wood chips spring under the rolling tires. This doubletrack trail leads to the last challenging section of singletrack that edges the perimeter of the fishing pond. The singletrack merges with a paved trail and meanders past the falls then back to the parking area.

Several trails northwest of the swimming pond are favorites for beginning riders, where a trace of the old Erie Canal can be ridden. Riders should take caution though—avoid this area during wet weather. This swampy section is rarely dry, and those nasty nettles grow strong and thick.

When you gotta go, you gotta go.

## **Miles**Directions

**0.0 START** at the parking area above the water falls. Turn right out of parking area and follow the main park road.

**0.05** Turn left before the park road splits, and cross to the Dry Quarry trailhead. True to its name, the trail descends to the bottom of the dry quarry.

**0.1** Pass a trail that goes off to the right. Continue straight, following the perimeter of the dry quarry.

**0.3** Ride across a limestone tabletop trail, then climb up a rock-studded ascent.

**0.4** Turn right onto a pea gravel path. Follow the well-groomed trail through the campsites and down to the Swimming Quarry beach.

**0.6** Trail merges with a gravel road. Follow the gravel road down to the beach area.

**0.8** Follow the road through the gravel beach parking lot.

**0.88** Take the road to the left out of the parking lot.

**0.9** Shift into your granny gear and take a quick right onto singletrack Perimeter Trail.

**1.1** Pass a trail to the right that descends to the beach.

**1.18** Pass a trail that leads to the quarry's edge.

**1.2** Turn right off the main trail to the ledge overlooking the Swimming Quarry.

**1.3** This scenic trail merges back to the main trail. Take the trail to the right at the Stairway Sign. There is a tricky descent just after the trails merge. Limestone lining this singletrack is similar to the cobblestones of old European farm roads.

**1.4** Trail splits at Prairie Trail Sign. Follow the Prairie Trail arrow and trail to the right.

**1.5** After passing a handful of small trails that lead to vistas of the quarry, the trail splits near the edge of the quarry. Follow the main trail to the right.

**1.65** Arrive at a trail intersection. Turn left. Turning right leads back to the swimming area.

**1.9** Arrive at a trail intersection. Turn left on a doubletrack path. This trail descends.

**2.1** Turn right at the bottom of the descent before the trail goes into an open field. Immediately arrive at a gravel trail intersection. Continue straight taking the singletrack trail.

**2.1** Pass a trail and campsite on the right. Come to a trail intersection. Take the trail to the left, then take an immediate right, and pass the red outhouse. The trail now travels along flat, easy terrain.

**2.5** Arrive at a trail split marked by the green outhouse. Take the doubletrack split to the left.

**2.55** Turn right on Georgetown Road.

**2.6** Turn right onto the gravel driveway across from the France Park Access Site for the Wabash River. Cut across the gravel parking lot, pass a wooden gate, and climb the Gravel Access Road.

**2.6** Turn left on Whispering Pine Trail at the top of the climb. The singletrack cuts through the woods.

**2.9** Pass a trail that takes a 120-degree turn to the right, and take the next right. This is a nice run through pine trees with a

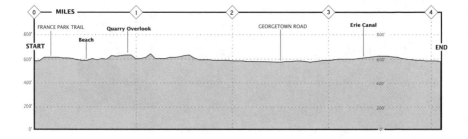

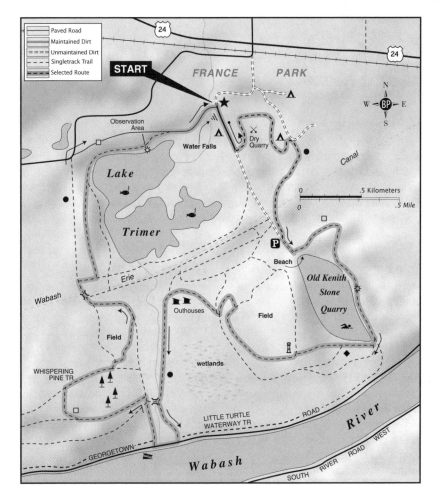

pine-needle carpet. The trail crosses a small field.

**3.1** Arrive at a trail intersection. Continue straight.

**3.2** The trail arrives at a "T." Turn left.

**3.5** Cross a wooden bridge over the old Erie Canal and pass a singletrack trail to the right.

**3.6** The trail arrives at a "T." Turn left.

**3.75** Arrive at a trail intersection. Go straight at the trail intersection onto technical singletrack. Now following the north rim of the fishing quarry.

**3.85** Come to a trail intersection. Continue straight onto technical singletrack. You should now be following the north rim of the Fishing Quarry.

**4.0** Cross the paved path to the observation area. Continue straight on singletrack.

**4.2** The Main Trail merges with the paved path. Take a right on the path and follow it back to the falls and parking area.

**4.25** Arrive back at the waterfalls.

# 7

# Oakbrook Valley

## Ride Summary

Oakbrook's short singletrack loop threads through flat, grassy fields and eventually leads to the technically demanding sections in the woods near Wildcat Creek. Two miles of trail is not enough to lure tourism dollars, but it does provide area cyclists with a decent outlet to satisfy their singletrack fix. In the past, the DINO (Do Indiana Off-Road) organizers thought enough of the course to award the property two races. Maybe the new owners will continue the tradition.

## Ride Specs

**Start:** Trailhead near caretaker's home
**Length:** 1.9-mile loop
**Approximate Riding Time:** 20 to 40 minutes
**Difficulty Rating:** Moderate due to challenging sections in the woods
**Trail Surface:** Singletrack and doubletrack
**Lay of the Land:** The beginning is grassy and flat; the singletrack in the woods has challenging climbs and descents
**Land Status:** Private Property
**Nearest Town:** Kokomo
**Other Trail Users:** Hikers and joggers

## Getting There

**From downtown Kokomo:** Take Sycamore Road/IN 22 west nine miles to County Road 900 West. Turn left on CR 900 West and travel one mile to CR 00 North/South. Turn right on CR 00 North/South and travel 0.5 miles to CR 950 West. Turn left on CR 950 West and travel 0.5 miles to the Oakbrook Valley Park Entrance. Turn right into the park and follow the Park Entrance Road to the parking area. *DeLorme: Indiana Atlas & Gazetteer:* Page 32, E-6

N amed after Miami Chief Kokomoko, the city of Kokomo is better known as the "City of Firsts." The pneumatic rubber tire, the carburetor, the American Howitzer, the all-transistor car radio, and the first commercially built gasoline-powered car in Indiana all were born in this city.

One man in particular was a driving force in this invention-crazed city. In 1894, Elwood Haynes drove into history when he took his first test drive around the streets of Kokomo. Actually, his car was towed three miles outside the city so not to disturb the horse-drawn carriages within the city limits. The first drive in was successful and Haynes went on to invent a number of other items.

His primary interest, though, was metallurgy. Haynes has a claim to the invention of stainless steel, as well as the invention of stellite—a high performance nickel chromium alloy. The development of this alloy led to the construction of the Stellite Corporation.

Haynes has a museum named after him, his house is a historical monument, and Oakbrook Valley Park was once his own. The recreational area was built in 1957 and used by the employees of Haynes International—what used to be the Stellite plant.

They built a softball diamond, basketball courts, horseshoe pits, a putt-putt golf course, and the buildings located on the site, all of which are still here today.

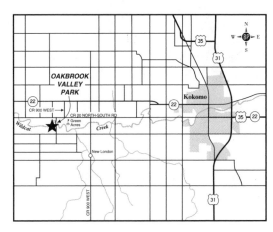

As younger employees moved up through the company, the park received less support and was abandoned. In the early 1980s, a group of firemen and policemen initiated a corporation to buy and refurbish the park, which was to be dubbed the Law Enforcement/Firefighters

Recreational Park. But since the majority of investors were civilians, the investors voted for the name Wildcat Valley Park.

A handful of years ago a local mountain bike enthusiast approached the caretakers of Wildcat Valley Park about constructing off-road bicycling trails in the park. Working together, the caretakers and mountain bikers cut a loop that follows the perimeter of the property. The property changed owners again in the summer of 1997 after construction of the trail was com-

Lamplighter bicycles, standing seven and one half feet tall, never adapted well to mountain biking. They did, however, work well for what they were designed for—lighting natural gas street lamps.

plete. Now the Oakbrook Community Church, the park's current caretaker, continues the tradition of allowing mountain bikers to use the property.

Starting near the caretaker's house, the trail hides just behind the treeline and leads to the front gate. Winding down the edge of the trees and the tennis court, the trail remains flat and acts as a nice warm-up for the singletrack.

Approaching the creek, the trail dips quickly and becomes more challenging. Using the most of a limited landscape, the trail has multiple creek crossings in addition to many climbs and descents on the hill that edges Wildcat Creek. On the ridgetop, and just behind the main lodge, the trail edges a swampy area. Past caretakers first believed this area was an environmental problem surfacing on their property. As it turns out, it was a natural spring once used to water one of the original landowners plow horses.

Look at that chainring! This land-speed-record-setting Schwinn was used back in 1939. Check it out at the Victory Bike Shop "museum" in Kokomo.

The trail then dives back to the creek's bank and follows the low path. A short climb leads to the trailhead, which completes the loop in just under two miles.

The caretakers hope to add more trails in the future. In the meantime, local cyclists have been given a moderate course to enjoy where they can prepare for upcoming mountain bike races.

After the ride, take IN 22 back into town and make a stop at the Victory Bike Shop—a bicycle museum of sorts. The shop opened in 1936 and Charles Sullivan started working there three years later. Charles now acts as the shop's curator, owner, and expert mechanic. Lining the walls of the shop are bicycles of a bygone era. Some of the exhibits include a 1937 Monarch Silver King Deluxe, a 1939 Schwinn used to set the former land speed record, a chromeless Victory bike, a boneshaker, and a seven-foot-tall lamplighter's bicycle. The only other antique, boasts the owner, is Charles himself.

## Ride Information

### ● Trail Contact:
**Oakbrook Valley Park**, Russiaville, IN
(219) 883-5758

### ● Schedule:
Open dawn to dusk, year-round

### ● Fees/Permits:
None

### ● Local Information:
Kokomo's comprehensive website;
www.inkokomo.com

### ● Local Events/Attractions:
**Elwood Haynes Museum**, Kokomo, IN
(765) 456-7500

### ● Accommodations:
**EconoLodge**, Kokomo, IN (765) 457-7561 • **Comfort Inn**, Kokomo, IN (765) 452-5050

### ● Restaurants:
**Mancinos Pizza and Grinders**, Kokomo, IN (765) 457-1800 • **Gordos Taco Shop**, Kokomo, IN (765) 453-9073

### ● Other Resources:
*Indiana: A New Historical Guide*,
Taylor/Stevens/Ponder/Brockman

### ● Local Bike Shop:
**Victory Bike Shop**, Kokomo, IN
(219) 452-9717

### ● Maps:
**USGS map:** Russiaville, IN

Other sites to see before leaving Kokomo include Old Ben and the Sycamore Stump. It seems Old Ben was a crossbred Hereford that weighed 4,270 pounds and stood six feet, four inches tall. The town so loved Ben that they had him stuffed. Paul Bunyan's Babe has nothing on Ben. The Sycamore Stump is what remains of a great Sycamore tree with a circumference of 51 feet. The tree was damaged during a storm in 1915. The stump was later hollowed out, placed in a park, and used as a telephone booth.

If the phone were still there, you could use it to call home, because with all of this riding and sightseeing, you will surely be running late!

## **Miles**Directions

**0.0 START** at the trailhead near the caretaker's home. Leave the parking area and ride across the grassy field next to the caretaker's house.

**0.05** Find the trailhead at the treeline. Immediately arrive at a trail intersection. Take the trail to the right.

**0.2** The trail bends to the right, paralleling CR 950 West. Roll straight across a grassy field and cross the paved entrance to the camp.

**0.3** Continue across the grassy field and find the trailhead at the treeline.

**0.4** The trail bends to the right.

**0.5** The trail heads off to the left just before emptying out into a grassy field.

**0.55** The trail bends to the right and straddles the treeline and a cornfield.

**0.6** The trail rolls behind the tennis courts.

**0.7** The actual trail is faint here. Turn left at the storage building and follow the edge of the grassy area. The trailhead is straight ahead.

**0.75** The trail heads off to the right. An old Coke machine on the left marks the trailhead.

**0.8** The trail splits. Take the left split.

**0.9** Leave the wide grassy trail and turn right onto singletrack.

**1.0** The trail crosses a creek.

**1.2** The trail crosses the creek a second time.

**1.3** The trail splits. Take the left split.

**1.4** The singletrack dumps out into an open area. Turn left along the treeline to find the trailhead.

**1.5** The trail heads off to the right. Continue straight on the main trail. The trail that heads off to the right leads to the bathhouse.

**1.6** The trail splits. Take the left split and begin a climb. The trail tops out with the parking lot in sight. Turn left and follow the treeline to the trailhead.

**1.7** The trail empties out into an open area with the parking lot in sight. Follow the treeline to the left toward the trailhead.

**1.8** The trail bends to the right, climbs, and tops out at the beginning of the loop. Cyclists have the option of riding back to parking area or taking another loop around the Oakbrook Valley Park trail.

**1.9** Reach the end of the ride.

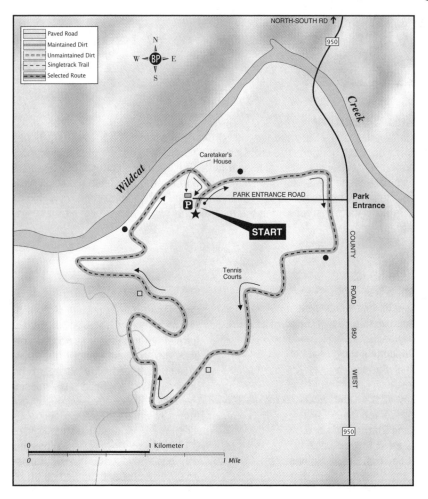

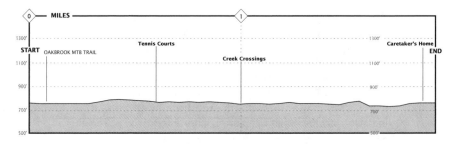

# Prairie Creek Reservoir

## Ride Summary

Motorcycles and ATVs have long used this trail system. The result is a honeycomb of paths bent on criss-crossing each other. The good news is that Muncie-area mountain bikers have trails near town. The bad news is that motorbikes still dominate these trails, so take caution. The rough terrain hones technical skills and definitely enhances bike-handling skills. The flatlander system, though, harbors no climbs, instead offering a multitude of short, steep pitches that prove difficult to master.

## Ride Specs

**Start:** Trail parking area
**Length:** 5-mile trail system
**Approximate Riding Time:** Rider's discretion
**Difficulty Rating:** Moderate
**Trail Surface:** Singletrack and double-track
**Lay of the Land:** Rocky, scrub, motorcyle-carved trails
**Land Status:** City Land
**Nearest Town:** Muncie
**Other Trail Users:** Motorcycles

## Getting There

**From downtown Muncie:** Go east on West Jackson Road, traveling 0.8 miles to Ohio Street and turn right. At the next intersection, Ohio Street becomes Burlington Street. Continue straight on Burlington Street. Drive 3.6 miles and turn left on Inlow Springs Road, following signs for Camp Munsee and Prairie Creek Reservoir. Inlow Springs Road becomes Windsor Road after crossing the White River. Drive 2.1 miles and turn right on CR 475 East. Follow CR 475 East 2.1 miles, then turn left on CR 500 South. Drive 0.1 miles and turn right on CR 462 East. Travel 1.4 miles on CR 462 East and turn left on CR 50 South. Drive 0.1 miles and turn left into the Prairie Creek Trailhead Parking Area. Follow the dirt road to the widened parking area. **DeLorme: Indiana Atlas & Gazetteer:** Page 40, C-6

Named after the "Munsee" clan of the Delaware Indians, Muncie became a hotbed of activity when natural gas was discovered for the second time just north of town. When natural gas was tapped for the first time in 1876, it had little economic value because few people knew its potential, and the site was closed. Ten years later, the Eaton Well was reopened when natural gas was deemed a worthy fossil fuel. By 1890, 226 industries had flocked to Delaware County and the city of Muncie.

Adopting the moniker "Gas City of the West," Muncie attracted glass-jar manufacturer Frank Ball to move his business from Buffalo, New York, after a fire destroyed his family's factory. Over 100 years later, the Ball Corporation is the oldest, continuously operating home canning jar manufacturer in the world.

In 1918, this philanthropic family went on to purchase the 64 acres and two buildings of the failing Muncie Normal Institute and presented it as a gift to the state. Four years later, the state thanked the family by naming

the school in their honor, calling it Ball State Teachers College. By 1965, the college had widened its class offering, gained university status, and is now known as Ball State University.

The statue of "Beneficence" stands on campus as a tribute to the Ball's generosity. Known as "Benny," the winged angel holds a gift of jewels with five columns standing behind her. Each column represents one of the five Ball brothers.

Ball State is also known for one of its most famous alumni, David Letterman. In the spirit of our favorite hometown comedian, alumni, and local boy turned good, please see the Top Ten list for mountain biking the Prairie Creek trail system (*see sidebar on page 75*).

As you enter the trail area, there is a sign that lists the charges for trail use. This sign is for motorcycles only. Mountain biking is free!

Prairie Creek's trails represent another example of a spider-webbed maze of singletrack and off-road wonder. Make your own loop or attempt to follow the elusive DINO route. The Do INdiana Off-road race series makes two stops here during their season and somehow manages to squeeze a racing loop from this labyrinth of trails.

The trails cover ground where there once was a gravel pit. The terrain is rough, stony, and full of scrub brush. Small growth trees, briars, and other low-lying shrubs seem to be the only vegetation capable of growing here.

A two-mile perimeter loop can be run by always choosing the farther-most left trail when traveling clockwise. This loop winds around the perimeter of this network of trails and follows the edges of the 1,250-acre reservoir. This loop is preferred when there aren't many motorcycles using the trails. Motorcycle riders seem to stay on the wider trails and avoid this tight section. If they do venture back on this loop, they seem to ride it at a reduced speed, which makes passing a less frightening experience.

One interesting site, found at the northeast end of the trail system over-looking the reservoir, is the remains of what appears to be a root cellar. It is little more than a hole cut in the side of the hill supported by a stone entrance. The structure stirs the imagination to wonder what stood on this point in years past.

Prairie Creek is a convenient and somewhat challenging loop for Ball State students and Muncie residents. It is also a prime example of how quickly an unmanaged trail system can be destroyed. Mountain bikers can thank ATV and motorcycle riders for creating the trails, but these motor-ized vehicles could also slowly be destroying their own creation.

This is a sensitive area and can really accommodate only a few trails crisscrossing through it. The problem, though, is honeycombing and continuously widening trails that result whenever puddles form in the middle of the trail. The trails are so tight that a trail intersection is

## Ride Information

**Trail Contact:**
Muncie Parks and Recreation Office, Prairie Creek Parks Department, Muncie, IN (765) 747-4776

**Schedule:**
Open dawn to dusk, year-round

**Fees/Permits:**
None

**Local Information:**
www.onlinecities.net/usa/in/muncie

**Local Events/Attractions:**
Ball State University, Muncie, IN (765) 289-1241 • Prairie Creek Reservoir

**Accommodations:**
Days Inn, Muncie, IN (765) 288-2311
Lees Inn, Muncie, IN (765) 282-7557

**Restaurants:**
Greek's Pizzeria, Muncie, IN (765) 284-4900 • Tony's Lockeroom, Muncie, IN (765) 288-9938

**Local Bike Shop:**
B&B Campus Bike Shop, Muncie, IN (765) 282-6389

**Maps:**
USGS map: Mount Pleasant, IN

crossed every 20 feet. There is some singletrack here, but trails that could allow a truck to pass through seem to be the most predominant.

Already erosion is in high gear and is particularly noticeable on the climbs at the northeast corner of the trail system. Two-foot trenches have been carved into the top of each of the four climbs now cutting into the hill.

With the state's limited trail systems, especially in the northern portion of the state, a trail adoption program would serve as an option to keep this system open and rideable. Cyclists could work with ATV and motorcycle riders to preserve Prairie Creek before it becomes another trail-closure statistic.

Besides, do you want to be the one to tell David Letterman that these trails are closed?

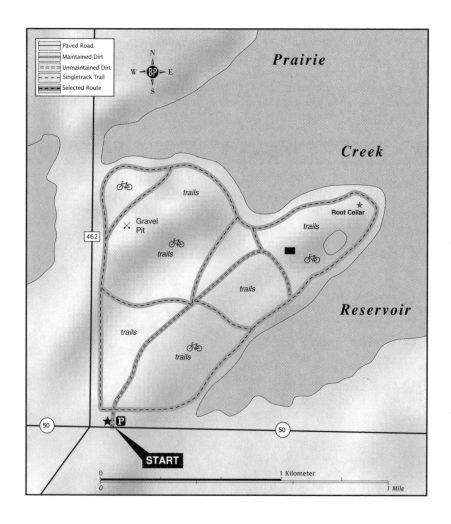

## Top Ten Reasons for Riding the Prairie Creek Trail System

10. *Optional motorpacing sessions offered by local ATV trail riders.*

9. *Can earn nursing credits from Ball State for dressing a gravel wound.*

8. *Professors encourage students to ditch class and go mountain biking at Prairie Creek.*

7. *Can earn cartography credits from Ball State for attempting to map every trail at Prairie Creek.*

6. *Delapidated root cellar at the northeast section of the trail system doubles as a walk-in beer cooler.*

5. *Munsee Clan based tribal hierarchy on annual Prairie Creek mountain bike race.*

4. *Great testing grounds for off-road equipment bought with textbook money.*

3. *Charlie Cardinal unwinds here after big games.*

2. *Dodging pesky motorcycles increases agility.*

1. *Frank Ball rode to Prairie Creek's highest point and proclaimed, "This is where I will rebuild my family's business!"*

# Town Run Trail Park

## Ride Summary

Even with losing its premier northern trails (gaze affectionately at the glistening strip mall), Town Run Trail Park still offers Indy cyclists the best singletrack in town. The remainder of the trail has been adopted as a city park and is now protected from development. The trail harbors some twisting singletrack found south of the bridge on White River's west bank. The trail offers few breaks, insistently winding through the wooded bottomland. The most exciting feature is the roller coaster. Trail builders laced the path over a forgotten levee to create a singletrack joy ride. Like the Beast at King's Island, this section is worth riding again and again.

## Ride Specs

**Start:** West Bank of the 96th Street Bridge
**Length:** 8-mile system
**Approximate Riding Time:** Rider's discretion
**Technical Difficulty:** Moderate due to flat but challenging singletrack
**Trail Type:** Singletrack
**Terrain:** Flat trail follows threads through White River corridor
**Land Status:** City park
**Nearest Town:** Indianapolis
**Other Trail Users:** Hikers, joggers

## Getting There

**From the northeast side of Indianapolis:** Take Allisonville Road north from I-465 1.2 miles to 96th Street. Turn left on 96th Street and drive across the White River bridge. Turn left into Town Run Trail Park's parking area. *DeLorme: Indiana Atlas & Gazetteer:* Page 39, F-9

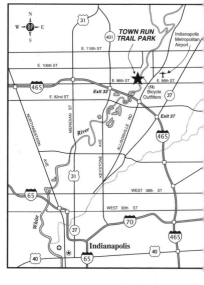

J ohn Matthews, owner of Bicycle Outfitters, had some insight when he opened his bike shop at 96th Street Station Shopping Center. From the parking lot of his store, customers can ride across the bridge and to the best legal trail system in the city of Indianapolis. If cyclists are interested in an introduction to the Town Run Trail Park loop or simply looking to ride with other cyclists, group rides leave the shop every Sunday at 5:30 P.M., daylight providing. Extending his version of Hoosier hospitality, John even has an air hose just inside his bike shop so cyclists can top off tires before heading out.

In recent years, cyclists scored a bittersweet victory in the land-use battle over these trails. Cyclists have watched as these trails were cut in half. The population growth around Fishers and Castleton has been such that seemingly every acre of land has been developed.

When this section of 96th Street was simply a dead end dirt road behind the shops at 96th Street Station, mountain bikers enjoyed the prosperity of this forgotten property. These were the best trails in Indianapolis with enough singletrack to provide fat-tire enthusiasts hours of cycling. The majority of the trails were flat with the most challenging section being the solitary hill occupied by an old cemetery and covered with trees. Here were a number of descents and climbs to raise heart rates and adrenaline levels. At the top of one such pitch, a bench was constructed to rest weary legs and watch other cyclists tackle challenging, root-strewn climb.

But as the Onceler, the faceless philosopher of Dr. Seuss' "The Lorax" fame so duly noted, "Progress is progress, and progress must grow." The quiet dirt road was transformed into a four-lane road and bridge spanning the White River. Forgotten property soon became prime waterfront, and cyclists cried behind their Oakleys as they lost their own "truffula-tree" covered paradise.

One of the proposals was to build a city park for the town of Fishers. Mountain bikers were the largest recreational group attending the Fishers town meeting. But sadly, even if the land had been developed into a park, a feeble ¼-mile trail was the only bone to be thrown to off-road riders.

As outdoor enthusiasts clamored for a voice in the park's development, the entire game changed. Big business stepped in, and suddenly instead of a park, the once-quiet land is now graced with another strip mall. Just as Indy mountain bikers were pushed off the trails of Ft. Benjamin Harrison, they had lost another battle and another great set of trails.

But all was not lost. Three private owners of the land south of the 96th Street bridge—Martin Marietta Aggregates, R.N. Thompson & Associates, and Oliver Daugherty—donated their land to Indy Parks for the creation of a mountain bike park. Thanks to their generosity, mountain bikers now have 126 acres of legal mountain bike trails. There are also plans to extend the corridor north of the bridge. And if all goes well, other city parks are considering allowing the activity on their property.

To ensure responsible land management policies, which include mountain biking, cyclists should enlist their efforts to keep these trails open. There are a number of national and statewide lobbying groups working hard to maintain a positive light on mountain biking. They work to construct rails to trails, open public lands to mountain biking, volunteer for trail maintenance projects, and lobby state and city legislators. (*Check out the Trail Clubs and Organizations list in the Appendix, which lists both local and national bike and trail organizations involved in trail maintenance and legislation. Get involved on a local or national level or both.*)

## Ride Information

### ● Trail Contact:
Bicycle Outfitters, Indianapolis, IN 46250, (317) 842-BIKE (2453)

### ● Schedule:
Open daily, year-round

### ● Fees/Permits:
Not yet determined

### ● Local Information:
Indianapolis Convention & Visitors Association, Indianapolis, IN (317) 639-4282 or www.indy.org

### ● Local Events/Attractions:
Castleton Square Mall (317) 849-9993

### ● Accommodations:
Courtyard By Marriott (317) 576-9559 • Sheraton Indianapolis North Hotel (317) 846-2700

### ● Restaurants:
D'Amicos Bagels (317) 845-4434 • 96th Street Sports Bar and Grill (317) 594-9696

### ● Group Rides:
Sundays at 5:30 P.M., daylight providing

### ● Organizations:
Indiana Bicycle Coalition, Indianapolis, IN 1-800-BIKE-110, (317) 327-8356

### ● Local Bike Shop:
Bicycle Outfitters, Indianapolis, IN (317) 842-BIKE (2453)

### ● Maps:
USGS map: Fishers, IN

The singletrack, which laces through the park is predominantly flat and winds its way through the cull trees along the flood plain. Riding these trails will no doubt increase bike-handling skills. The trails continue past Interstate 465 and leads to another field of trails just beyond the interstate.

One particularly pleasing section along this riverside ride is the roller coaster. This portion really takes advantage of the abandoned farmer's levee. If ridden correctly, the speed of the descents will carry cyclists up the steep pitches on the other side. Like King's Islands wood coaster, the Beast, this section is worth riding again and again. Unlike the Beast, however, this coaster allows two-way traffic. So, thrill-seekers be forewarned.

After the ride, cyclists may be faced with a difficult decision—deciding whether to enjoy a cold brew at the 96th Street Sports Bar and Grill or grab a chicken salad bagel sandwich at D'Amicos Bagels. Choosing between the two can be as difficult as racing for the lead on narrow singletrack.

Post-ride disputes aside, this trail system provides Indianapolis cyclists a challenging ride without a lengthy commute. During the week, area cyclists can easily drive to the trailhead, ride a couple of loops, grab a beer or bagel, and be home by eight o'clock.

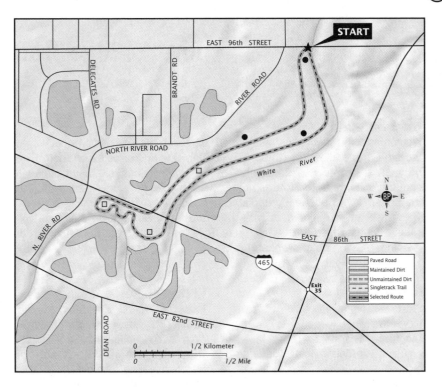

# River's Edge Trail

## Ride Summary

Welcome to introductory singletrack 101. The trails are basic enough that Bicycle Garage allows customers to actually test-ride bicycles on them. The rudimentary route has no climbs and is a great location to introduce a spouse, child, or friend to trail riding. The chances of crashing are slim, but the possibility of becoming addicted to the euphoria of trail riding is great. There are few straight sections; therefore improvements in bike-handling skills will be noticed after a few rides. River's Edge is great for a lunchtime, evening, or even quick weekend ride.

## Ride Specs

**Start:** Parking lot on the east side of Bicycle Garage
**Length:** 8-mile system
**Approximate Riding Time:** Rider's discretion
**Difficulty Rating:** Easy to moderate due to no hills and mild singletrack
**Trail Surface:** Singletrack
**Lay of the Land:** Flat, river bottomland
**Nearest Town:** Indianapolis
**Other Trail Users:** Hikers and joggers

## Getting There

**From I-465 and Keystone Avenue (Exit 33):** Go south on Keystone Avenue 0.6 miles to 82nd Street. Travel east on 82nd Street approximately one mile to the River's Edge Shopping Center. Turn left into the parking lot and park at the east end of the shopping center next to the Bicycle Garage of Indianapolis (bike store). *DeLorme: Indiana Atlas & Gazetteer: Page 39, F-8*

I ndianapolis is in a dilemma when it comes to mountain biking. It holds the highest number of mountain bikers in the state, yet holds the least number of legal trail systems. Granted, Indianapolis is topographically challenged, but there are a few geological wrinkles on the northeast side of town that provide good terrain for mountain bikes. The challenge, however, is in getting the approval needed to open some of these public and private lands to mountain biking. And this burden can be attributed, in great part, to cyclists themselves.

The trails of Fort Benjamin Harrison are a prime example of a trail system closed down because of cyclists' disregard for the property on which they rode. Officials have documented separate incidents in which cyclists washed their muddy bikes in the fort's showers and taunted troops during military maneuvers.

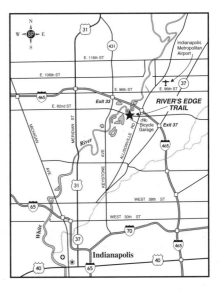

Now that the Fort has been transformed into a state park, there is talk that mountain biking may be allowed once again. This news, combined with the emergence of a higher level of responsibility among cyclists, increases the chance that these trails will be reopened to mountain biking in the future. One reason for the increasingly responsible cyclist is the recently acquired political power gained through representation in the Indiana Bicycle Coalition. Political force coupled with the fashionable insurgence of low-impact riding will hopefully lead to more land opening up to off-road cyclists in the future.

In the meantime, local cyclists must be content to ride such places as the River's Edge trails. Located behind the River's Edge Shopping Center, these trails serve more as a mountain bike test-ride for customers and employees at the Bicycle Garage than a long ride in the national forest. In

Marshall "Major" Taylor was born in Indianapolis in 1878 and went on to become the city's most fabled bicyclist. Taylor earned his nickname as a child when he performed bicycle tricks while donning a military uniform. The black sprinter became the first African-American to win the world championships in 1899. Marshall also won the American sprint championships in 1899 and 1900 all while overcoming racism from both the general public and his fellow competitors.

fact, the owners of the Bicycle Garage helped design this trail system and host rides here every Wednesday at 5:30 P.M. Please call in advance for more details.

There are a few miles of single-track that wind behind the store and lead up to Riverbend Apartments, located on the north side of I-465. Enthusiastic cyclists can take Allisonville to 96th Street and ride the trails up there as well.

For beginners, this is a non-threatening loop where cyclists can get their feet wet with some basic singletrack. There are no substantial climbs, but very few straight sections. Thus, bike-handling skills can be improved as cyclists pedal through this short course. There is also a jogging path edging Lake Allisonville that has been incorporated into the trail system, offering a break from the singletrack.

For cyclists working on the northeast side of town, this trail system serves as a perfect lunchtime or evening workout loop. Carve the trails for 45 minutes, then grab some food from one of the many area eateries.

On the north side of I-465, cyclists will come across a number of fitness stations. Fitness fanatics can dismount their bicycles and perform the recommended fitness activities if the trails don't provide enough stimulation.

For a more difficult ride, some challenging obstacles are found on the trail directly behind the Bicycle Garage. There are two ditches that offer short steep drops which bottom out and are immediately followed with a short climb. Test your skills while attempting to ride over a downed tree, and finish this technical section with a short climb up to the parking lot. This section can either be avoided or sought out, depending on the level of difficulty for which you are looking.

Overall, the trail is tight, winding, and surrounded by tall weeds. There is two-way traffic throughout, and accidents can be avoided by simply keeping your speed in check.

## Ride Information

**Trail Contact:**
Bicycle Garage of Indianapolis, Indianapolis, IN (317) 842-4140

**Schedule:**
Open daily, year-round

**Fees/Permits:**
None

**Local Information:**
Indianapolis Convention & Visitors Association, Indianapolis, IN (317) 639-4282 or www.indy.org

**Local Events/Attractions:**
Castleton Square Mall (317) 849-9993
• Borders Books, Music, and Café (317) 574-1775

**Accommodations:**
Courtyard By Marriott (317) 576-9559
• Sheraton Indianapolis North Hotel (317) 846-2700

**Restaurants:**
Uno Pizzeria (317) 594-4865

**Group Rides:**
Bicycle Garage of Indianapolis, Indianapolis, IN (317) 842-4140—rides hosted every Wednesday at 5:30 P.M.

**Local Bike Shop:**
Bicycle Garage of Indianapolis, Indianapolis, IN (317) 842-4140

**Maps:**
USGS map: Fishers, IN

The author, looking smug atop this bale of hay.

## **Miles**Directions

*This trail system has many criss-crossing trails. Cyclists may attempt this route or simply explore as they go.*

**0.0 START** at the Bicycle Garage of Indianapolis. There are two trailheads. One is directly behind the Bicycle Garage and the other is located at the far east end of the parking lot. Take the trailhead at the far east end.

**0.31** The trail splits. Take the right split.

**0.45** Pass a trail on the right. Stay on the main trail to the left.

**0.5** Arrive at a multi-trail intersection. Take the main trail straight through this intersection.

**0.55** The main trail bears to the right.

**0.6** The main trail intersects with a larger trail. Turn left. Lake Allisonville and I-465 now in view. Pass a bridge on the right and continue straight on the main trail.

**0.7** Pass under I-465. Continue straight on the trail.

**0.75** The trail splits. Take the main trail to the right.

**0.8** A small trail splits off to the right. Stay on the main trail to the left. Pass many small trails on the left and right. But continue on the main trail.

**1.2** The trail splits. Take the left split. The right split leads to the tennis courts of Riverbend Apartments.

**1.3** The trail splits. Take the right split. Travel 0.3 miles and soon thereafter take a 180-degree turn. The trail passes many small trails and splits, but the main trail is easy to identify. Take the main trail back under I-465.

**2.0** The trail splits just as it passes the wooden bridge. Take the left split around the lake. The right trail leads back to the Bicycle Garage.

**2.4** The trail splits. Take the left split following the perimeter of Lake Allisonville.

**2.5** Cross a wooden bridge. The trail becomes a paved path.

**2.8** The trail intersects with a corporate park road. Turn left on the corporate park road.

**2.82** Look for the "Fitness Trail" sign on the right. Take a right onto the Fitness Trail.

**3.0** The jogging path splits. Take the left split. Now paralleling I-465.

**3.5** Cross a wooden bridge and arrive at a trail intersection. Turn left then an immediate right onto the singletrack path. Pass many small intersections and splits, but stay on the main trail.

**3.9** The trail splits. Take the right split. Now approaching the challenging section of the loop.

**4.1** Cross a ditch and arrive at a trail intersection. Take the main trail to the right.

**4.15** The trail splits. Take the right split and climb a hill to return to the parking lot of the Bicycle Garage.

**4.2** Ride complete.

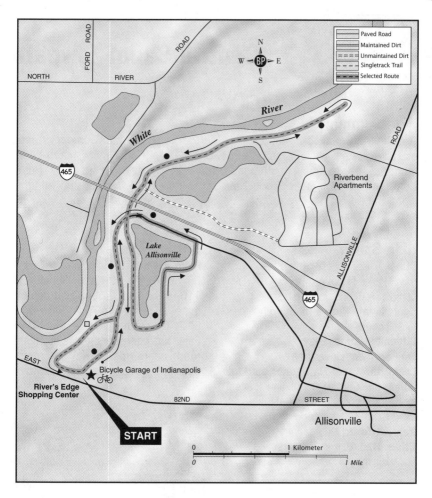

Legend:
- Paved Road
- Maintained Dirt
- Unmaintained Dirt
- Singletrack Trail
- Selected Route

N
W — BP — E
S

FORD ROAD

ROAD

NORTH          RIVER

White          River

465

Riverbend
Apartments

Lake
Allisonville

ALLISONVILLE

ROAD

465

EAST

Bicycle Garage of Indianapolis

River's Edge
Shopping Center

82ND                STREET

Allisonville

START

0                1 Kilometer
0                              1 Mile

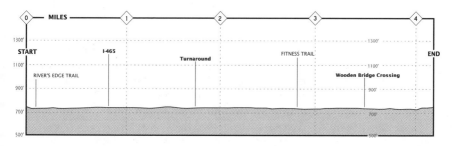

MILES
0        1        2        3        4

START                                                              END

1300'                                          1300'
I-465
RIVER'S EDGE TRAIL          Turnaround          FITNESS TRAIL
1100'                                          1100'
                                   Wooden Bridge Crossing
900'                                            900'

700'                                            700'
500'                                            500'

87

# Central Canal Towpath

## Ride Summary

The Central Canal Towpath, formerly the Indianapolis Water Company Canal, starts at Heslar Naval Armory and cuts a flat path past many notable Indy tourist sights. The gravel path passes the Indianapolis Museum of Art, Butler University, and ends at Broad Ripple's Monon Trail. Cyclists can hammer along the trail or make a day of it, stopping to do some sightseeing.

## Ride Specs

**Start:** Trailhead off 30th Street, just past Heslar Naval Armory
**Length:** 5.6-mile point-to-point
**Approximate Riding Time:** 45 minutes to 1½ hours
**Difficulty Rating:** Easy
**Trail Surface:** Linear trail
**Lay of the Land:** Flat, gravel path following the Central Canal and leading past many notable tourist sights
**Land Status:** City park
**Nearest Town:** Indianapolis
**Other Trail Users:** Joggers, walkers, and anglers

## Getting There

**From downtown Indianapolis:** Take I-65 north to 29th/30th Street (Exit 116). Take West 30th Street approximately 1.5 miles to White River Drive East. Go north on White River Drive East and park along the side of the road near Heslar Naval Armory.
***DeLorme: Indiana Atlas & Gazetteer:*** Page 39, H-7

Cruising along the towpath.

Transportation in Indiana's early days was difficult at best. Not yet established as the crossroads of America, Indiana had only the National Road (the road to the West) crossing through to connect it with the rest of the Union.

During this era of river transportation, dignified riverboat pilots like Mark Twain steered majestic steamboats through the state's major rivers. Riverboats paddling along the Ohio and Wabash Rivers brought commerce to sleepy river towns and turned them into glitzy social centers.

Therefore, local legislators believed digging canals, which would host slow-moving, horse-drawn barges, would connect Indiana with these river towns and the rest of the country.

In fact, the Central Canal, constructed in Indianapolis, was originally designed to be a connector route to the Wabash and Erie Canals. The goal was to link Indiana with New York City and New Orleans. If connected to these major commerce centers, Hoosiers could trade goods and cutting edge ideas, and, more importantly, become a contributing factor in the country's industrial rise.

Unfortunately, only nine miles were completed before the project was abandoned. The completion of the canal depended on revenues generated from canal commerce. The lack of revenue, political fraud and embezzlement, and the emergence of railroads killed the fanfare surrounding this grand project.

Other than a grand ceremonial voyage back in 1837, the Central Canal has seen little boat traffic. It has seen its share of recreational traffic, though. Years ago, members of the now defunct Wheelway League pedaled along the towpath while young lovers paddled their canoes through the slow-moving water.

For a period of time, the Central Canal was called the Indianapolis Water Company Canal. As the canal's ownership has changed, so have the challenges of today's cyclists. One such challenge is finding a parking space.

The best chances for parking is at the Heslar Naval Armory at the southern end of the maintained canal trail. There is less traffic and plenty of free parking, and no time is lost searching for limited, costly parking at the other end of the path in Broad Ripple.

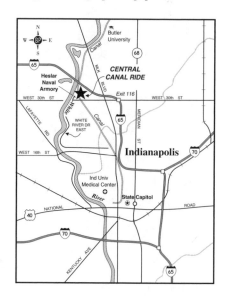

Once on the trail, cyclists will pass many notable sites, including the canal itself. How ironic it is that this botched canal project is one of the longest stretches of canal left in the state. Even the mighty Erie Canal, which we sung about as children, has been reduced to mere traces and empty indentions.

Near the trailhead, Marian College and the Major Taylor Velodrome are just a stone's throw away. Marian is noteworthy for cyclists in that it is one of only two colleges in the country to offer bicycle racing scholarships.

A distinct advantage for the Marian team is having the Major Taylor Velodrome right across the street. This homecourt advantage has raised Marian to one of the country's top bike racing schools, including having the distinction of being the four-time National Track Champions.

As the trail crosses under 38th Street, cyclists have a decision to make: continue along the trail, visit the Indianapolis Museum of Art, or visit James Whitcomb Riley's gravesite at Crown Hill Cemetery. While the museum is just on the other side of the canal, Crown Hill Cemetery is a little farther east on 38th Street, past Michigan Avenue. If you have the time, take in a little culture, or bask in the spectacular view of the city from Riley's hilltop gravesite at the county's highest point. Tradition also warrants that you leave a few pennies on the grave.

## Ride Information

### 🕻 Trail Contact:
Indy Parks and Recreation (Greenways) (317) 327-7431

### 🕐 Schedule:
Open daily, year-round

### 🕐 Fees/Permits:
None

### ❓ Local Information:
Indianapolis Convention & Visitors Association, Indianapolis, IN (317) 639-4282 or www.indy.org

### 💡 Local Events/Attractions:
Crown Hill Cemetery (tours) (317) 920-2726 • Indianapolis Museum of Art; (317) 920-2660 • Major Taylor Velodrome (317) 327-8356

### 🍴 Accommodations:
Residence Inn By Marriott (downtown, but on the canal) (317) 822-0840

### 🍴 Restaurants:
Bazbeaux Pizza (317) 255-5711 • C.T. Peppers (317) 257-6277

### 👥 Organizations:
Indy Parks and Recreation (Greenways) (317) 327-7431

### 📖 Other Resources:
*Indiana: A New Historical Guide,* Taylor/Stevens/Ponder/Brockman

### 🚲 Local Bike Shops:
Bike Line (317) 253-6211 • Bicycle Garage (317) 253-7433

### 🗺 Maps:
USGS map: Indianapolis, IN

## Pennies for the Poet

The tradition of leaving one-cent donations on James Whitcomb Riley's gravesite dates back to when the grave was first built in 1916. The original purpose of the money was to finance the Romanesque-looking monument. Today the money is collected and donated to Riley Children's Hospital. Another interesting fact about Riley's gravesite is this prime resting spot was awarded to the poet and not the politician. Away from the hill in a less favorable site in Crown Hill, the late Hoosier president, Benjamin Harrison, also rests. It just goes to show, politicians don't get all of the best perks—in life or death.

## **Miles**Directions

**0.0 START** at the Heslar Naval Armory. Leave your parking space and ride to the intersection of White River Drive East and West 30th Street. Turn left and travel east on WEST 30th Street.

**0.2** Turn left before crossing the canal onto the Central Canal Towpath, marked by a blue gate.

**0.8** Pass under I-65.

**1.2** Pass under East 38th Street.

**1.5** Pass the Indiana Museum of Art on the opposite side of the canal. During the summer you may often find jazz concerts on the back steps of the museum.

**1.52** Pass a trail on the left. There is a loop back there, but mountain biking is prohibited.

**1.7** Pass another trail to the left that leads to the trail loop. Continue straight.

**1.8** Take wooden bridge under Michigan Avenue. On the east side of Michigan Avenue, both the canal and the White River are in full view.

**2.4** Pass a trail on the left. This is another trail that runs parallel to the canal.

**2.6** Pass a bridge on the right. Cyclists can take this bridge to Butler University.

**2.9** Pass another bridge on the right. Cyclists can take this bridge into Butler University. Possible stops include Hinkle Fieldhouse or Holcomb Observatory.

**3.1** The Canal Towpath crosses 52nd Street. Continue straight. There is a sign here dedicated to the runners who helped raise money for the homeless.

*"For generations, The Indianapolis Water Company Canal has hosted thousands of runners, walkers, and bikers along its picturesque banks. Each year, hundreds of runners participate in the annual Turkey Trot run and help feed and clothe the homeless. This plaque is dedicated to those generous runners who have given, so others may have."*

**3.2** The Canal Towpath crosses 53rd Street. Continue straight. Roll past the "Do Not Enter" sign. You are now on a paved, one-way street. This is an access road for the homes that face the canal. Beware of cars in this section.

**3.4** Pass 54th Street on the left. Continue straight.

**3.4** Pavement ends as the Canal Towpath passes Ripple Street.

**3.7** Pass a singletrack trail to the left. This leads to private property. Stay on the main path.

**3.8** Pass a singletrack trail to the left. This leads to private property. Stay on the main path.

**3.9** On the opposite side of the canal is the Butler-Tarkington area. This intersection is not far from the Atlas Supermarket where David Letterman worked as a teenager.

**4.0** The trail crosses Illinois Street. Continue straight. Now on singletrack. This is a deviation from the official trail. Use the official, gravel path on opposite bank when singletrack is muddy.

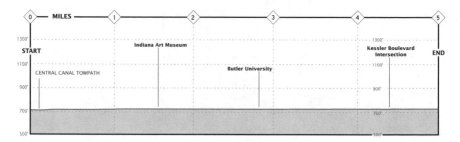

## **Miles**Directions *continued*

**4.3** The trail crosses Meridian Street. Continue straight.

**4.5** The trail crosses Kessler Boulevard. Continue straight.

**5.0** Singletrack trail crosses Central Avenue. Continue straight. This is where the canal's largest gaggle of geese and flock of ducks reside. If you happen to have a spare loaf of bread in the back pocket of your jersey, consider stopping to feed the waterfowl.

**5.2** The trail cuts through the CVS Pharmacy parking lot at the intersection of 63rd Street and College Avenue. Take

63rd Street across College Avenue. 63rd Street becomes Laverock Road.

**5.4** Laverock Road ends at the sidewalk. Continue straight on the sidewalk.

**5.6** The sidewalk crosses Guilford Avenue. Continue straight on the sidewalk.

**5.65** Central Canal Towpath intersects with the Monon Trail. But the ride doesn't have to end here. The Village of Broad Ripple has many eccentric shops and wonderful eateries. Another choice is riding along the Monon Trail, Indy's most popular rail trail. It's a great trail— albeit a paved one.

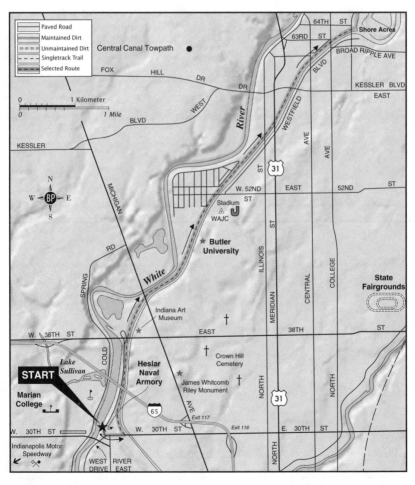

# Southern

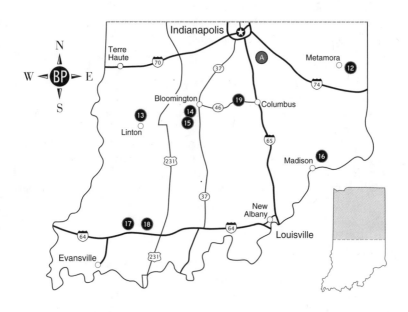

N
W BP E
S

Indianapolis ★

Terre
Haute ○ 70

A

Metamora
○ 12

37

74

Bloomington ○ 14 46 19 Columbus
15

13
Linton ○

231

65

Madison 16
○

37

New
Albany

17 18 64

64 Louisville

Evansville ○

231

Indiana

# Southern Indiana

Southern Indiana has all the necessary elements needed to play host to mountain bikers. The area is blessed with miles of rolling woodlands and challenging terrain. The striking beauty of this region has even earned one county the nickname of "The Little Smokies."

Spice that geographical mixture with a few open-minded landowners, some politically savvy cycling advocates, and tons of off-road enthusiasts and you have a recipe that has helped the sport boom in the Hoosier southlands.

The model for private landowners embracing the sport of mountain biking has a name as unique as its mission—Gnaw Bone. Fred and Alice Lorenz became pioneers when they started allowing fat-tires to tread across their privately owned trails. Seeing that mountain bikers can be a responsible, revenue-generating bunch helped spur the movement to open trails within Hoosier National Forest, convert city property into mountain-bike playgrounds, and turn abandoned rail corridors into popular biking and hiking trails.

Southern Indiana also hosts the first town park dedicated solely to mountain biking. Bloomington's Wapehani Mountain Bike Park serves as a blueprint for cyclists working with city officials to convert abandoned property into off-road bicycling playgrounds. The challenging singletrack at Wapehani has hosted many DINO (Do Indiana Off Road) races and affords Bloomington cyclists the luxury of a trail system within city limits.

The cities of Linton and Shelbyville followed Bloomington's lead and opened Linton Conservation Club and Roger Shaw Memorial Park, respectively. Both parks had long been neglected before local cyclists seized the opportunity to make something more of the land. By working with city officials and overseeing the cleanup of the park and cutting of trails, cyclists have given their hometowns a wonderful gift of off-road opportunities.

Rails-to-trails advocates also have two trails to brag about. Clear Creek and the Whitewater Canal Trail are both scenic, flat-lander favorites. The straight and easy paths allow cyclists to spend less time shifting and grinding and more time for gazing at the flora and fauna of the surrounding countryside.

Near the town of Madison, lands ideally suited for mountain biking—Clifty Falls State Park and the Jefferson Proving Ground—have yet to open their trails to mountain biking. Instead of whining about their loses, area cyclists have taken to the county roads. These dirt- and gravel-road routes harbor some of the longest climbs listed in the state. Never mind that some of these sections are paved. The scenery, steep climbs, and screaming descents make Madison's County Roads a "must ride" while visiting this historic river town.

Whether cyclists are looking for flatlands or flat-out screaming descents, weekday "get-me-by" rides or weekend getaways, rides that traverse reclaimed strip mines, or the pristine forests of Brown County, the trails of southern Indiana await.

# Whitewater Canal Trail

## Ride Summary

This rail-trail is as much a tourist destination as a mountain bike ride. The flat trail begins at historic Metamora, past the grist mill, then follows the Whitewater Canal east. This easy-grade path provides a nice way to work off a fried chicken dinner from the Hearthstone or the homemade fudge from one of the local fudge shops. Hopefully, in the near future, this trail will double in length and give cyclists twice the reason to come here for a ride.

## Ride Specs

**Start:** Free parking area east of Duck Creek Aqueduct
**Length:** 4.2-mile point-to-point of proposed 8-mile trail
**Approximate Riding Time:** 30 minutes
**Difficulty Rating:** Easy
**Trail Surface:** Rail-trail
**Lay of the Land:** Flat, grass and dirt rail trail follows the Whitewater Canal
**Land Status:** Rail trail corridor
**Nearest Town:** Metamora
**Other Trail Users:** Hikers

## Getting There

**From Brookville:** Take U.S. 52 west approximately nine miles to Metamora and **Pennington Road.** Turn left on Pennington Road and drive one mile to the free parking lot east of Duck Creek Aqueduct. Pass the shops and Duck Creek Aqueduct before coming to the parking area.
**From Indianapolis:** Follow U.S. 52 east all the way to Metamora. Follow directions from Metamora below.
**From downtown Metamora:** Simply follow Pennington Road east through town until it ends at the trailhead.
*DeLorme: Indiana Atlas & Gazetteer:* Page 47, F-8

When young Balser, from Charles Major's *Bears of Blue River*, traipsed around Shelbyville and picked up those notorious bear cubs, chances are he walked along the Whitewater Canal Trail near Brookville. As he trekked across the eastern portion of the state, he would surely have passed through Metamora. Mrs. John Matson gave Metamora its name based on an Indian princess from a popular New York City play. Metamora was plotted in 1838 with the canal cutting right through the middle of town. This center-line artery contributed to the life, death, and eventual rebirth of the town.

The original glory days were short lived during the river-travel boom that swept the Midwest. After 20 years, river travel was replaced by railroads, and many booming river and canal towns busted. And though a railroad was built directly next to the canal, Metamora still faded into obscurity. Passenger trains eventually stopped traveling along the line, and Interstate 74 became the main thoroughfare connecting Indianapolis to Cincinnati, bypassing Metamora altogether.

In the 1940s, new life arrived in the form of local and state funds. They were used to restore the town's aging buildings. Twenty years later, craftsmen, boutique owners, and antique dealers settled here and transformed the area into a tourist attraction similar to that of Nashville, Indiana. They began selling their wares and created a blossoming economy of crafts, antiques, handmade gifts, and homemade fudge, with the Metamora Grist and Roller Mill as the town's keystone.

Cincinnati—only 52 short miles away!

This functioning mill was built in 1845 and rebuilt in 1900. Distinguished by its large waterwheel, the mill still uses the canal's water power to pummel the grain. Visitors can purchase a bag of corn meal and admire the tools of a bygone grain-grinding era.

Another attraction is the 14-ton Ben Franklin barge. Visitors can take a half-hour slow-moving boat tour through the area. Don't forget to thank the "horse power" (draft horses Rex and Tony) that pulled you along on your tour.

On the way to the trailhead, you will pass the Duck Creek Aqueduct. A wooden shed covers this 60-foot, water-filled bridge. Featured in *Ripley's: Believe it or Not*, it is believed to be the only covered bridge aqueduct in existence.

Like many rails-to-trails projects across the state, the Whitewater Canal Trail is just in its infant stage. Only two miles of the trail have been cut, and it should be classified as not yet ready for prime time. The trail is wide and grassy and doesn't see much traffic.

Since the path is wide and flat, cyclists can focus more on the area's surroundings and less on pedaling. In the fall, the colors surrounding Metamora along the rolling hills fill the eyes with wonder. This full-color foliage show has few rivals in the state. In the hues of the dropping leaves, hiding far from the noise of the tourists, cyclists may also spot the elusive great blue heron.

Just past the end of the railroad line, the canal becomes more of a creek. In this back section of the route, hidden in the high brush near the canal's edge, a blue heron has made a home.

The proposed trail will eventually connect Metamora with Brookville and has the potential of becoming one of the most scenic rail-conversion projects in the state. But judging by the sturdy construction of the gate at the trail's end, it appears it will be some time before the remainder of the trail is opened. If you would like to help to open the rest of this trail, or help out with other rails-to-trails projects around the state, contact the Hoosier Rails-to-Trails Council.

Metamora's historic grist mill.

As it stands now, the trail provides a great opportunity to burn off the calories of a delicious fried chicken dinner with all the trimmings from the Hearthstone as well as the delicacies from the homemade fudge shops. In fact, by using U.S. 52, a loop can be made from the restaurant, to the trail, and then back again to the homemade fudge shop—a perfect ride!

## Ride Information

**❶ Trail Contact:**
Hoosier Rails-to-Trails Council, Indianapolis, IN (317) 237-9348 • Rails-to-Trails Conservancy, Washington, DC (202) 797-5400 • Indiana Department of Natural Resources (317) 232-4070

**🕐 Schedule:**
Open daily, year-round

**❸ Fees/Permits:**
None

**❓ Local Information:**
The official Metamora website; www.metamora.com

**❾ Local Events/Attractions:**
Historic Metamora, grist mill, fudge, antique, and knick-knack shops • Canal Days—First full weekend in October

**🍴 Accommodations:**
Macyln Campground, Metamora, IN (765) 647-2541 • Hop On Inn, Metamora, IN (812) 933-0052

**🍴 Restaurants:**
Hearthstone Restaurant, Metamora, IN (765) 647-5204

**👥 Organizations:**
Indiana Department of Natural Resources, Indianapolis, IN (317) 232-4070

**👥 Other Resources:**
*Indiana: A New Historical Guide,* Taylor/Stevens/Ponder/Brockman

**🚲 Local Bike Shop:**
Bike Shop, Connersville, IN (765) 825-8458

**Ⓝ Maps:**
USGS maps: Metamora, IN Brookville, IN

## **Miles**Directions

**0.0 START** at the free parking area east of Duck Creek Aqueduct. Leave the parking lot and turn right on Pennington Road.

**0.05** Pennington Road turns to gravel. Continue straight.

**0.1** Pass a big red barn and the "Whitewater Canal Trail" sign. Continue straight, being careful to avoid the electric fence on your right. Now on a wide, grassy canal towpath.

*The Duck Creek Aqueduct is listed in* Ripley's Believe It Or Not *as the only covered bridge aqueduct in existence.*

**0.5** The canal towpath switches to gravel and cuts between two fences. Whitewater Canal crosses a driveway and changes back to a grassy canal towpath.

**1.2** Cross a gravel driveway leading to the Moster Turf Farm. Continue straight on the towpath.

**1.6** Pass the end of the train tracks. Great blue herons nest near this section of the canal.

**2.1** Come to the "Trail Closed" sign. The Whitewater Canal Trail ends here. The remainder of the trail is currently under development. Return to Metamora from which you came.

**4.2** Arrive back in Metamora for some homemade fudge.

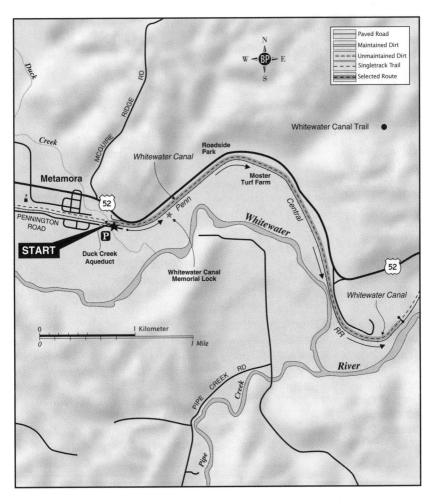

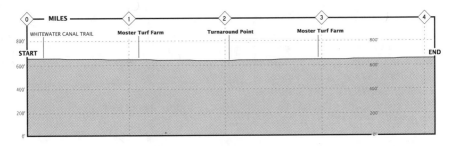

# 13

# Linton Conservation Club

## Ride Summary

Quite a lot of action is packed into the four-mile system at Linton. Technical skills can only be enhanced after a few trips to this reclaimed strip pit. The trails resemble more of an enduro course than a mountain bike trail. An example of the resemblance can be found in the thrilling section called the "roller coaster." This stretch rolls over a series of small spines and short pitches. The momentum of each descent will carry cyclists up each subsequent climb.

## Ride Specs

**Start**: Conservation Club parking lot
**Length:** 1.9-mile loop, part of a 4-mile system
**Approximate Riding Time:** 30 minutes
**Difficulty Rating:** Moderate
**Trail Surface:** Singletrack and dirt roads
**Lay of the Land:** Trail twists, climbs, and descends numerous pitches over remnants of the reclaimed strip mine
**Land Status:** City park
**Nearest Town:** Linton
**Other Trail Users:** Hikers and anglers

## Getting There

**From Bloomington:** Take IN 45 south approximately 14 miles to IN 445. Take IN 445 west four miles to IN 54. Take IN 54 west approximately 24 miles into Linton. Pass the McDonald's and take the next right at the "Sunset Park: Camping and Diving" sign (CR 1100 West). Take CR 1100 West 0.7 miles to the Linton Conservation Club. Turn right into the Conservation Club and park in front of the main building. *DeLorme: Indiana Atlas & Gazetteer:* Page 49, D-8

**B**efore this town became the city of Linton, it was known as the village of Jerusalem. In 1835, a post office was established and the village honored General Linton of Terre Haute by adopting his name.

In 1865 the town's population stood at a mere 200. By the turn of the century, the town had become a coal city and the population grew to 3,100. And during the 1930s, Linton boasted of being the population center of the United

States. But as much of the nation moved west, the center of population moved with it and now rests in St. Louis, Missouri.

Being the center of the country's population was not taken lightly by Linton, and that era is commemorated by a stone historical marker situated on the trails of the Linton Conservation Club.

As the population moved, so did the industrial focus of Linton. Like many of the trail systems in the southwestern section of the state, the Conservation Club was once a strip mine. Maumee Collieries operated the mine until 1927. After that, the land stood vacant for 17 years until 1942, when its 600 acres were turned over to the city of Linton.

The city worked to reclaim the land by planting trees and stocking fish in the 27 man-made lakes created by the mining company. But after the initial cleanup, for reasons unknown, the land was neglected and improvement projects abandoned.

In 1993, Jay Gainey read in the local paper that the city council was looking for something to do with this land behind the Conservation Club. Jay then talked with his friend and business partner, Mike Murphy, about the possibility of building a mountain bike park.

In prior years, Jay had searched for places to ride his mountain bike. Though he had jogged on the trails at nearby Shakamak State Park, he believed the park would also be ripe for mountain biking.

## Ride Information

**◐ Trail Contact:**
Jay Gainey, (812) 847-7682

**◐ Schedule:**
Open dawn to dusk, year-round

**◐ Fees/Permits:**
None

**◐ Local Events/Attractions:**
Greene-Sullivan State Forest, Dugger, IN (812) 648-2810

**◐ Accommodations:**
Camping—Sunset Park, Linton, IN (812) 847-8513 • The Park Inn, Linton, IN (812) 847-8631

**◐ Restaurants:**
Pizza City; (812) 847-2207 • Stoll's Country Inn, Linton, IN (219) 847-2477

**◐ Local Bike Shop:**
Bicycle Garage, Bloomington, IN (812) 339-3457

**◐ Maps:**
USGS map: Linton, IN

These newfound lovers of the sport soon discovered what many cyclists had known for some time. Many of the best trails in the state are off-limits. They rode at the park until the rangers kicked them out.

But Jay and Mike didn't give up; they created their own trails instead. In 1993, they presented their plan to the Linton City Council for the Conservation Club's land, which had no trails, was overgrown with weeds, and had become an illegal dumping ground. They offered to clean up the dump, cut some trails, and maintain the area with the stipulation that mountain biking be allowed. The city accepted the proposal and the pair went to work immediately.

They spent a week marking trees with ribbons and eyeballing where future trails would be constructed. Jay sought the help and ideas of Norman Gage, Superintendent of City Parks. He explained to Jay the County Corrections Work Program, in which lawbreakers, sentenced to hours of community service, were available for hire.

After the work dates were coordinated, the project was awarded a sizable workforce. On some days as many as 20 men showed up to cut the trails—many of whom brought their own tools.

They worked through the winter and were able to clear four miles of trails in the first season. And with a $1,000 donation from a kickboxing tournament sponsored by Fitness One and American Karate, trail signs were constructed, bridges were built, and a new marquee was placed at the entrance. Now that they have a better understanding of the work involved, Jay and Mike hope to clear seven more miles of trails. The completion of such a circuit will connect the Conservation Club with Sunset Park to the north. Sunset Park offers camping and has both primitive campsites and sites with electrical hookups. The park also boasts of having one of the clearest lakes in the state, offering scuba diving and snorkeling.

Testimony for the trails has come from city officials, race coordinators, and other cyclists. The mayor even showed his support of the trail effort by attending the park's inaugural DINO race, and past DINO Coordinator Rick Cox called the course one of the top three in the state.

Does your city have an abandoned parcel of land that is suitable for mountain biking? Contact your city council and volunteer to clean up and manage the land or cycling rights. It may take weeks, months, or even years to accomplish, but cities like Linton, Shelbyville, and South Bend have proven that it's worth the effort.

If the first four miles of trails are any indication, the Linton loop is worthy of the praise. The overall topography of the area is flat, with mounds produced from mining activity as the area's only hills. These climbs and descents lack in length but are still technically pleasing. Most of the trails straddle ridges or run along the ravines, but two trails serve as the system's roller coaster. A series of whoop-de-doo's are found at the ride's halfway point on trails 8 and 9. Here the trail dives from ridge to ravine and back to the ridge. Cyclists have little time to recover from each climb, but enough momentum is gained to carry cyclists through the entire up-and-down run.

If your stomach is not too queasy from Trails 8 and 9, Linton has two great eateries—Stoll's Country Inn and Pizza City. Stoll's buffet is guaranteed to ease any bonking pangs, while Pizza City fills the bill for pizza and beer.

Driving away from Linton, cyclists will have a satisfying feeling that can't be fully credited to the area's food. Riding on an old abandoned coal pit, since transformed by two men into a viable trail system, truly takes the cake around here.

## **Miles**Directions

There are many trails criss-crossing this system. Cyclists can forge their own loop or attempt to follow the one below.

**0.0 START** at the Conservation Club Parking Lot. Find the trailhead at the west side of the parking lot on the left side of the trailer. Follow the trail through an open field.

**0.05** The trail splits. Take the left split.

**0.1** Arrive at the Main Trail intersection. There are two signs. Follow the main trail to the left.

**0.2** Arrive at a trail intersection with the "Trail 11" sign straight ahead. Take a 180-degree turn to the right, staying on the Main Trail.

**0.5** The Main Trail intersects with a dirt road. Turn right on the dirt road.

**0.6** Turn left off the dirt road onto the Main Trail. Now at the Historical Marker for the United States Center of Population from 1930-1940.

### **Trail Rules:**

*No motorized vehicles.*
*Trails for hiking and biking only.*
*Hikers have right of way.*
*Bicyclists must stay on trails.*
*Bicyclists must wear helmets.*
*Hikers and bicyclists must use caution and enter at own risk.*

**0.7** The Main Trail intersects with Trail 8. Turn left on Trail 8.

**0.71** Atop the first climb, Trail 8 intersects with Trail 9. Turn right on Trail 9. This is the roller-coaster section of the trails. Instead of straddling the ridges, Trail 9 dives up and down, giving riders enough momentum to roll to the top of the upcoming ridge with little effort.

**0.8** The trail splits. Take the left split.

**0.9** Arrive at a trail intersection and the "Trail 8" sign. Turn left.

**0.95** Trail 8 intersects with the Main Trail. Now back at the same point where you started Trail 8. Turn left on the Main Trail.

**1.0** The Main Trail intersects with a dirt road. Turn left on the dirt road.

**1.05** Follow the "Main Trail" sign and turn right onto singletrack.

**1.08** Arrive at the intersection of Trail 5. Continue straight on Trail 5.

**1.1** Trail 5 splits. Take the right split following the "Trail 5" sign and the stack of four car tires.

**1.3** Trail 5 intersects with the Main Trail. Turn left at the "Main Trail" sign.

**1.4** The Main Trail intersects with a dirt road. Continue straight on the Main Trail.

**1.5** The Main Trail intersects with Trail 4. Follow the Main Trail to the left. Immediately arrive at a trail split. Continue to follow the Main Trail to the *left*.

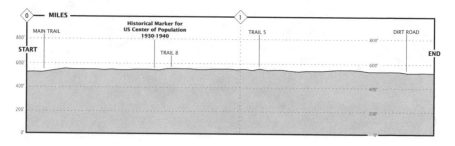

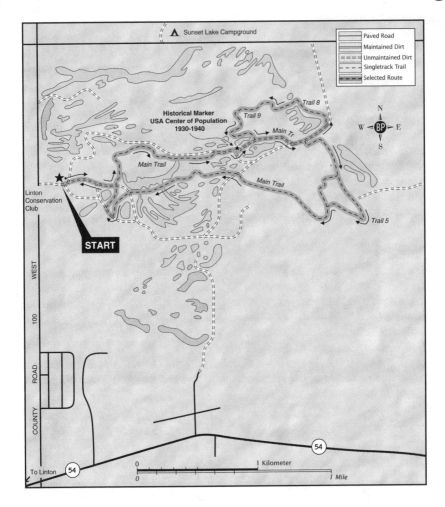

**Miles**Directions *continued*

**1.7** The Main Trail passes Trails 1,2, and 3. Now you're at an intersection with a dirt road. Continue straight on the Main Trail.

**1.8** The Main Trail intersects with a dirt road. Turn right on the dirt road and follow it back to the main parking area or take another lap.

**1.9** Arrive at the Conservation Club Parking Area. Ride complete.

# Wapehani Mountain Bike Park

## Ride Summary

This is the first park in Indiana to be designated solely as a mountain bike park. The property, formerly a Boy Scout camp, harbors many challenging, twisting trails. The park is also a popular stop for the DINO Series, which holds numerous races here. This trail system is great for area cyclists, but not really a destination spot. Unless, of course, you're looking to preview the course before a race.

## Ride Specs

**Start:** Wapehani parking area
**Length:** An estimated 7-mile system
**Approximate Riding Time:** Rider's discretion
**Difficulty Rating:** Moderate
**Trail Surface:** Singletrack
**Lay of the Land:** This singletrack playground makes use of seemingly every cranny of the park's limited acreage
**Land Status:** City park
**Nearest Town:** Bloomington
**Other Trail Users:** Hikers

## Getting There

**From downtown Bloomington:** Take 2nd Street approximately two miles to Wiemer Road. Follow Wiemer Road south 0.7 miles to the entrance of Wapehani Mountain Bike Park. Turn right into the park and drive 0.3 miles to the parking area. *DeLorme: Indiana Atlas & Gazetteer:* Page 50 B-3

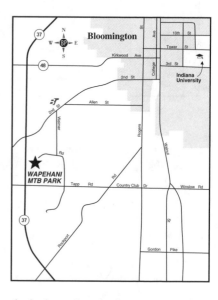

Until 1968, Highway 37 was a narrow winding road that made travel difficult even on a good day. Add some foul weather and a dark night, and the road was downright treacherous. But with Bedford attorney and Highway Commissioner Ruel W. Steele at the helm, that would soon change.

Two decades of traveling along the highway from his hometown to the capital city inspired the commissioner to upgrade the road into a safe, major thoroughfare and connect southern Indiana with Indianapolis.

The state raised funds for the project by placing a two-cent per gallon tax on gasoline, and Highways 37, 31, and 1 were all improved and near completion before Steele's term was complete. He became a hometown hero and received accolades for his political achievement. He was awarded an Indiana University football jersey with the number 37, and years later the highway itself was named after him.

But the widening of the highway brought with it some growing pains. In Bloomington, the widened byway effectively cut Camp Wapehani, a Boy Scout summer camp, in half. Adhering to their motto, the local Boy Scouts were prepared and moved their 30-year-old summer camp to a better location, one farther away from the city with more natural surroundings.

The abandoned Camp Wapehani was given to the city around 1980 and was soon thereafter converted into a mountain bike park, managed by Bloomington Parks and Recreation. Other parks cater to mountain biking, but Wapehani is the only designated mountain bike park in the state.

Some of the cool trails you'll find while here.

Using only the land east of Highway 37, the trails in Wapehani Park are packed tight. Local mountain bikers designed seven miles of trails in this 35-acre park. And while hikers, joggers, and wildlife enthusiasts are welcome, mountain biking holds the reins here.

Bloomington Parks and Recreation requires all cyclists to wear helmets, and also encourages cyclists to register and sign a waiver at local bike shops.

The park's design makes it virtually impossible for cyclists to get lost in this maze of trails that encircles Wapehani Lake. It is possible, though, to get a great workout without having to ride far from your vehicle. On the map from Bloomington Parks & Recreation there looks to be a simple loop, but this is definitely a create-your-own-loop ride. This spider-web system is a plus for Bloomington-area cyclists who want to put in some rugged miles to prepare for the Little 500 (see In Addition on page 116). Few out-of-towners ride this course unless they desire to preview it before the annual DINO mountain bike race (see DINO sidebar).

If you do lose your bearings, use these references: The grassy field is on the north side of the lake and closest to the parking lot; the dam is on the east side of the lake; and the biggest climbs are on the south side of the lake.

## Ride Information

### 🏵 Trail Contact:
**Bloomington Parks and Recreation,** Bloomington, IN (812) 349-3700

### 🕐 Schedule:
Open dawn to dusk, year-round

### 💲 Fees/Permits:
None

### ❓ Local Information:
**Bloomington/Monroe County Convention & Visitors Bureau,** Bloomington, IN 1-800-678-9828 or www.visitbloomington.com

### 🎯 Local Events/Attractions:
**Indiana University** •

### 🛏 Accommodations:
**Best Western,** Bloomington, IN (812) 332-2141 • **College Motor Inn;** (812) 336-6881

### 🍴 Restaurants:
**Burritos as Big As Your Head,** Bloomington, IN (812) 332-5970 • **Hinkles Hamburgers,** Bloomington, IN (812) 339-3335

### 🏢 Organizations:
**DINO,** Indianapolis, IN (317) 856-0489

### 🚲 Local Bike Shop:
**Bicycle Garage,** Bloomington, IN (812) 339-3457

### 🅝 Maps:
**USGS map:** Bloomington, IN • **Bloomington Parks and Recreation** trail map

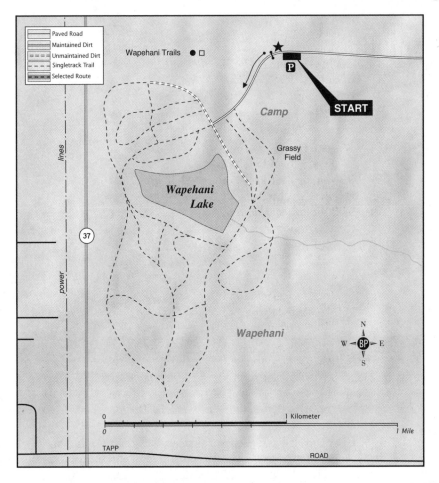

## DINO MOUNTAIN BIKE RACE SERIES

*DINO (Do INdiana Off-road) is a series of mountain bike races that are sanctioned by NORBA (National Off-Road Bicycle Association) with the majority of the races held in Indiana. A few other races are hosted by surrounding states.*

*In years past, more than 20 races made up the series with categories from beginner to expert, as well as many age-group categories. There were also four childrens' races for kids 12 and under. The youngsters' races varied from one-half mile to two miles, the entry fee was waived, and all participants received an award.*

*So, whether you are yearning to become the state champion or you just want to introduce your kids to mountain bike racing, DINO has something to offer you. And with many race courses throughout the state, there is probably a race less than one hour from your home.*

For more information, call or write:
K.C. Racing, 5250 Mannon Ct., Indianapolis, IN 46221 (317) 856-0489

In 1825, Baynard Hall was, in essence, Indiana University. As the university's sole professor, he taught Greek and Latin to an entire student body consisting of 10 men. Indiana University has since grown to become one of the largest state schools in the country.

Academics aside, Indiana University is most famous for its sporting endeavors. While most Hoosiers revel at the sight of Bobby Knight marching his team to the NCAA Final Four, cyclists pay their homage to the cinders of Bill Armstrong Stadium and the Little 500. Indiana University's annual bicycle race, the Little 500, was created in 1951 and soon grew to become one of the Midwest's most famous bicycle races.

The race is held in April and consists of two separate races for men and women. Both are contested on the cinder track at Bill Armstrong Stadium; the women race 100 laps and the men race 200 laps. Each field is made up of 33 teams of four riders and two alternates, with the men vying for the William S. Armstrong Championship Trophy and the women competing for the Borg Warner Trophy.

Cyclists race around a quarter-mile running track, but much of the excitement happens in the pits as riders attempt their exchange. The incoming

rider races in, dismounts, and throws the bicycle to his teammate. The teammate jumps on the passing bicycle and speeds up to the field of racers. If they're both lucky, they stay upright and avoid sliding across the harsh cinders.

In 1979, the Little 500 was featured in the movie, *Breaking Away*. Actors Dan Stern, Jackie Earle Haley, Dennis Christopher, and Dennis Quaid rode to victory on their cycling team, the Cutters. This movie escalated the Little 500 into the national spotlight, won an Oscar for "Best Original Screenplay," and gave cyclists a cult film that any rider worthy of shaving his legs watches at least once a year. The fame, the bike race, campus dances, ice-cream socials, golf outings, and, of course, the partying has earned the Little 500 weekend the worthy title of "The World's Greatest College Weekend."

## Little 500 Facts
- All of the bicycles are donated by the Roadmaster Corporation
- The inaugural race started at 11:00 A.M., just like the Indianapolis 500
- Celebrities such as David Letterman, Bob Hope, the Smothers Brothers, Rich Little, the Jackson Five, and Dionne Warwick have performed at the Little 500-even before *Breaking Away* was filmed
- *Breaking Away* was written by Indiana University alumnus, Steve Tesich, who rode on the winning Little 500 team in 1962.

# Clear Creek Rail-Trail

## Ride Summary

This rail-trail provides Bloomington residents and I.U. students a nice alternative to the singletrack at Wapehani. The easy, flat trail grade allows cyclists to maintain a high-tempo spin unencumbered by hills, downed trees, or serpentine singletrack. Crossing Clear Creek where a trestle once was proves to be the trail's only obstacle. Hopefully the trail will double in length in the near future.

## Ride Specs

**Start:** Trailhead on southside of the parking area
**Length:** 3.3-mile point-to-point of proposed 6.2-mile trail
**Approximate Riding Time:** 30 minutes
**Difficulty Rating:** Easy
**Trail Surface:** Rail-trail
**Lay of the Land:** Flat, grass and gravel-covered rail-trail
**Land Status:** Rail-trail corridor
**Nearest Town:** Bloomington
**Other Trail Users:** Joggers and hikers

## Getting There

**From downtown Bloomington:** Take College Avenue south 0.7 miles to Walnut Street. Continue south on Walnut Street 1.5 miles to Country Club Road. Turn right on Country Club Road and drive 0.2 miles to the Rails-To-Trails parking area. Turn left at the "Rails-To-Trails/City of Bloomington Parks and Recreation" sign. *DeLorme: Indiana Atlas & Gazetteer:* Page 50, C-3

> *Pioneers built it.*
> *Abe Lincoln worked for it.*
> *Jesse James robbed it.*
> *And America grew on it.*
>
> Rails-to-Trails Conservancy

The literature provided by the National Rails-to-Trails Conservancy asks cyclists to envision an emerald necklace or a greenway of trails linking America. This is a fine fantasy and one that could be accomplished, but there are some hurdles that must be overcome before it can be completed.

According to the Hoosier Rails-To-Trails Council, one of the primary stumbling blocks is some very stubborn Hoosier landowners. Some of these residents show ill will because these corridors of land designated for railroads were taken away from them or their ancestors in the first place. The big muscle behind this argument is the Farm Bureau. This large lobbying group has

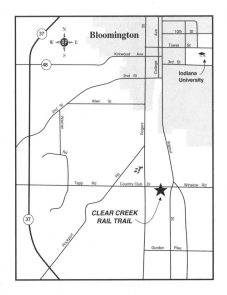

convinced many farmers this land should be returned to them.

Another argument states that criminals from bigger cities will use these backways to access private property and be given a quick escape route. Understanding that most crimes happen as a matter of convenience, I don't see too many criminals using a mountain bike as their escape vehicle of choice.

On the other hand, the arguments for establishing such trailways are numerous. Surveys have shown that more people would ride if safe routes were built. Other supporting arguments include fading business districts that could be revitalized by increasing traffic, a growing number of potential home buyers near such trails, decreased air pollution, and increased health benefits from riding and walking. And with the National Trail Systems Act of 1983 in hand, the Hoosier Rails-to-Trails Council is at the head of these arguments. This law encourages railroad companies to work with communities wishing to convert abandoned lines.

Sights along the rail trail corridor.

If the Hoosier Rails-to-Trails Council can win this battle, the dream will become a reality. The vision includes abandoned linear corridors converted into useful veins of transportation and miles of flat, well-groomed cycling routes connecting every major city in the state. Some of the paths could be paved, with others surfaced with gravel and perfectly suited for mountain bikes. As land access issues keep some of the best areas closed to cyclists, abandoned rail corridors provide the greatest potential for new trail networks.

There are more than 10 rails-to-trails projects in Indiana. The Clear Creek rails-to-trails is managed by Bloomington Parks and Recreation and is the best rail-trail for mountain bikers in the state. The path originates on the south side of Bloomington and heads southwest out of town. The beginning of the path is covered with pea gravel and later switches to larger gravel and grass.

Once the trail leaves the outskirts of town, the path is predominantly dirt. At a few points, five-foot walls of limestone border the path, giving it a tunnel effect. When not surrounded by stone, hardwoods surround the route.

## Ride Information

### Trail Contact:
Hoosier Rails-to-Trails Council, Indianapolis, IN (317) 237-9348 • Bloomington Parks and Recreation, Bloomington, IN (812) 349-3700

### Schedule:
Open daily, year-round

### Fees/Permits:
None

### Local Information:
Bloomington/Monroe County Convention & Visitors Bureau, Bloomington, IN 1-800-678-9828 or www.visitbloomington.com

### Local Events/Attractions:
Indiana University

### Accommodations:
Best Western, Bloomington, IN (812) 332-2141 • College Motor Inn (812) 336-6881

### Restaurants:
Burritos as Big As Your Head, Bloomington, IN (812) 332-5970 • Hinkles Hamburgers, Bloomington, IN (812) 339-3335

### Organizations:
Rails-to-Trails Council, Washington, DC (202) 797-5400

### Local Bike Shop:
Bicycle Garage, Bloomington, IN (812) 339-3457

### Maps:
USGS maps: Bloomington, IN; Clear Creek, IN

The trail is mostly flat with the only challenge occurring where a trestle used to be. A quick drop takes cyclists down to the creekbed. The descent is rideable, but you had better check your brakes first, for it drops quickly and offers no ford to cross the small stream. Once at the bottom, shoulder your bike and pick your way across the rocks. The preceding climb is also best undertaken with the bike still on the shoulder.

The trail ends at 3.3 miles and dribbles off into a resident's backyard. Hopefully this is only a temporary end to the trail. The goal is to stretch the trail another three miles to top out at 6.2 miles. There is no gate here and that is a positive sign that the additional three miles will soon be open.

## RAILS-TO-TRAILS FACTS

- A storefront area of Dunedin, Florida, was suffering a 35 percent vacancy rate until the Pinellas Trail was established. Now storefront occupancy is at 100 percent and business is thriving.
- In Idaho, parents now feel safe riding bicycles with their children and running errands along the 45-mile Wood River Trail that connects the towns of Bellevue, Hailey, and Sun Valley.
- A household can save up to $3,000 annually by giving up their second car and seeking alternate forms of transportation.
- Missouri's 235-mile Katy Trail traverses nine counties and adjoins 35 towns. Some of these communities have been in decline since the railroad's demise and were initially opposed to the trails, fearing vandals and rowdy trail users. To the contrary, restaurants, pubs, campgrounds, and bicycle rental companies experienced a boom in business. A survey of the trail's western half showed the trail visitors generated an estimated $3 million in local revenue.

—ISTEA and Trails: Enhancement Funding For Bicycling and Walking

## **Miles**Directions

**0.0 START** at the Clear Creek Parking Area. Find the trailhead at the south end of the parking area.

**1.0** Clear Creek Trail crosses Gordon Pike. Follow the perimeter of the gravel parking lot to the trailhead.

**1.3** Clear Creek Trail crosses South Rogers Street.

**1.5** Clear Creek Trail crosses That Road and skirts the parking lot of Bloomington Marine and Auto Trim.

**2.0** Come to a creek crossing where a trestle used to be.

**2.1** Clear Creek Trail crosses a trestle. Clear Creek Trail splits. Take the right split.

**2.5** Clear Creek Trail passes underneath IN 37.

**3.3** Clear Creek Trail ends at Dillman Road. Turn yourself around and head back to the start.

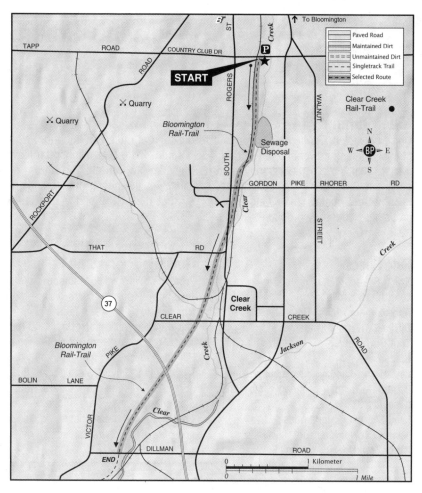

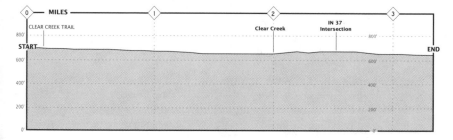

# Madison's County Roads

## Ride Summary

Don't be fooled. These county roads offer up a great mountain bike ride. Near Madison, these gravel and paved roads hold some long, steep climbs that leave cyclists shifting into their granny gears and grinding to the top. The reward for such climbs is some high-speed descents that get the heart rate up and the knobby tires humming. Cyclists should note that during the spring, the creek crossings could be too deep to traverse.

## Ride Specs

**Start:** Rykers Ridge Elementary
**Length:** 16.8-mile loop
**Approximate Riding Time:** 2 hours
**Difficulty Rating:** Moderate
**Trail Surface:** Gravel and paved county roads
**Lay of the Land:** Scenic county roads traverse a handful of steep climbs and descents
**Land Status:** County roads
**Nearest Town:** Madison
**Other Trail Users:** Automobiles

## Getting There

**From downtown Madison:** Take Jefferson Street north. Jefferson changes to U.S. 421. Take U.S. 421 half a mile to Aulenbach Road and turn right. At 2.6 miles, turn left on Telegraph Hill Road which later merges into Rykers Ridge Road. Take Rykers Ridge Road north 3.9 miles to Rykers Ridge Elementary and Rykers Ridge Baptist Church. Park at the school on weekends and park at the church on school days.

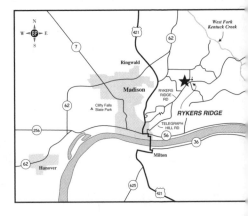

In November, the leaves fall and the hardwood trees go bare, leaving leach-white sycamores looking like mammoth skeletons. The weather throughout most of the winter in Madison, however, remains relatively warm.

The signs around town indicate what's in store for this scenic mountain bike ride. "Visit Historic Madison" is not just an empty tourism promise gauged to fill the bed and breakfasts. Madison is the only city in Indiana, and one of just seven in the country, whose entire downtown area is designated as an historic district.

As a key stop during the booming river transport days, Madison flourished from the 1840s to the 1860s. Once the riverboats were replaced by railroads, the town suddenly became very isolated. Distanced from the main highways and busy railways, the town nearly froze in time. Its economy sputtered during the next hundred years, with few changes made to keep up with the rest of the state.

As you travel through this historically preserved city, sightseeing may seem to take precedence over your intended off-road trek. Along the wide, turn-of-the-century main street you will pass many antique shops, quaint restaurants, and bed and breakfasts (some hosts go as far as greeting guests in period clothing). Several eateries and lodges are housed in the many historic, architecturally diverse buildings.

The 1885 Victorian home now known as the Cliff House sits atop the cliffs, overlooking Madison and the murky Ohio River. Many of the upstairs bedrooms offer a great view of the surroundings. Downstairs is a warm parlor and a large breakfast room. In the morning, the table is covered with croissants, pastries, fruit, coffee, and juices—the perfect send-off before a lengthy ride.

The area surrounding Madison is blessed with pleasing topography, miles of endless forests, and many challenging hiking trails, but no legal singletrack. Mountain biking is currently not allowed at nearby Clifty Falls State Park or the Jefferson Proving Ground. But cyclists should not fret: just riding on the rolling county roads is an ample workout for even the best cyclists. And as a bonus, there are many historical and scenic stopping points along the way.

One of the first sites that cyclists will pass is the Jacob Ryker home. With his namesake on the ridge, school, and the Baptist church, Jacob Ryker's heritage is marked for many generations to come.

With outcrops of limestone and shale as old as 400 million

years, there are numerous places along the ride to search for fossils. Take the time to pore over the rocks in search of fossilized spines, shells, and corral from the living creatures of the ancient shallow sea that once covered our land during the Precambrian period.

The area has a distinctive New England feel characterized by a shallow creek paralleling the road, waves of evergreen, and a sheep farm nearby.

Madison is one of seven cities in the country whose entire downtown has been designated as an historical district.

The climbs and descents that lace through this scenic country also evoke a mountain setting. There are two major descents on the ride that demand the rider's full attention, especially since they are both surfaced with gravel. The first one, at 4.9 miles, speeds cyclists to a creekbed and the first fossil stop. The second drop comes at the 12-mile mark. To fully enjoy this downhill, take a break at the top of the hill to

take in all directions of the view, catch your breath, and check your brakes. Speeds on this 0.3-mile run can reach as high as 40 miles per hour! The gravel and the bend at the creek crossing may unleash an adrenaline rush and a feeling of controlled fear possibly not exhibited since childhood.

Before the next climb, the loop rolls along the flats and beyond a pasture of Belgian horses before splashing through two creek crossings. In the spring, these fords are impassable, not to mention extremely cold.

These last climbs take riders back up to Rykers Ridge and the end of the ride. From here, cyclists can hurry back into town to see if there are any croissants at the Cliff House leftover from breakfast. But if you didn't stay there the night before, the owners might wonder why Lycra-clad individuals are pilfering their food!

## Ride Information

### ● Trail Contact:
Fizz Bike Shop, Madison, IN (812) 273-3499

### ● Schedule:
Open daily, year-round

### ● Fees/Permits:
None

### ● Local Information:
Madison Area Convention and Visitors Bureau, Madison, IN 1-800-559-2956, (812) 265-2956 or www.oldmadison.com

### ● Local Events/Attractions:
Madison Regatta (unlimited hydroplane racing), first weekend in July

### ● Accommodations:
Cliff House, Madison, IN (812) 265-5272 • Clifty Falls State Park (Inn and campground), Madison, IN (812) 273-5495

### ● Restaurants:
Key West Shrimp House, (812) 265-2831• Ye Olde Fashioned Soda Fountain (812) 273-1311

### ● Other Resources:
Indiana: A New Historical Guidebook, Taylor/Stevens/Ponder/Brockman

### ● Local Bike Shop:
Fizz Bike Shop, Madison, IN (812) 273-3499

### ● Maps:
USGS map: Canaan, IN • Indiana state road maps

## **Miles**Directions

**0.0 START** at Rykers Ridge Elementary School. Leave the school parking lot, riding north on County Road 300 East. Ride along the paved road past the Jacob Ryker house.

**0.5** Turn left on Jefferson Lake/Cross Road.

**1.7** Turn right on Cook/Old IN 62. There is no sign for this paved road.

**2.8** Arrive at an intersection with Cozy Acres Golf on the right. Turn right on IN 62. This paved road has a wide shoulder to ride on.

**3.1** Turn right on Olive Branch Road.

**3.8** Arrive at an intersection. Turn right on Geyman Hill Road. This paved road turns into Whippoorwill Road.

**4.4** Pass the Whippoorwill Girl Scout Camp.

**4.8** The road changes to gravel and descends sharply. Caution: there is a sharp turn that can be tricky if traveling too fast on the gravel.

**5.6** Cross a low bridge, carrying cyclists across West Fork Creek. This is the first fossil stop. Take some time to scour the rocks for branch and horn corral, shells, and spines from marine animals of eras past.

**5.6** Arrive at an intersection with a paved road. Turn left on China/Mannville Road.

**5.61** Cross Dry Fork Creek and take an immediate right on Dry Fork Road.

**5.7** Dry Fork Road turns to gravel.

6.5 Cross Dry Fork Creek and the second fossil stop.

**7.3** Come to intersection of Whippoorwill Road. Continue straight on Dry Fork Road.

**7.8** Dry Fork Road turns back to asphalt and ascends for the day's first major climb.

**8.6** Arrive at an intersection with a paved road. Turn right on Hall's Ridge Road.

**9.9** Arrive at an intersection with a gravel road. Turn left on Wright Hill Road.

**10.8** Enter the Wright Hill Wildlife Sanctuary.

**11.3** Wright Hill Road tops out on a high point with an incredible vista. Prepare for the fastest downhill of the day. Caution: the road bends near the end of the descent and crosses a creek.

**11.8** Wright Hill Road intersects with a paved road. Turn right on China/Mannville Road.

**13.3** China/Mannville Road intersects with a gravel road. Turn left on Jefferson Lake (IN 410). There is no sign at this intersection. The road quickly bends to the left. The right split is a private drive.

**13.4** Splash through the West Fork creek crossing. These fords are impassable during high water.

**13.45** Cross the second creek. The road turns to asphalt and begins the second major ascent.

**13.5** The road splits. Take Jefferson Lake, the paved road to the left.

**14.2** Pass a road on the left. Continue straight on Jefferson Lake.

**15.0** Come to the intersection with CR 320 North. Continue straight on Jefferson Lake.

**15.6** Arrive at an intersection. Turn left on CR 300 East.

**16.3** Back at school parking lot. Ride complete.

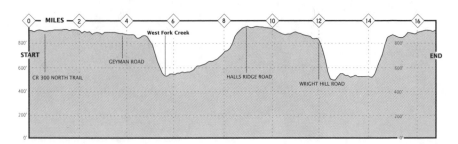

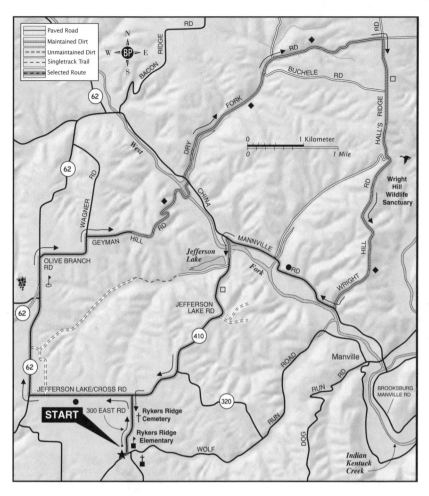

# 17

# Lynnville Park

## Ride Summary

Lynnville Park has few sections where cyclists can just relax and pedal mindlessly. There are hundreds of obstacles to ride over and around in this tight, labyrinth of trails—a place perfectly suited to Trials riders. Cyclists will either hone their bike handling skills here at Lynnville or throw their bikes into the strip pit out of frustration. This trail is definitely not for beginners.

## Ride Specs

**Start:** Main camping area
**Length:** 2.6-mile loop, part of a 6-mile trail system
**Approximate Riding Time:** 45 minutes
**Difficulty Rating:** Difficult due to so many technical obstacles
**Trail Surface:** Singletrack and dirt roads
**Lay of the Land:** Craggy, technical, twisting trails roll up and down the slag heaps, remnants of a strip mine
**Land Status:** County park
**Nearest Town:** Lynnville
**Other Trail Users:** Hikers

## Getting There

**From Evansville:** Take I-164 north approximately 12 miles to I-64. Take I-64 east 10 miles to the Lynnville/Boonville exit (Exit 39). Go north on IN 61 0.1 miles to IN 68. Go west on IN 68 1.5 miles to Lynnville Park. Turn right into Lynnville Park and find a parking spot at the camping area. *DeLorme: Indiana Atlas & Gazetteer:* Page 61, A-12

R on Pendley, of the Evansville Bicycle Club, described Lynnville Park best when he added the word "technical" to its title. Mountain bikers interested in challenging, rugged terrain can thank the Peabody Coal Company for this incredibly difficult and technical ride.

The park's ridges and ravines, that work the most hard-core cyclists into a frenzy, were created from Peabody's now defunct mining operation. After the mine closed in 1964, Peabody donated its 1,100 acres to the nearby city of Lynnville. The one-time slag heaps are now tree-covered ridges, producing some of the most challenging riding in the area.

Indiana can get cold. Temperatures this day reached a balmy 5° above zero! Brrr…

The evergreen forest growing here at Lynnville creates somewhat of a misplaced ecosystem as well, giving the trail a slightly western feel. Riding along the ravines while surrounded by evergreens evokes visions of riding in the Rocky Mountains of Colorado—only without the mountainous ascents.

Lynnville Park has few climbs that are rideable, and most of the descents are very challenging. With the multitude of obstacles, there are few points along the route that allow even one half-mile of continuous riding. This is not the place to introduce a beginner to this sport.

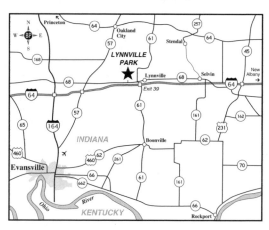

The trail system used to be part of the Black Coal Enduro, one of the most challenging motocross systems on the Enduro circuit. Even straddling a multihorse engine would not help on some sections of the trail.

The biggest challenges on this trail are the ruts left from ATV wheels and the chunks of limestone lining the trail. Either obstacle can lead to a two-point takedown into the dirt. The main benefit from riding this system comes from developing bike-handling skills similar to those of a "trials rider."

Trials riders show off their skills by riding up and over picnic tables, cars, or log piles, as well as delicately balancing themselves on their front tires with the finesse of an arterial surgeon. Frequent trips through the Lynnville system may raise cyclists' skills close to this level. However, these same challenges might frustrate a less-experienced rider to the point of wanting to sink his bike to the bottom of one of the strip pits.

## Ride Information

**Trail Contact:**
**Lynnville Park,** Lynnville, IN (812) 922-5144

**Schedule:**
Open dawn to dusk, year-round

**Fees/Permits:**
$2

**Local Events/Attractions:**
**Wahn Seidler Observatory** (812) 922-5681 • **Warrick County Museum,** Boonville, IN (812) 897-3100

**Accommodations:**
**Lynnville Park Campground,** Lynnville, IN (812) 922-5144

**Restaurants:**
**Locust Street Cafe,** Boonville, IN (812) 897-4724 • **Blimpies Restaurant,** Boonville, IN (812) 897-5653

**Local Bike Shop:**
**Bicycle World,** Evansville, IN (812) 473-2453

**Maps:**
**USGS map:** Lynnville, IN

One highlight of the park is the Wahn Seidler Observatory, sponsored by the Evansville Astronomical Society. The Seidler Observatory is one of the largest telescopes in Indiana. The observatory is far enough from big city lights to afford a detailed view of the stars. Information regarding group reservations and public viewing hours can be obtained by calling the observatory at (812) 922-5681.

Campers have two choices at Lynnville Park: for the social camper, there is the main camp area resembling a subdivision of tents and pop-up trailers, and for those seeking solitude, there are many satellite campsites around the lake and near the observatory. Be sure to look out for the wild turkeys at these satellite campsites.

Years ago, wild turkeys were eliminated from the state. Far away from the hustle and bustle of the main campground, though, the gobbler's amazing comeback can be witnessed as a sizable flock of wild turkeys make their rounds near the sites. If you remain quiet enough, they will wander within camera range and provide the morning's entertainment as you cook breakfast.

One travel tip for campers planning to stay overnight at Lynnville Park is to buy your supplies before you leave your hometown. There is one store in Lynnville, but their prices are pretty lofty. Gas prices are also about 20 cents more per gallon here. *Caveat emptor.*

## **Miles**Directions

*With so many trails criss-crossing this system, cyclists may opt to create their own loop or attempt to ride the following loop.*

**0.0 START** at the north end of the campgrounds, roll past the bathhouse, and travel west on the gravel road that cuts between two gravel pits.

**0.25** Turn right at the sign marked "Rough Road." The trail passes a few lakeside campsites then bends to the right.

**0.4** Turn left and cross a bridge.

**0.41** Once across the bridge, take the faint trail to the right. Follow the ridge overlooking a swamp-like overflow from the strip pits.

**0.7** Turn left on a dirt road.

**0.75** Pass a picnic area and dive right off the dirt road onto a creekbed trail.

**0.8** You now have a choice of three descents off to the right. The middle one looks less intimidating. After this quick descent, most cyclists will have to walk the bike up the following climb.

**0.82** Immediately turn right at the top of climb.

**0.9** Bear left at the trail split.

**0.95** Turn left at the top of the trail.

**1.0** Come to a faint trail split. Take the right split. A short drop puts you between three ridges. Arrive at a challenging descent. Stay close to the center

so as to hit the narrow bridge straddling the water and reeds. Now at one of the pit's horseshoe ends.

**1.1** Turn right on a dirt road.

**1.15** Take a sharp left onto another dirt road and climb to the observatory.

**1.2** Turn left off the dirt road onto a very faint trail. The trail is near the bend in the road, just before the power lines.

**1.28** Arrive in the backyard of the Wahn Seidler Observatory. Follow the perimeter of the grass yard to the next trailhead nearest the road.

**1.47** Turn left on the gravel road and ride approximately 100 feet to the trail on the right.

**1.5** Turn right off the gravel road onto singletrack. Follow the trail to the left.

**1.6** Come out of the valley floor and up another sharp, technical climb.

**1.7** After the short climb, turn right on the wide trail. Take an immediate right, attempting a steep, technical climb. This is followed by a steep downhill. Now traveling west, parallel to a dirt road.

**2.0** Turn right on the dirt road. You are now due east of the observatory. If you are ready to bale, you can take the main dirt road back to your car from here. Otherwise, head back toward the observatory and follow the road to the left.

*Cold feet? Try loosening shoe laces instead of stretching another pair of socks over your feet. Loose shoes (just not too loose) will increase circulation and help to warm your toes. Also, put on a stocking cap. An insulated noggin translates into warm fingers and toes.*

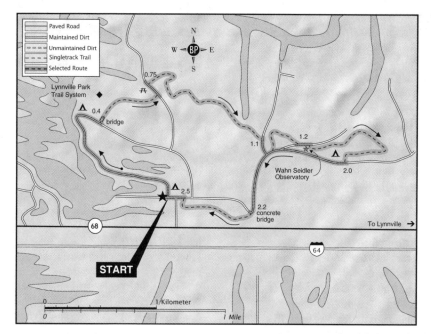

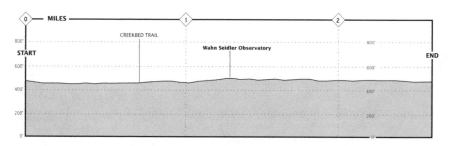

**2.2** At the next bend in the road, go straight toward the concrete bridge and follow the singletrack trail off the road.

**2.3** Follow the trail to the right. Now traveling parallel to IN 68, heading toward the entrance of the park.

**2.5** The trail splits. Take the right split just before coming to the entrance road.

**2.52** Arrive at a trail intersection. Continue straight. The trail descends toward the main road.

**2.55** Turn left on the main dirt road and head back toward the campground.

**2.6** Ride complete. Now go out and enjoy your own loops and trails in the park!

133

# 18

# Yellow Banks
# Recreation Center

## Ride Summary

The challenge of this trail system is navigation. There are so many trails criss-crossing each other, it's difficult to keep one's bearings. Cyclists can follow the suggested loop or make up their own keeping track of the keynote markers. *Cyclists beware: ATVs still frequently use these trails.*

## Ride Specs

**Start:** Big barn in Yellow Banks' parking area
**Length:** 4.4-mile loop, part of an estimated 10-mile trail system
**Approximate Riding Time:** 45 minutes
**Difficulty Rating:** Moderate
**Trail Surface:** Singletrack, doubletrack, and gravel road
**Lay of the Land:** Singletrack leads through woods and fields, then back to the recreation area
**Land Status:** Private property
**Nearest Town:** Dale
**Other Trail Users:** Hikers and ATV riders

## Getting There

**From Evansville:** Take I-164 approximately 12 miles to I-64. Take I-64 east 10 miles to the Lynnville/ Boonville exit (Exit 39). Go north on IN 61 at the Lynnville/Boonville exit (Exit 39). Go 0.1 miles to IN 68. Go east on IN 68 10.5 miles to Selvin. Go north on Yellow Banks Trail, marked by the Yellow Banks Recreation Center sign. Go approximately 0.7 miles to the Yellow Banks Recreation Center entrance. Turn left into the park and follow the Park Entrance Road to the parking area. *DeLorme: Indiana Atlas & Gazetteer:* Page 62, A-2

Y ellow Banks Recreation Center was founded along the buffalo trace on which wild herds used to travel from grassy meadows to the Ohio River. This path, cut through yellow clay, later served as a route for pioneer travelers.

Today, along that same path and less than one mile outside the town of Selvin sits the Yellow Banks Recreation Area—a mini-resort that offers a multitude of family activities. The Yellow Banks brochure promises an "Escape from Reality." And for only $1.50 per person, Yellow Banks does offer a most impressive list of activities for a day of family fun.

Read these next paragraphs in a single breath using the pitch of a used car salesman to get the full effect of these promos from the recreation center's brochure.

"Swimming! Fishing! Overnight Camping! Pottery Shops! Grocery Store! And much, much more! Relax and tan on the huge sand beach! Including diving, trapeze, and playground (lifeguards on duty)!

Picnic under the cool shelter houses! Enjoy a game of horseshoes or volleyball! Or bring your bicycle for a peaceful ride on the bicycle trails!

Cool off with homemade ice cream made daily at Yellow Banks Grocery Store and Bait!" *Let's just hope they don't confuse the groceries and the bait when churning the ice cream.*

"Facilities include restrooms, hot showers, electric and sewer hookups, water, and picnic tables! Cabins now available to rent! Holiday World only minutes away!"

"Events include the famous Yellow Banks Craft Show! Second and third weekends in September! Featuring hundreds of

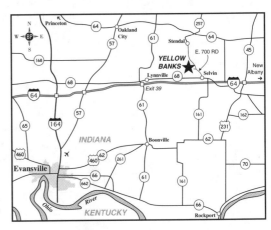

booths, pony rides, buggy rides, antique machinery at work, live music, breakfast, corn bread, BBQ, and bean soup! Flea markets!" Wow!

One word of caution, though. The brochure also warns patrons to beware of "thrown clay." It appears that this happens frequently near the Pottery Shop. Cautiously watch as artisans shape flowerpots, dinnerware, and jack-o'-lanterns from Yellow Banks' clay. Understand that neither

Yellow Banks nor the publisher of this book will assume any liability as a result of injuries sustained from thrown clay.

Now that you've had an aerobic workout from reading the promos, and assuming that you haven't been struck by flying clay, you're warmed up and ready to ride the trails.

Originally, the trails were open to lot owners who had motorcycles and ATVs. But as that trend passed, the owner decided to expand his operation and open the trails to mountain biking. Although motorized bikes cut the trails, the owner has reduced the number of permits offered to motorcycle riders with the hopes that mountain biking will become the mainstay.

Yellow Banks is a moderate trail system that is in somewhat of an infant stage. The route is enjoyable to ride, but there are a few confusing sections in which a number of trails intersect. Even a map may not be of great assistance. On a positive note, if you do lose the exact route that was mapped, keep heading in the same general direction and you will come across the trail loop a little farther along.

The confusing portions of the trail are a result of ATVs cutting too many trails in a small area. There is a clearly visible keynote marker at each of these sections, though, that should indicate that you are heading in the right direction.

The climbs at Yellow Banks are not overly difficult and the trail is predominantly singletrack. There are a few swampy sections, but these seem to be isolated.

## Ride Information

**🌑 Trail Contact:**
**Yellow Banks Recreation Center,** Dale, IN (812) 567-4703

**🕐 Schedule:**
Open dawn to dusk, year-round

**💲 Fees/Permits:**
Mountain biking is free. $1.50 per person for swimming and use of showers

**📍 Local Events/Attractions:**
**Yellow Banks Craft Show,** 2nd & 3rd weekends in September • **Warrick County Museum,** Boonville, IN (812) 897-3100

**🍴 Accommodations:**
**Yellow Banks Recreation Center** Campground, Dale, IN (812) 567-4703

**🍴 Restaurants:**
**Locust Street Cafe,** Boonville, IN (812) 897-4724 • **Blimpies Restaurant,** Boonville, IN (812) 897-5653

**🚲 Local Bike Shop:**
**Bicycle World,** Evansville, IN (812) 473-2453

**🅝 Maps:**
**USGS map:** Holland, IN

(**Note:** *Because Yellow Banks Recreation Area has become such a labyrinth of trails from heavy ATV use, it would be unreasonable to consider accurately mapping every trail in the system. Instead, both author and publisher have attempted to show that a loop through this network of criss-crossing trails is possible, but that detailed directions for this particular loop would require an unbearable amount of labeling for all of the many twists and turns involved. Cyclists are encouraged to use the forest map provided and to follow both the SIMBC (Southern Indiana Mountain Bike Club-now defunct) and DINO (Do INdiana Off-road) arrows and trail markings to help guide them through this sometimes crazy, but always fun network of off-road bicycling trails. For this reason, there are no detailed mile-by-mile directions available. However, keynote directions and a profile map of the connecting trails making up this loop are provided for useful trail and terrain references. Have fun and try not to get too lost!*)

## **Miles**Directions

**0.0 START** from the trailhead at the south end of the parking lot. Look for the grassy trail below the dam.

**0.2** Arrive at a trail intersection. Take the SIMBC (Southern Indiana Mountain Bike Club) trail to the left.

**0.5** Follow the SIMBC sign and trail to the left.

### KEYNOTE MARKER 1

**1.1** Trail arrives at a "T." Turn left. Now at an open area close to a strip pit.

**1.2** Arrive at a "T." Stay on the trail that follows the perimeter of the pit.

**1.3** Follow the trail leading through the two strip pits.

**1.4** Turn left on the farthestmost right trail and begin your first climb of the ride.

**1.5** Arrive at a trail intersection. Turn left and descend toward the pits.

### KEYNOTE MARKER 2

**1.6** At the end of a quick descent, look for a small trail to the right. Dive off the main trail to the smaller trail. Now entering a confusing section of unmarked trails. Many ATVs continue to cut new trails, constantly changing the system's layout.

### KEYNOTE MARKER 3

**3.2** The trail arrives at a "T" at a gravel road. Turn left on gravel road.

**3.9** Arrive at a trail intersection. Continue straight. Pass a house on your right.

### KEYNOTE MARKER 4

**3.91** The trail crosses a paved road. Continue straight on the trail.

**4.0** The trail splits soon after it crosses the road. Take the left split.

**4.4** The trail ends at the Recreation Center.

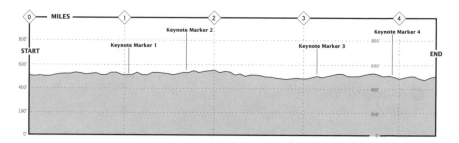

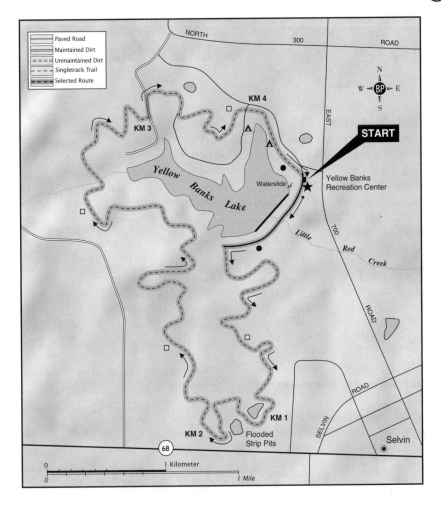

Legend:
- Paved Road
- Maintained Dirt
- Unmaintained Dirt
- Singletrack Trail
- Selected Route

NORTH 300 ROAD

EAST

N
W ⟵ BP ⟶ E
S

START

Yellow Banks
Recreation Center

KM 4

KM 3

Yellow Banks Lake

Waterslide

Little Red Creek

700 ROAD

KM 1

KM 2

Flooded
Strip Pits

SELVIN ROAD

Selvin

68

0                1 Kilometer
0                              1 Mile

# Gnaw Bone Camp

## Ride Summary

Many Hoosier mountain bikers were introduced to the sport at Gnaw Bone. Indiana's best private-property trail system has been welcoming fat-tire visitors for years. The 25-mile system harbors challenging singletrack, mostly moderate climbs and descents, and a few granny-grinders thrown in to boot. A great descent provides a fast finale. Make sure to call first. Gnaw Bone is closed when summer camp is in session or when the trails are too muddy to ride.

## Ride Specs

**Start:** Gnaw Bone Camp main lodge
**Length:** 7.1-mile loop; part of 25-mile trail system
**Approximate Riding Time:** 45 minutes to 2 hours
**Difficulty Rating:** Moderate
**Trail Surface:** Singletrack and double-track
**Lay of the Land:** Singletrack trails traverse rolling hills and descend the camp's many ravines. Many technical descents and climbs can be found on the camp's northeast corner.
**Land Status:** Private property
**Nearest Town:** Gnaw Bone
**Other Trail Users:** Hikers, campers, and cross-country skiers

## Getting There

**From Columbus:** Take IN 46 west approximately 13 miles to IN 135 south. Take IN 135 south 1.9 miles to Gnaw Bone Camp. Turn left into Gnaw Bone Camp. Park at the general store. *DeLorme: Indiana Atlas & Gazetteer:* Page 51, B-7

F or many years, the Gnaw Bone trails defined Hoosier mountain biking. Area cyclists knew this 1,560-acre camp to be one of only a few legal and challenging places to ride—and for the most part, they were right.

But even with many new legal mountain bike trail systems opening to cyclists each year in Indiana, Gnaw Bone Camp will likely always rank as one of the state's better systems. It is also the award winner for having the most unique name. In typical Hoosier fashion, there is a tale for how the camp and nearby town earned its moniker.

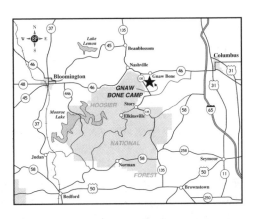

A local sheep farmer was having trouble with the onslaught of wild dogs regularly raiding his herd and feeding on his sheep. With no other solutions in sight, the farmer killed all the sheep, and his family feasted on mutton. A local storyteller sat at the grocery store and told all who would listen that "they have been gnawing sheep bones over at Sally's all summer."

On arrival at Gnaw Bone Camp, your first course of action, like it or not, will be to pet the pack of golden retrievers suddenly surrounding your vehicle. The hounds can get fairly feisty if you ignore their request. Also set aside some time to talk with Alice Lorenz, part owner/caretaker of the camp. Alice asks that you call before showing up to ride (*see Ride Information*) since she does not open the camp when the trails are muddy.

Alice's father, Fred Lorenz, spent much of his life in Indianapolis as an industrial arts teacher at Country Orchard Day School. In 1944, he took the first step to fulfilling his lifelong dream of running his own camp. He bought a substantial plot of land in Brown County and eventually accumulated over 1,560 acres. He claims that the first 1,000 acres cost substantially less than the last 560 acres because of the increased interest in Brown County property.

Fred allowed Boy Scouts and other campers to enjoy his land, and in 1943 the Lorenzes sponsored their own summer camp. These two-week sessions were open to both boys and girls, but recently they've switched to all-girl sessions.

Recently, Gnaw Bone's summer camp celebrated its fiftieth anniversary with 500 camp alumni attending the party to swap campfire stories and drink Gnaw Bone's legendary beverage—sassafras tea. Campers claim the tea is less than tasty, but since it is the product of Gnaw Bone's very own sassafras trees, sipping this drink stirs fond memories.

## Ride Information

### Trail Contact:
**Gnaw Bone Camp,** Nashville, IN (812) 988-4852

### Schedule:
Open dawn to dusk, year-round. *Exceptions: When summer camp is in session or the trails are too muddy to ride*

### Fees/Permits:
$3

### Local Information:
**Brown County Convention & Visitors Bureau,** Nashville, IN 1-800-753-3255 or *www.browncounty.com*

### Local Events/Attractions:
Nashville's quaint shops, Brown County State Park, Nashville, IN (812) 988-6406

### Accommodations:
**Story Inn,** Nashville, IN (812) 988-2273 • **Brown County State Park Campground,** Nashville, IN (812) 988-6406 • **Comfort Inn** (812) 988-6118

### Restaurants:
**The Story Inn,** Nashville, IN (812) 988-2273 • **Hotel Nashville Resort Dining** (812) 988-8400

### Group Rides:
**CIBA** (Central Indiana Bicycle Association) rides here occasionally

### Organizations:
**CIBA, Central Indiana Bicycle Association,** Indianapolis, IN (317) 327-BIKE or *www.spitfire.net/ciba/*

### Other Resources:
**Tales and Trails of Brown County,** Fears/McDonald/Sturgeon

### Local Bike Shop:
**Bicycle Station,** Columbus, IN (812) 379-9005

### Maps:
**USGS map:** Nashville, IN • **Gnaw Bone Camp trail map** available at check in

After signing in for your ride and paying the $3 trail fee, pick up a map detailing the 25-mile trail system, and take the north trail from the parking lot. The trail rolls past the eloquent "Gnaw Bone Hilton," which is merely a screened-in cabin. The first climb rolls up Wahoo Trail. At the top of the climb, take Lake Ridge Trail for a short distance to Copperhead Ridge. This becomes a walk-only section when crossing paths with hikers or ATV riders.

Roll along Raspberry Ridge to the Downey Trail and check out the Lorenz's hilltop spread. Sitting majestically atop a high clearing, the house has one of the highest views in Gnaw Bone.

After passing the estate, cyclists soon come upon the most technical sections of the trail system. A steep twisting descent bottoms out at a creekbed, bringing cyclists to the low point of the area's topography. That can mean only one thing—the trail must ascend. These climbs are rideable, assuming you are a techno-master with large anaerobic capacity and durable legs.

On the backside of the property, hardwood forest gives way to magical evergreen woods. Ferns, moss-covered logs, and a canopy of pine needles reveal a surreal scene. As you wind through the fairy-tale forest, the trees break and the woods turn to pasture. A mural-inspiring scene unfolds as the backdrop of a forested ridge accents the waving pasture grass that surrounds an aging pole barn.

As the trail turns south, you will break back toward the main lodge and enter the hardwood forest again. Here you will find the historic cabin of Chief Eaglefeather. Consider taking a short rest here because the next climb requires fairly strong legs. For every climb, though, there is an equally rewarding descent, and the following hill takes you all the way back to the main lodge.

After the ride, if you choose to stay, you have the option of playing checkers on tabletop boards or watching the hummingbirds fight for the feeder. If you relax on the homemade furniture of the covered porch long enough, you might even spot a blue-tailed skink. And don't forget to ask Alice about Gnaw Bone and its fantastic past.

## **Miles**Directions

*There are many miles of trails at Gnaw Bone. This is just one possible route.*

**0.0 START** Take the trailhead at the north end of the parking lot. Walk across the footbridge, pass the Gnaw Bone Hilton, and head north on Haunted House Trail.

**0.45** Come to a grassy area just past the cabin. Continue straight on Wahoo Trail.

**0.75** The trail splits at the top of the hill. Take the right split following the sign to Lake Ridge Trail. You should now be on Lookout Trail.

**0.8** The trail splits. Take the Lake Ridge Trail to the left.

**0.9** Bear left, following the Copperhead Ridge Trail. This is an easement trail that crosses the neighbor's property. Stay on

## **Miles**Directions *continued*

the trail and walk your bikes if you come upon hikers or ATV riders.

**1.45** Roll past Tioga Pass.

**1.65** Pass a trail on the right. Continue straight on Copperhead/Raspberry Ridge. Here, cyclists can turn right down Cemetery Hill and visit the graves dating back to the 1850s at Pittman Cemetery.

**2.3** Pass an unmarked trail on the left. Continue straight. Now back on Gnaw Bone property.

**2.35** Arrive at the Tulip Trail/Downey Trail split. Turn right and follow Downey Trail.

**2.45** The trail empties into an open field where you can see the incredible house built by Alice's father. You are still on Gnaw Bone property here. Return to Downey Trail.

**2.6** Bear right on Tulip trail at the southeast corner of Gnaw Bone property. Big chainring time.

**3.0** Technical riders rejoice as the trail leads to the steepest and most challenging descents and ascents. Take a left at Walkers Hill and descend rapidly. Follow an unnamed creekbed trail past Best Hill and Lloyd's Hill.

**3.3** Arrive at a trail intersection. Take a left up Tulip Hill. Shift as you turn on the trail to prepare for 145-foot climb. If you want to focus on technical riding only, riders can create a loop on this northeast section of the property.

**3.5** The trail splits. Take the right split along Lloyd's Loop. Soon after, follow the trail to the left and pass the gate on your right.

**3.75** Bear to the left. Now you're at the top of the climb.

**3.75** The trail splits. Take the left split following the sign to Middle Hill. Pass Best Hill Trail immediately after the trail split. Continue straight.

**3.85** Veer right onto Middle Hill Trail. Do not go left. The left trail takes you off Gnaw Bone property.

**4.2** Pass Hoot 'n Holler on the left. Continue straight. Now you're on Mulcahy.

**4.3** Arrive at a trail intersection. Turn left. (Lloyd's Hill is off to the right.) This is one of the few places in Indiana where you can ride through waist-high grass and not feel the sting of nettles. You might pick up a few chiggers, but that's another story.

**4.6** Come to a trail intersection. Follow Mulcahy to the left. (Outer Banks is the trail to the right.)

**5.0** Cross Mulcahy Bridge. Follow the trail along the northern perimeter of the camp.

**5.2** Go through the gate. Please close the gate behind you to keep the horses in their pasture. You will now be riding across a picturesque field. Waving grass, aging barn, and a rising ridge in the backdrop creates a classic Indiana scene.

**5.5** Pass a barn, cross Gnaw Bone Creek, then pedal into another field. Turn left on Raccoon Ridge Trail.

**5.65** The trail bends to the left at an old barn and rolls past a gate.

**5.85** Ride past Chief Eaglefeather's cabin. Technical climb ahead, following the sign to Lookout Cabin.

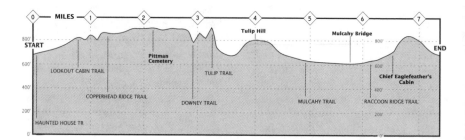

## **Miles**Directions *continued*

**6.2** Arrive at a trail intersection. Turn right onto Haunted House Trail.

**6.3** Bear right at the split. Pine Ridge Trail is a big chainring descent all the way to the bottom.

**6.4** Bear left at the split. (Dallas Lake Trail is on the right.)

**6.5** Pass the trail on the left. Continue straight.

**6.55** Pass Harrison Trail Loop on the right. Continue straight.

**6.63** Follow Pine Ridge Trail as it bends to the left. A faint trail goes straight.

**6.67** Pass Westenedge and Hillside Trails. Continue on Pine Ridge Trail.

**6.85** Come to Three-Trail Downhill. Cyclists' choice (I took the farthestmost left trail).

**7.0** Take This Way split to the left.

**7.1** Trail ends in the grassy field near parking area. Ride complete.

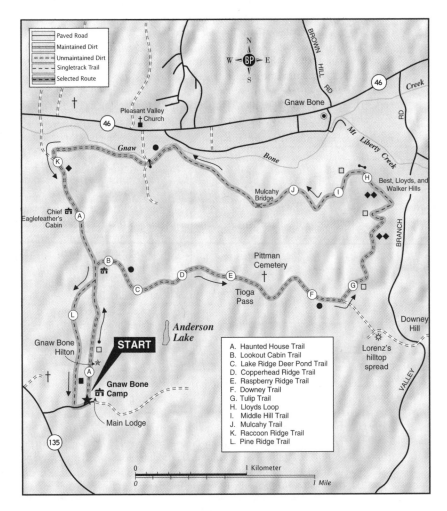

Legend:
- Paved Road
- Maintained Dirt
- Unmaintained Dirt
- Singletrack Trail
- Selected Route

A. Haunted House Trail
B. Lookout Cabin Trail
C. Lake Ridge Deer Pond Trail
D. Copperhead Ridge Trail
E. Raspberry Ridge Trail
F. Downey Trail
G. Tulip Trail
H. Lloyds Loop
I. Middle Hill Trail
J. Mulcahy Trail
K. Raccoon Ridge Trail
L. Pine Ridge Trail

## Southern Indiana

Listed here is a great ride in Southern Indiana that didn't make the A-list this time around but deserves recognition. Check it out and let us know what you think. You may decide that it deserves higher status in future editions or, perhaps, you may have a ride of your own that merits some attention.

### (A) Roger Shaw Memorial Park

The singletrack trails of Roger Shaw Memorial Park are perched on the banks of the Blue River. A section of the three-mile system is part of The Bears of Blue River Trail and area Boy Scouts helped to clear and maintain the section. Marshall Shaw donated the land to memorialize his son Roger Shaw who was killed in an automobile accident. Scouts still help to maintain the trails.

Not much was done with the property when it was first given to the city, and it quickly fell into disrepair. Local bike shop owner, Tim McKenney approached the city in the summer of 1996 with a plan. He offered to cut and maintain some trails if the city agreed to maintain the grassy park entrance area and continue with trash pickup. McKenney also requested that mountain bikers be allowed to use the park.

The town approved the plan in the fall of 1996, and McKenney with a crew of five others, cut the first two miles of trail in January of 1997. Most of the path was cut

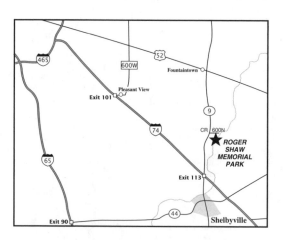

with lawnmowers and weed whackers. Surprisingly, McKenney didn't use a chainsaw. Instead of cutting down trees, McKenney chose to wind the trail around them. The creation has given Shelbyville-area cyclists a flat serpentine course that is a mere five to ten minutes from their homes.

With the help of Indiana Mountain Bike Association, McKenney eventually added another mile of trail. In fact, an IMBA maintenance crew makes an annual trek to Shelbyville to clean up the trails. The annual trek is as much a social event as it is a workday. IMBA also comes out to put on mountain bike skills and bicycle safety clinics. Much of the credit of the international off-road organization's interest can be credited to McKenney's personal connections, proving the adage that one person can truly make a difference.

The trails that were cut in the park are physically easy, but technically it's rated as moderate with a few difficult sections. Instead of shifting gears, cyclists will have to focus on weaving past trees, riding over plenty of logs (intentionally left on the trail), speeding past walls of brush, and navigating through minefields of hedge apples and walnuts. It may sound silly, but these oversized apples and nuts have the same effect as marbles. If these don't take down cyclists, the cull trees probably will. More times than not, riders will buzz by the cull trees cleanly or simply graze a hip or shoulder. Other times handlebars tangle with a tree, and the cyclist executes a most unexpected and unstylish William-Nealy-cartoon inspired dismount.

To get to Roger Shaw Park, which by the way is open year-round, follow Indiana 9 North from Shelbyville for 4.2 miles. Turn right onto County Road 600 North, and drive one mile to the Roger Shaw Memorial Park entrance. Turn right into the parking area. For more information, contact Tim & Gaye McKenney at The Bicycle Shop in Shelbyville, (317) 392-6853. **Delorme: Indiana Atlas & Gazetteer:** Page 45, C-12

REST HEADQUARTERS

STOWN RANGER DISTRICT

HOOSIER

National Forest

# Hoosier

DEPARTMENT OF AGRICULTURE

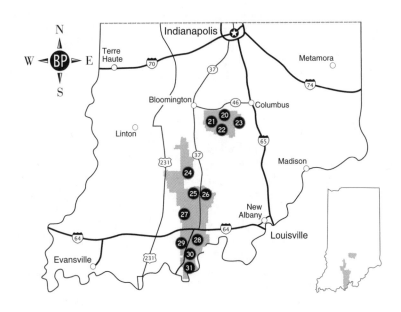

# National Forest

# Hoosier National Forest

*An Act to empower the United States of America to acquire lands in the State of Indiana by purchase or otherwise, for establishing, consolidating, and extending national forests, and to grant the United States all rights necessary for proper control and administration of lands so acquired, and legalizing certain acts and proceedings connected therewith.*

—Chapter 29 of Senate Bill 39

In the 1930s, southern Indiana farmers were in a dilemma. Their land was marginally productive at best, and the markets at which they could sell their crops were miles away. Low crop prices, several droughts, and the Depression aggravated farmers' efforts and prompted many of them to leave their homesteads in search of a better life.

These delinquent properties in turn created a concern with state legislators. Indiana's governor Paul McNutt asked the Forest Service to convert these abandoned farms into a national forest. His request was approved, and in 1935, Indiana bought the first parcels of land that would be called the Hoosier National Forest.

Over the next few decades, more land was bought with the immediate goal being to control erosion and wild fires. Manpower for many of the projects was provided by the Civilian Conservation Corps. These unemployed workers not only rehabilitated much of the damaged and abandoned land by reforesting, but they also helped develop many of Hoosier National Forest's recreation areas.

Today, the Hoosier National Forest spans over 193,000 acres, with trails running from Bloomington to the Ohio River. With state parks drawing much of the weekend tourist traffic, the forest trail areas enjoy less congestion, lower costs, and sites that perhaps only a relative few Hoosiers have seen. With regards to mountain biking, the forest is truly the Graceland of Indiana off-road bicycle riding.

Seemingly endless miles of trails serve to entertain cyclists of all abilities. For beginners or cyclists wanting to spend more time watching wildlife, Hardin Ridge, Tipsaw Lake, Birdseye, or the Oriole Trail are fulfilling options. For hardcore cyclists anxious to spend hours grinding granny gears or scrubbing brake pads down to metal, Youngs Creek, Nebo Ridge, and Hickory Ridge serve up more challenging rides. Ability aside, cyclists can find short loops or all-day rides at many locations in Hoosier National Forest.

The Forest Service recently introduced trail-use permits as a pilot program. Tags are now required to be purchased and displayed by all mountain bikers. The cost is $3 per day or $25 for an annual pass. Tags can be purchased at the Bedford and Tell City HNF offices (Hoosier National Forest Headquarters, Bedford, IN (812) 275-5987), through the mail, or from more than twenty vendors located near the trails. A list of local vendors is displayed at most HNF trailheads. One example of the beneficial program can seen at the Nebo Ridge trailhead. The newly constructed parking area was paid in part from trail-use permit revenue.

Cyclists would be remiss if they came to the forest only to ride, though. At the developed recreation areas, fishing, boating, hiking, and viewing wildlife are only a handful of activities that can be enjoyed. As an added bonus, camping is free on the majority of the forest's property.

In the near future, more mountain bike trails will be opened. In fact, forest officials are always looking for individuals or groups to volunteer for trail improvement or trail construction projects. Imagine the fulfillment of riding on a trail that you helped construct. For more information on volunteer projects, call one of the Hoosier National Forest Offices.

In the meantime, tread softly and enjoy some of the finest trails Indiana has to offer.

# Nebo Ridge Trail

## Ride Summary

Formerly known as the Knobstone Trail, Nebo Ridge Trail has long been a popular spot amongst mountain bikers. The hills are rolling, not excruciating, but challenging nonetheless. Since most of the singletrack follows ridgetops, it remains relatively dry throughout the year. And so you don't think too unfavorably toward paying to ride here, keep in mind that the new parking area was paid for with the trail access fees.

## Ride Specs

**Start:** Nebo Ridge parking area
**Length:** 8.3-mile point-to-point
**Approximate Riding Time:** 1 hour to 1½ hours
**Difficulty Rating:** Moderate due to length and many rolling hills
**Trail Surface:** Singletrack, doubletrack
**Lay of the Land:** This primarily ridgetop trail rolls over many moderate climbs
**Land Status:** National Forest
**Nearest Town:** Story
**Other Trail Users:** Hikers and horseback riders

## Getting There

**From Columbus:** Travel west on IN 46 for 13 miles to IN 135 south. Take IN 135 south nine miles to Story. Veer off IN 135 at the Story Inn (this is Elkinsville Road, but it is unmarked). Travel 2.7 miles and pass a gravel road on your right. Take the left bend in the road and cross a bridge. Go 0.3 miles, then take a left into the parking area. This newly constructed parking area was paid for with trail access fees. *DeLorme: Indiana Atlas & Gazetteer:* Page 51, D-7

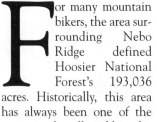

For many mountain bikers, the area surrounding Nebo Ridge defined Hoosier National Forest's 193,036 acres. Historically, this area has always been one of the most popular off-road bicycling locales, but its only legal mountain bike trail, Nebo Ridge Trail (formerly Knobstone Trail), was rarely the only path followed.

At many intersections you will see U.S. Forest markers branching in multiple directions. Nebo Ridge is part of a much larger trail, with the majority of the area's paths dedicated solely to hikers. In fact, one section is being designated strictly as a rare vegetation area. More trails should be

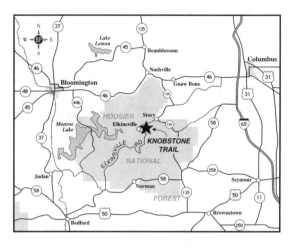

open
s o o n
here, but the out-and-back Nebo route is currently this area's only choice for off-road cyclists.

Seemingly endless miles of hardwood forest surround the trail on all sides, and the forest's distinctive layers are visible from every angle. Here cyclists can envision what much of state looked like during the frontier days.

The forest's canopy acts as a thick umbrella shielding much of the ground from the sun. The large trees steal sunlight from the next layer of smaller trees and shrubs called the "understory." These plants then act as a subcanopy for the forest floor. Here, leaves, sticks, and fallen trees decompose, leaving mosses, ferns, wildflowers, and mushrooms to flourish.

The author, his truck, and his faithful steed.

At the trailhead, the closest town is Elkinsville, which, during the 1850s, was quite a trading hub. Today, though, Elkinsville is better known as a town that was bought out by government. When plans were made to flood the area for Monroe Reservoir, the town was purchased by the state and most of the residents moved away. A cluster of houses still remains in the area, as do some ill feelings toward the buyout and government intervention.

In the past, residents went as far as placing a fence across the county road that led to one of Nebo Ridge's old trailheads. Rangers hesitated to intervene, and the town was isolated enough that the county officials tended to ignore that the fence was built. The fence has since come down, but the defiant attitude still abounds. So cyclists beware.

For the most part, the Nebo Ridge Trail follows the ridgetops. There are a few climbs, but all are within reason and are rideable for intermediate cyclists. Since this trail takes you nine miles away from your vehicle, it's a good idea to carry tools, plenty of food and water, and additional layers of clothing.

## Ride Information

### ● Trail Contact:
Hoosier National Forest Headquarters, Bedford, IN (812) 275-5987 or www.fs.fed.us/r9/hoosier

### ◐ Schedule:
Open daily, year-round

### ⑤ Fees/Permits:
$3

### ❓ Local Information:
Brown County Convention & Visitors Bureau, Nashville, IN 1-800-753-3255 or www.browncounty.com

### ⱽ Local Events/Attractions:
Nashville's quaint shops, Brown County State Park, Nashville, IN (812) 988-6406

### ⊜ Accommodations:
Story Inn, Nashville, IN (812) 988-2273 Brown County State Park, Nashville, IN (812) 988-6406 • Comfort Inn (812) 988-6118

### ⑪ Restaurants:
Story Inn, Nashville, IN (812) 988-2273 Hotel Nashville Resort Dining (812) 988-8400

### ⑪ Group Rides:
Bicycle Garage, Bloomington, IN (812) 339-3457

### ⑪ Organizations:
CIBA, Central Indiana Bicycle Association, Indianapolis, IN (317) 327-BIKE or www.spitfire.net/ciba/

### ☃ Local Bike Shop:
Bicycle Garage, Bloomington, IN (812) 339-3457

### Ⓝ Maps:
USGS maps: Story, IN; Elkinsville, IN • HNF trail map available at HNF headquarters

## Ten o'clock Treaty Line

*The Ten o'clock Treaty Line crosses the state near the trailhead at Nebo Ridge. This line marks the portion of southern Indiana opened to white settlers in 1809 by the Fort Wayne Treaty.*

One of the area's highlights, though not yet open to mountain biking, is Browning Mountain. This ridgetop features several rectangular-shaped slabs of limestone. The spectacular view from these stone benches conjures up images of the Appalachian mountains to the east. With pockets of steam dividing the layers of distant ridges, climbing up to view the "Little Smokies" is definitely worth the hike.

In typical Hoosier fashion, many tales have been spun over the origin of the stones. One such story explains that Native Americans dragged the stones from the lowlands and built a castle on the hilltop. Today many Native Americans still make annual pilgrimages to worship on the hilltop.

Another tale has it that a farmer piled the stones away from his farmland in order to clear a field. The geological explanation seems most likely, though. Water from an ancient sea exposed the rock and shaped it over the years, and as the water receded, the stones were left piled on the hilltop.

The perfect finale for this ride is a weekend stay at the Story Inn. The inn features hot showers, antique-decorated rooms, and a variety of gourmet meals—all within three miles of the trailhead. Who says mountain bikers don't like to be pampered?

## MilesDirections

**0.0 START** from the gravel trailhead at the end of the parking area. Begin the trail's first climb.

**0.5** Arrive at a trail intersection. Follow the main trail straight across.

**1.0** A small trail splits off to the left. Stay on the main Nebo Ridge Trail to the right.

**1.6** Nebo Ridge Trail splits to the left and changes from doubletrack back to single-track.

**2.7** Pass a deer pond on the left. The logs make perfect benches.

**3.3** The trail splits. Take the right split.

**3.4** Nebo Ridge Trail runs parallel to the gravel Berry Road.

**3.75** Arrive at a trail intersection. Continue straight.

**6.6** Enter the pine forest. Nebo Ridge Trail becomes covered in a carpet of pine needles.

**6.7** Nebo Ridge Trail bends to the left. A faint trail strays off to the right.

**8.3** Nebo Ridge Trail ends at County Road 1000 North. Turn around and head back to the start. Hope you brought some food with you!

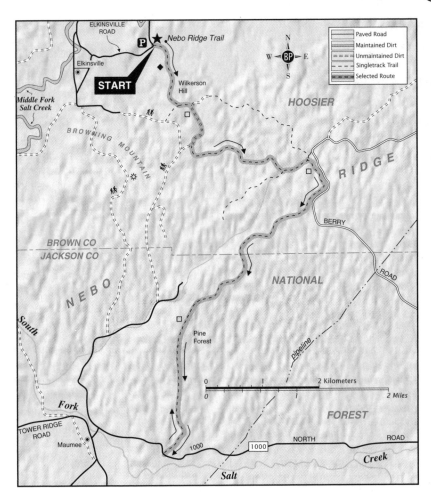

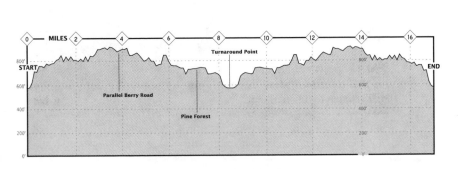

# 21

# Hardin Ridge

## Ride Summary

Hardin Ridge is Hoosier National Forest's shortest trail. It's not a destination spot by any means, but it is a nice alternative activity for campers, boaters, and beach-goers. The trail has one major climb at the beginning that then leads to two miles of easy grade singletrack. Once at the top, cyclists can enjoy a spinning-gear gallivant past the entrances to many of the recreation area's campgrounds. This is a great trail on which to introduce kids to mountain biking.

## Ride Specs

**Start:** At the gravel-covered trailhead across from beach overflow parking lot
**Length:** 1.9-mile point-to-point
**Approximate Riding Time:** 15 to 45 minutes
**Difficulty Rating:** Easy with one moderate climb
**Trail Surface:** Gravel-covered double-track and singletrack
**Lay of the Land:** The mostly flat trail parallels the service roads and has one moderate climb
**Land Status:** National Forest
**Nearest Town:** Bloomington
**Other Trail Users:** Hikers

## Getting There

**From Bloomington:** Follow East 3rd Street to the intersection with IN 46 Bypass. Continue east on IN 46 for 1.3 miles, then turn right onto IN 446 South. Drive 11.4 miles to Chapel Hill Road. Turn right onto Chapel Hill Road and drive 1.8 miles to Hardin Ridge Entrance. Turn right onto the entrance road and drive 2.3 miles to the road that leads to the beach parking lot. Turn left down the beach parking lot road and follow it to the parking area.
***DeLorme: Indiana Atlas & Gazetteer:*** Page 50, D-4

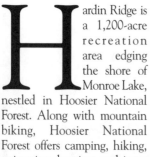

Hardin Ridge is a 1,200-acre recreation area edging the shore of Monroe Lake, nestled in Hoosier National Forest. Along with mountain biking, Hoosier National Forest offers camping, hiking, swimming, boating, and interpretive programs. The recreational area also has six camping loops with 200 campsites—a handful of which are walk-ins—and a swimming beach that offers the choice of sand or grass. The trail

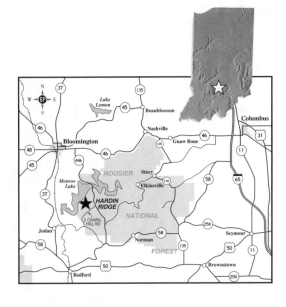

at Hardin Ridge is akin to the Tipsaw Lake Trail (see Ride 29), with one minor difference, Monroe Lake is 80-times larger than Tipsaw Lake.

When the reservoir was proposed in 1954, a newspaper headline read, "5,600-Acre Lake, State's Largest, Proposed For Monroe County." By the time the U.S. Army Corps of Engineers and Indiana Department of Natural Resources finished the project in 1964, they had created a body of water nearly twice that size. The 10,750-acre reservoir now serves as a water supply for Bloomington, a flood control for Monroe County, and a water playground for boaters, water-skiers, and anglers around the state. The reservoir has some of the best fishing in the state. Anglers can hook a variety of fish from bluegill, catfish, hybrid striped bass, largemouth bass, and walleye. Hunting is also allowed with special permits on nearby property. Deer, rabbit, grouse, turkey, and waterfowl are some common game hunted during the designated seasons.

Cruising along Hardin Ridge.

For those looking to pack in a weekend filled with as many of these activities as possible, boats can be rented from one of the marinas on the lake. The caffeinated outdoors enthusiast can fish and mountain bike in the morning, eat some lunch (fresh fish, if you're lucky), swim, water-ski, sunbathe, breeze through a magazine, and quaff a couple of ales on one of the lake's cocktail coves. As the sunlight fades the bedraggled outdoors enthusiast can pitch a tent in one of the area's many campgrounds, and collapse on top of a fluffy sleeping bag dreaming of the long summer day. (I can think of at least one outdoorsmen who calls a day like that "Nirvana.")

Cyclists can bathe in an unabated view of the body of water on the way to Hardin Ridge. Just past the Paynetown Recreational Area and John Mellencamp's luxurious lakeside digs cyclists can take pause on the causeway and gaze longingly upon Indiana's largest body of water.

# Ride Information

## ◐ Trail Contacts:
**Hoosier National Forest**, Bedford, IN (812) 275-5987 or *www.fs.fed.us/r9/hoosier*

## ◐ Schedule:
Open daily, year-round

## ❓ Fees/Permits:
**Gate Fee:** $3 • **Camping:** $9 non-electric sites, $13 electric sites

## ❓ Local Information:
**Bloomington/Monroe County Convention & Visitors Bureau**, Bloomington, IN 1-800-678-9828

## ◉ Local Events/Attractions:
**Lake Monroe**, Bloomington, IN (812) 837-9546

## ▤ Accommodations:
**Hardin Ridge Campground**, Bloomington, IN 1-800-280-CAMP (2267) • **Paynetown Campground**, Bloomington, IN (812) 837-9546 • **Fourwinds Resort**, Smithville, IN (812) 824-9904

## ⓘ Restaurants:
**Burritos as Big as Your Head**, Bloomington, IN (812) 332-5970 • **Hinkles Hamburgers**, Bloomington, IN (812) 339-3335

## ⓘ Other Resources:
**Monroe Lake**, Bloomington, IN (812) 837-9546—*boat rentals and other information*

## ⚙ Local Bike Shops:
**Bicycle Garage**, Bloomington, IN (812) 339-3457

## Ⓝ Maps:
**USGS maps:** Allens Creek, IN • **HNF trail maps** available from HNF headquarters, (812) 275-5987

While the recreation area trail, just a few miles on the other side of the vista, will not be a travel destination for most cyclists, the campground path does serve as an alternate activity for campers and boaters. The singletrack and doubletrack is easy, save for the moderate climb at the trailhead. The trail parallels the main entrance road and provides many bailout points to flat smooth asphalt.

This combination makes Hardin Ridge a great introductory trail for kids, spouses, and friends. After the ride, a swim in the lake is a great reward for rookies that complete the introductory course. So, come down for the cycling and stay the weekend doing everything else.

## **Miles**Directions

**0.0 START** at the trailhead across the street from the entrance to the beach overflow parking lot. It is a well-groomed, gravel doubletrack path that climbs uphill.

**0.4** Finish the moderate climb and cross the main entrance road. The trail then crosses the entrance to Pine Campground.

**0.7** The trail intersects with the Twin Oaks Visitor Center parking entrance. Cut through the parking lot that parallels the main entrance road.

**0.8** The trail resumes at the other end

of the parking lot, near the main entrance road.

**0.9** The trail crosses the entrance to White Oak Campground.

**1.1** The trail crosses the entrance to Blue Gill Campground.

**1.4** Pass a trail on the right, which leads to Southern Point Campground.

**1.5** The trail crosses the entrance to Holland Campground.

**1.9** The trail ends at the entrance to Eads Campground.

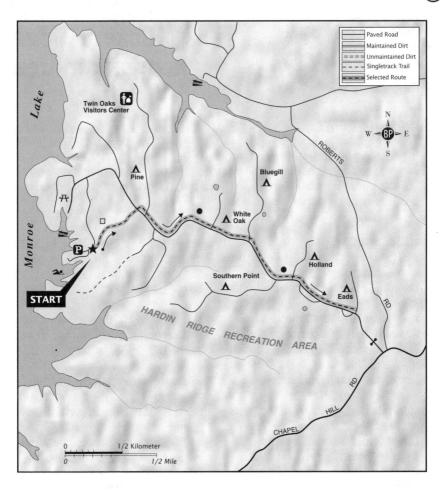

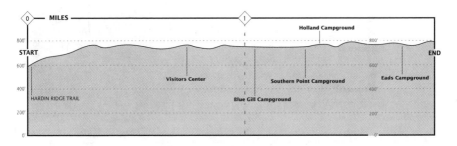

# 22

# Hickory Ridge
# Recreation Area

## Ride Summary

This forty-three mile trail system is the largest and best mountain biking trail system in the state. The variety of terrain will satisfy all levels of cyclists. And maps at major trail intersections help to maintain bearings on the expansive property. Dirt, gravel, and paved roads offer plenty of bailout points if bonking appears imminent.

## Ride Specs

**Start:** Trailhead on NW side of the campground/parking area
**Length:** 12.2-mile loop, part of a 43-mile trail system
**Approximate Riding Time:** 2-3 hours
**Difficulty Rating:** Moderate
**Trail Surface:** Singletrack, forest road, and gravel roads
**Lay of the Land:** Expanse of single-track and forest roads make up Indiana's best trails. Trails vary from easy to difficult.
**Land Status:** National forest
**Nearest Town:** Norman Station
**Other Trail Users:** Hikers, horseback riders, and hunters

## Getting There

**From Columbus (Exit 68 on I-65):** Take I-65 south approximately four miles to IN 58 (Exit 64). Go west on IN 58 and drive 15.2 miles to the junction of IN 258/58. Take IN 58 to the right. After 17 miles on IN 58, IN 58 merges with IN 135. Take IN 58/135 to the left. At 18.2 miles, take a right on IN 58 west as it splits from IN 135. At 26 miles take a right on County Road 1250 west (marked by the Hickory Ridge sign). CR 1250 west turns into Route 650 north. At 27.5 miles, the road splits and turns to gravel. Take the right split following the small U.S. Forest Service sign. At 28 miles turn left into Hickory Ridge's parking/camping area. **DeLorme: Indiana Atlas & Gazetteer:** Page 50, E-6

Hickory Ridge Trail

You are here ➤

E arly settlers first viewed these large tracts of forest as an obstacle to their progress, and soon clearcut much of it to make way for farmland. From 1870 to 1910, sawmills harvested much of the vast forest that blanketed a large part of the state, tearing down black walnut, tulip poplar, black cherry, and white oak. The remaining cull trees were deemed useless and were cut and burned.

The Depression forced many farmers to abandon their property, causing a concern among officials over the growing number of delinquent homesteads. In 1934, Governor Paul McNutt approached the Forest Service to buy this land and set it aside as a national forest.

They accepted his proposal and the initial plots were purchased one year later. To replenish the barren ground, the Civilian Conservation Corp was brought in. These unemployed workers began reforesting and controlling the massive erosion problems. In fact, over the next seven years, the Conservation Corp was a major work force behind many of the Hoosier National Forest projects, and since then the base has expanded considerably.

The result is that thousands of wooded acres are being preserved and portions of Indiana returned to a pristine state, a reminder of a time when pioneers first crossed our borders.

Around Hickory Ridge, acres of wooded hills cover and surround outcrops of limestone. And as Indiana writer Scott Russell Sanders discovered in this area of southern Indiana, limestone is a topic that can break the glare of any stony-eyed local and quickly change terse responses into hour-long ramblings.

For his book, *Stone Country*, Sanders interviewed many stone men and passed on the collective passion inspired from the limestone that dominates the landscape of the southern third of Indiana.

*"I am glad to live in this pocket of rumpled hills where the crust of the earth shows through. When the fog of human voices grows too thick for my lungs, and the ticking of my own inner clock rattles my soul, and I feel the winds of momentariness whistling through my ribs, I go out to climb a cliff or splash down a stony creekbed or dangle my legs over a quarry's lip."*

Sanders, also a cyclist, may have edited out the line, *"...or climb the leg-breaking hills carved from glaciers that crumpled the land and the limestone beneath."* If Sanders ever needed inspiration to write *Mountain Bike Country*, I would introduce him to Hickory Ridge.

Hickory Ridge holds the largest expanse of mountain bike trails in the state. In this 43-mile system, there are several loops from which to choose. Each intersection of this system has trail signs, and the distances between the markers, based on the Hoosier National Forest maps, are accurate. It is easy to gauge fitness by choosing a distance and a trail that matches your skill.

Whatever trail you choose, or however long you plan to ride, you may be hard pressed to ride all of these trails in a single weekend. However, there are few other amenities or activities offered at this recreation area. This combination may appeal to hard-core cyclists who want to combine two full days of riding seemingly endless trails with some very primitive backcountry camping.

One bit of advice: whenever tackling these longer, backwoods routes, it's best to carry tools, spare tubes, and plenty of food and water. And with the fickle weather often found down here in southern Indiana, be sure to carry a few extra layers of clothing.

With the variety of loops, ride times can vary from 45 minutes to all day long. Examine the map in this book to see which loop you want to tackle. While some trails follow the land's contours with rideable descents and ascents others are a bit more challenging. Instead of following the contours, these routes climb and descend the area's hills and valleys. The northwest paths lead to the vicinity of the observation tower.

Here, on the backside of the property, just off Tower Ridge Road, stands the tower. Mountain biking is not allowed here, but the view is worth the hike. Climb to the top and preview the land you're about to ride, or gaze at the hills you've already climbed. To fully appreciate the view, take a pair of binoculars. During the summer, turkey vultures and hawks can be seen circling above the treetops.

## Ride Information

### 🌜 Trail Contact:
**Hoosier National Forest Headquarters,** Bedford, IN (812) 275-5987 or *www.fs.fed.us/r9/hoosier*

### 🕐 Schedule:
Open daily, year-round

### 💲 Fees/Permits:
$3

### ❓ Local Information:
**Brown County Convention & Visitors Bureau,** Nashville, IN 1-800-753-3255 or *www.brown-county.com*

### 💡 Local Events/Attractions:
**Brown County State Park,** Nashville, IN (812) 988-6406

### 🛏 Accommodations:
**Hickory Ridge Campground** (primitive) • **Story Inn,** Nashville, IN (812) 988-2273 • **Brown County State Park,** Nashville, IN (812) 988-6406 • **Comfort Inn** (812) 988-6118

### 🍴 Restaurants:
**Story Inn,** Nashville, IN (812) 988-2273 • **Hotel Nashville Resort Dining** (812) 988-8400

### 🚴 Group Rides:
**CIBA (Central Indiana Bicycle Association)** rides here occasionally

### 👥 Organizations:
**CIBA, Central Indiana Bicycle Association,** Indianapolis, IN (317) 327-BIKE or *www.spitfire.net/ciba/*

### ❓ Other Resources:
**Stone Country,** Scott Russell Sanders

### 🔧 Local Bike Shop:
**Bicycle Garage,** Bloomington, IN (812) 339-3457

### Ⓝ Maps:
**USGS maps:** Norman, IN Elkinsville, IN • **HNF maps** available at HNF headquarters

The tower isn't the only place to spot wild birds, though. Along the trail, grouse are sometimes stirred and will run as fast as cyclists can ride. They will run to a clearing, then break into flight.

## **Miles**Directions

**0.0 START** from the Trail 1 trailhead at the northwest corner of the parking/camping area. Don't be fooled by the large "Hickory Ridge" information sign. That is not the trailhead.

**0.3** Arrive at the intersection with Trail 8. Take the right split (still on Trail 1).

**0.48** Arrive at the intersection with Trail 9. Continue straight on Trail 1.

**0.7** Pass Trail 11 on the right. Continue straight on Trail 1.

**0.95** Arrive at the intersection with Trail 10. Take Trail 10 to the left.

**1.48** Pass an unmarked trail and building set back in the woods on the right.

**1.7** Arrive at the intersection with Trail 4. Take a right on Trail 4.

**1.8** Trail 4 crosses a gravel road and becomes doubletrack.

**2.85** Arrive at the intersection with Trail 18. Take a right on Trail 18.

**3.55** Pass a trail on the left (leads to Hoosier Horseman Campground). Follow Trail 18 as it bends to the right.

**4.9** Trail 18 crosses a gravel road and passes a parking area.

**5.05** Trail 18 widens to doubletrack. This trail is leading to challenging descents and climbs.

**7.8** Trail 18 tops the climb and intersects with Trail 20. Take Trail 20 to the right.

**8.1** Trail 20 ends at CR 725 north. Turn right on the pavement, then take an immediate left on gravel CR 1225 west.

**9.2** CR 1225 splits (marked by the Hickory Ridge map at the intersection). Take the right split.

View along the pipeline section of Hickory Ridge.

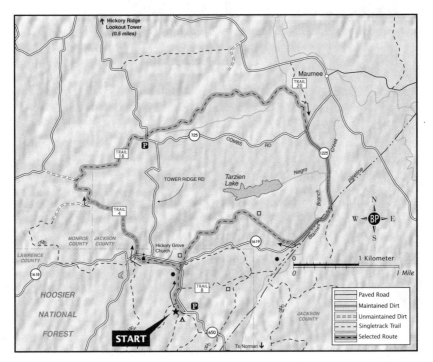

**9.85** Arrive at the intersection with Trail 13/3. Take Trail 3 on the right. (It's currently marked Trail 13, but Hoosier National Forest will soon correct this error.)

**11.9** Trail 3 ends at a gravel road. Continue straight, picking up Trail 1 on the opposite side of the road.

**12.3** Pass Trail 11 on the left. Continue straight on Trail 1.

**12.4** Arrive at the intersection with Trail 9. Continue straight on Trail 1.

**12.5** Pass Trail 8 on the right. Follow Trail 1 as it bends to the left.

**13.0** The ride finishes at parking area.

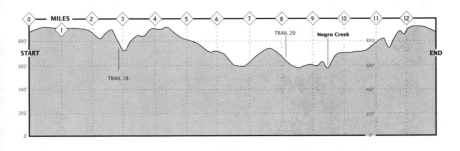

# Bicycle Camping

I f you consider your mountain bike saddle the most comfortable seat in the house and crave an opportunity to prove your self-sufficiency, try bicycle camping. It does require more planning and preparation than a standard day trip, but the particular satisfaction gained from reaching a campground or a remote outdoor destination on two wheels, knowing you're ready for a cozy night outdoors, makes the extra effort worthwhile.

If you plan on doing a lot of bicycle camping/touring, it's a good idea to invest in quality equipment. Everyone should have a pair of medium-to-large size panniers that can be mounted on a rear rack (if you are planning a long trip, you might consider a front rack). A lightweight backpacking tent, sleeping pad, and sleeping bag can be attached to the rear rack using two or three bungie cords. We all have a tendency to over-pack, but the extra weight of unnecessary equipment may cause you to tire more easily. Here are some tips to help you find the appropriate amount of gear:

- Bring a multi-purpose tool that has a can opener, bottle opener, scissors, knife, and screwdriver.
- Pack only one extra change of clothes, plus any necessary layers such as a polypropylene shirt and tights, polar fleece, wool socks, and rain gear. If you are on a multi-day trip, bring extra shorts and t-shirts, and if it's winter, bring an extra pair of polypropylene tights and shirt, as well as a few extra pairs of wool socks.
- Bring a tin cup and spoon for eating and drinking and one lightweight pot for cooking.
- Invest in a lightweight backpacking stove, tent, and sleeping bag.
- Bring along freeze dried food. You can buy many pre-packaged rice and noodle mixes in the grocery store for half of what you'll pay at backpacking stores.
- Bring the minimum amount of water needed for your intended route. Anticipate if there will be water available. Invest in a water filter that can be used to filter water from water sources along the trail.

## Equipment List

Use the checklist of equipment below when you are planning for a single or multi-day trip. You can develop your own equipment list based on the length of your trip, the time of year, weather conditions, and difficulty of the trail.

### Essentials

- bungie cords
- compass
- day panniers
- duct tape
- fenders
- pocket knife or multi-purpose tool
- rear rack
- front rack
- trail map
- water bottles
- water filter
- tool kit
- patch kit
- crescent wrench
- tire levers
- spoke wrench
- extra spokes
- chain rivet tool
- extra tube
- tire pump

### Clothing

- rain jacket/pants
- polar fleece jacket
- wool sweater
- helmet liner
- bicycle tights
- t-shirts/shorts
- sturdy bicycle shoes/boots
- swimsuit
- underwear
- bike gloves
- eye protection
- bike helmet/liner

### First Aid Kit

- bandages (various sizes)
- gauze pads
- surgical tape
- antibiotic ointment
- hydrogen peroxide or iodine
- gauze roll
- ace bandage
- aspirin
- moleskin
- sunscreen
- insect repellent

### Personal Items

- towel
- toothbrush/toothpaste
- soap
- comb
- shampoo

### Camping Items

- backpacking stove
- tent
- sleeping bag
- foam pad
- cooking and eating utensils
- can opener
- flashlight/batteries
- candle lantern
- touring panniers
- pannier rain covers
- zip-lock bags
- large heavy duty plastic garbage bags
- citronella candles (to repel insects)
- small duffels to organize gear

### Miscellaneous Items

- camera/film/batteries
- notebook/pen
- paperback book

### Tip:

Zip-lock bags are a great way to waterproof and organize your gear. Large, heavy-duty plastic garbage bags also make excellent waterproof liners for the inside of your panniers.

# Ogala MTB Trail

## Ride Summary

Solitary cyclists will enjoy the Ogala Trail. This seven-mile system has easy to moderate stretches over a variety of terrain. The singletrack and forest roads cut through plenty of unkept sections that can become unruly during the summer. At the end of the ride, a paved descent allows cyclists to finish with a high-speed, knobby-tire humming descent.

## Ride Specs

**Start:** Gate at north end of parking area
**Length:** 6.3-mile loop; part of a 7-mile system
**Approximate Riding Time:** 1 to 1½ hours
**Difficulty:** Moderate
**Trail Surface:** Singletrack, forest roads, and county roads
**Lay of the Land:** Traverse small ridges and ravines that offer a variety of easy to moderate-grade paths
**Land Status:** National forest
**Nearest Town:** Freetown
**Other Trail Users:** Hikers and horse-back riders

## Getting There

**From Columbus:** Take IN 46 west approximately 13 miles to IN 135 south. Take IN 135 south 16.3 miles to County Road 1190 North. This is the first road you can turn left on once you cross the Jackson County Line. Turn left on CR 1190 North (follow CR 1190 North as it bends to the right and to the left) and travel 1.1 miles to the gravel road parking area. *DeLorme: Indiana Atlas & Gazetteer:* Page 51, D-8

The Ogala Trail System is one that seems to thrive on the edge. Situated at the southern border of Brown County and away from the hubbub of Nashville and Brown County State Park's tourist traps, Ogala resides peacefully in the quiet fringe of nature.

Ogala also seems to exist on the fringe of the Forest Service. Sitting like a diamond in the rough, this trail system is mostly undeveloped with many trails sparsely marked; fallen timber crossing some of its cut paths. Ogala's tranquil existence draws the solitary cyclist and will show off its gems only to the most peaceful trail users. Tucked back along these faint paths, wild turkey, grouse, many species of wood-pecker, and deer all call the Ogala area home. On still winter afternoons,

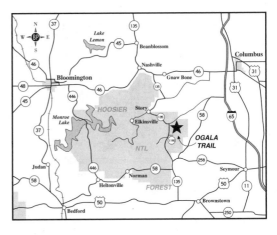

distant tapping of pileated and blackback woodpeckers are the forest's only sounds. While on the snow-covered ground, three-toed turkey tracks seem to saunter in all directions.

At one time, one could access the Ogala property by forest roads. But these wide service routes have not been maintained and today have been reduced to mere single-track trails. These one-lane routes make up the majority of the loop and cut through high grass where the dirt roads used to exist. Ogala is classified as easy to moderate primarily because the trail rolls along without any major climbs and the route is fairly easy to navigate. There are a couple of challenging climbs at the east end of the route that help to make the ride a little more intense.

One of the first points of interest cyclists will come across is Sundance Lake (*you actually pass the entrance leading to Sundance Lake*). Named after a Native American purification ceremony, the lake plays host to an annual gathering in late spring. Indians travel from around the country to attend this ancient dance. Strict rules apply and no photographs or video may be taken. Guards are even posted throughout the woods to enforce this rule. A local resident tells of a TV crew that was escorted out of the woods when they were caught with their cameras and equipment. Strict policies aside, guests are welcome to attend. More information can be obtained from the Hoosier National Forest Offices.

Sundance Lake is also known for its supreme fishing. If you can tote a pole while you ride, it might be worth the effort. This 5.3-acre lake was built in 1992 with the cooperation of Indiana's B.A.S.S (Bass Anglers Sportsman Society) Chapter Federation, Indiana's Department of Natural Resources, Soil Conservation Service, and the Forest Service. This consorted effort created one of Hoosier National Forest's most productive lakes. Stocked with redear, bluegill, bass, and channel catfish, almost anyone can catch a fish here.

Once past Sundance, cyclists will ease off the dirt road and return to singletrack. Dropping down into a hollow, cyclists must bypass a series of recovering ravines. These gullies reveal the sad shape this land was in before being purchased by the Forest Service. The four-foot gullies have stabilized from the grass and small trees that have dropped roots here. However, this section is still unrideable, and trailblazers wisely rerouted the path here.

From here the trail flattens out for a short while leading to the route's notable climbs. At the east end of the trail, the path rolls over two ridges before turning back to the west. Just past this bend, the path passes an abandoned storage building and bends back to the north. Soon after this turn, the trail steadily climbs and turns, continuing its trek west. In the winter, when the brush is low, cyclists are afforded a scenic view of the adjacent ridge from the top of this climb.

The final leg of Ogala follows County Road 1190 North. As a bonus, a high-speed downhill offers a grand finale that carries cyclists into the parking area.

Once the bikes are on the rack, relaxation is found just one mile from the trailhead. Comfortable beds and a continental breakfast await at the Blossom Hollow Bed and Breakfast. The downside to these quarters is that there are only two rooms. Therefore, it's best to call ahead for reservations. The upside, however, if you are lucky enough to get a room in

## Ride Information

### 📞 Trail Contact:
**Hoosier National Forest Headquarters,** Bedford, IN (812) 275-5987 or *www.fs.fed.us/r9/hoosier*

### 🕐 Schedule:
Open daily, year-round

### 💲 Fees/Permits:
$3

### 💡 Local Information:
**Jackson County Visitors & Convention Bureau,** Seymour, IN *www.indico.net/counties/jackson*

### 💡 Local Events/Attractions:
**Sundance Lake**

### 🛏 Accommodations:
**Primitive camping along Ogala trail • Blossom Bed and Breakfast,** Freetown, IN (812) 988-9374

### 🍴 Restaurants:
**Crossroads Restaurant,** Seymour, IN (812) 522-6767 • **Gerth Cafe,** Seymour, IN (812) 522-3860

### 🚲 Local Bike Shop:
**Bicycle Station,** Columbus, IN (812) 379-9005

### 🅝 Maps:
**USGS map:** Waymansville, IN • **HNF trail maps** available at HNF Headquarters

May, comes when the local dogwoods are in full-bloom. The white blooms of the trees fill the hollow and paints a glorious springtime scene.

Ogala is open to hunters, has great fishing, hosts a large Native American gathering, is home to a number of feathered friends for bird watchers to enjoy, and has a quaint bed and breakfast close by, yet it remains fairly anonymous. I guess word of this outdoor jewel just hasn't gotten out to the public—yet.

## **Miles**Directions

**0.0 START** from the parking area off CR 1190 North. Leave the parking area and roll past the gate at the north end of the parking area.

**0.1** The trail crosses a small creek.

**0.2** The trail splits. Take the left split.

**0.25** The trail splits. Take the left split.

**0.8** The trail splits. In the summer, this split is difficult to see. Take the left split and cross a creek. A blue marker is on the near side of the creek. A white diamond can be seen on the opposite side of the creek.

**1.1** Come to a faint trail split. Take the right split. The left split crosses Little Salt Creek and leads to Becks Grove Road.

**1.4** Arrive at a trail intersection marked by a brown HNF sign. There is an arrow to the left and two unmarked trails to the right. Continue straight through this intersection.

**1.5** The trail bends to the left and crosses a small creek. After a small climb, the trail bends to the right, then bends to the left again. These switchbacks are not on the map.

**1.8** The trail passes a deer pond on the left.

**2.0** The trail intersects with CR 1190 North at a bend in the road. Turn left on CR 1190 North.

**2.2** The trail passes the entrance to Sundance Lake.

**2.4** Turn right off CR 1190 North into an unmarked parking area for a small unnamed lake. Take an immediate left on a faded, downhill forest road heading east.

**2.4** The trail bypasses a series of deep gullies. This is an example of the massive erosion that occurred before HNF purchased the land.

**2.5** Arrive at a trail intersection. Turn left. The trail immediately bends to the right and parallels an abandoned forest road. The trail basically follows the old forest road to a dirt road.

**3.1** The trail fades as it leads to an open grassy area. Follow the ruts across the opening to the trail.

**3.2** The trail crosses over the end of a dirt road. Cross the dirt road and follow the jeep trail that borders the private property on the left (marked by two ten-foot posts, each with "No Trespassing" signs). Pass a lake and climb over a ridge.

**3.4** Pass a trail on the left at the top of the climb. Continue straight.

**3.5** Arrive at a trail intersection marked by a rusty gatepost at the top of the climb. Turn right.

**3.6** Pass an abandoned storage building on the left. The trail bends right, heading north. A short climb leads to a bend to the left and to a steeper climb.

**4.3** The trail merges into another trail.

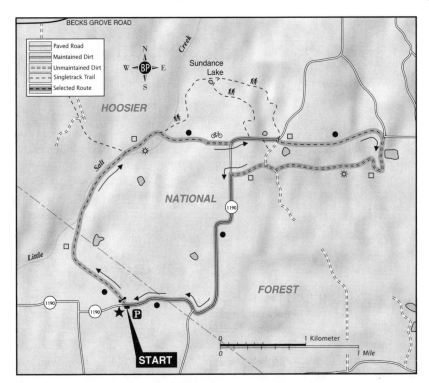

## **Miles**Directions *continued*

Take the trail and HNF trail signpost to the right.

**4.4** Come to a faint trail split. Take the faint trail to the left. The trail to the right leads back to the unnamed lake that was passed at 2.3 miles. This section is very faint.

**4.75** The trail intersects with CR 1190 North. Turn left.

**5.0** The road bends to the right.

**5.1** The road bends to the left.

**5.3** The road turns to asphalt.

**5.6** The road bends to the right.

**5.8** The road bends to the right and intersects with CR 400 West. Continue straight on CR 1190 North.

**6.3** A great downhill run finishes at the parking area. Turn right into the parking area. Ride complete.

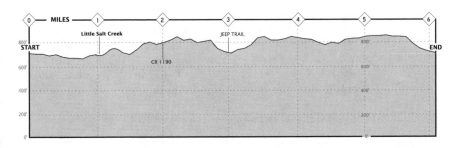

# Shirley Creek

## Ride Summary

Shirley Creek is used predominantly by horseback riders. For mountain bikers who don't mind sharing the multi-use trail, challenging rides await. Away from the hitching racks, more than 11 miles of singletrack, challenging descents, and granny-gear climbs merit the "moderate to difficult" rating.

## Ride Specs

**Start:** Trailhead on the north end of the campground, across the gravel road from the restrooms

**Length:** 8.75 mile-loop of an 11.3-mile system

**Approximate Riding Time:** 2 hours

**Difficulty Rating:** Moderate to difficult

**Trail Surface:** Singletrack and double-track

**Lay of the Land:** Once past the climb out of the campground, the trail is fairly level. Soon thereafter, the level path leads to challenging descents and climbs until just past Felknor Hollow

**Land Status:** National forest

**Nearest Town:** French Lick

**Other Trail Users:** Equestrians and hikers

## Getting There

**From Bloomington:** Take IN 37 south approximately 25 miles to IN 50 just south of Bedford. Take IN 50 west 9.6 miles to the intersection of IN 50 and IN 60. Continue west on IN 50 0.1 miles to the first county road on the left. Turn left on this county road and immediately cross some railroad tracks. Drive 0.9 to CR 825 west. Turn right on CR 825 west. Drive 3.4 miles to the split in the road. Take the left split (CR 810 north) and pass Bonds Chapel and a cemetery on the right. Drive 1.3 miles to CR 775. Turn right on CR 775 and drive 1.2 miles to the "Shirley Creek Trailhead" sign on the left. Turn left into the property and follow the road to the campgrounds. *DeLorme: Indiana Atlas & Gazetteer:* Page 57, B-9

Two things are unique to the Shirley Creek trail system. The first is the Lost River. In this karst that surrounds the trail, sinkholes, caverns, and underground waterways are common. As one of the longest subterranean waterways, the Lost River flows underground southeast of Orleans and runs south of Orangeville, eventually flowing into the East Fork of the White River.

The second thing unique to Shirley Creek is NBA Hall of Famer Larry Bird. Deemed the "Hick from French Lick," Bird did not actually grow up

in French Lick. Just down the road a piece from Shirley Creek is Bird's real hometown of West Baden. In fact, Bird's mom still resides in their hometown. It's rumored that Larry still stops by sometimes to mow his mother's grass.

Since Bird attended the area's high school, the resort town of French Lick adopted Bird as their own hometown boy with high hopes of filling more rooms. Every town needs a hook, and what better hook could a Hoosier town have than a living basketball legend.

Away from the resorts is the campground for Shirley Creek Recreation Area. Like most Hoosier National Forest campgrounds, no fees or permits are needed for camping. The grounds include primitive sites, pit toilets, and hitching racks at each site to tie off your weary bicycles or to air out your musty sleeping bag. Unfortunately, there is no drinking water here.

Generally, there is little activity in the campground except for the few equestrians who come to enjoy the trails. This is a group, though, that is friendly and approachable. So take the opportunity to talk to the people with whom you share the trails. A friendly conversation and an invitation to share a campfire will go a lot farther to enhance relationships than any legislative hearing ever will. Talk about the trail, show them the maps from this book, and pass on some of the trail's highlights or caution areas.

The idea behind this stretch of national forest is to escape civilization for a while, breathe fresh air, and enjoy the untouched, undeveloped beauty of the forest. The only difference between you and equestrians is your choice of transportation.

A positive attitude will be helpful at the start of this ride. Shift into your granny gear to begin this predominantly singletrack system, as the trailhead is marked by a quick ascent that climbs to the ridgetop and away

# Ride Information

## 📞 Trail Contact:
**Hoosier National Forest Headquarters,** Bedford, IN (812) 275-5987 or *www.fs.fed.us/r9/hoosier*

## 🕐 Schedule:
Open daily, year-round

## 💲 Fees/Permits:
$3

## ❓ Local Information:
**French Lick/West Baden Chamber of Commerce,** French Lick, IN (812) 936-2405 or *www.frenchlick.com*

## 🅥 Local Events/Attractions:
**Ski Paoli Peaks,** Paoli, IN (812) 723-4696

## 🛏 Accommodations:
**Shirley Creek Campground (primitive) • French Lick Springs Resort,** French Lick, IN 1-800-457-4042, (812) 936-9300

## 🍴 Restaurants:
**The Mineral Springs,** Paoli, IN (812) 723-4648

## 🚲 Local Bike Shop:
**Thornes Bedford Bicycle Center,** Bedford, IN (812) 275-4656

## 🅝 Maps:
**USGS maps:** Huron, IN; Georgia, IN • **HNF trail map** available at HNF headquarters

from the campground. After this climb, the path levels off and crosses County Road 775. The route then rolls under a thick forest canopy and past a small deer pond. Cyclists are now just south of Hindostan. With the Hindostan Whetstone Company as its keystone, the town was a thriving stone-cutting hub until the 1820s. But when an unknown disease swept through the area, Hindostan was transformed into a ghost town.

After passing the trail that leads to Hindostan, the path bends to the west. As the singletrack heads toward Bonds Chapel, it holds a series of challenging climbs and descents that finish at County Road 810. The loop follows the county roads and offers a nice scenic break before heading back into the woods.

Just off the dirt road, the trail descends to a gate. A quick climb then takes cyclists back to the ridgetop. The trail takes a challenging descent into Felknor Hollow at the southwestern corner and lowest point of the route. The climb out of the lower landscape proves to be challenging as the trail ascends from 500 feet to the 800-foot ridge. After the climb, the route crosses back to County Road 775 and heads toward the campground, where it leaves most cyclists horse tired.

## **Miles**Directions

**0.0 START** at the Shirley Creek Campground. Find the trailhead at the north end of the campground.

**0.25** The trail splits. Take the right split.

**0.55** The trail splits. Take the left split.

**0.60** The Trail splits. Follow the main trail to the right. (The trail to the left dumps out to CR 775.)

**0.95** The trail intersects with CR 775. Take a right on CR 775.

**0.97** Trail turns left off CR 775 just past the Orange County NW Dumpsite. You're now on singletrack.

**1.45** The trail bends to the right.

**1.55** Pass a deer pond on the right.

**2.0** The trail splits. Take the right split and a pass a deer pond on the left.

**3.0** The trail crosses CR 810 north. Continue straight on singletrack. The trail bends to the left and follows a utility easement.

**3.2** The trail intersects with CR 810 north. Turn right onto CR 810.

**3.35** Turn left on CR 860 West. Now riding on a gravel road.

**3.8** Pass a driveway on the left. Continue straight on CR 860 West.

**4.0** CR 860 West ends. Arrive at a trail split overgrown with weeds. Take the right split.

**4.2** Come to an open area. Find the trail on the left. Roll past the gate and continue on the trail.

**4.3** Pass a faint trail heading off to the left. Continue straight on the main trail.

**4.8** The trail splits. Take the left split. Now entering a section of challenging descents.

**6.3** Arrive at a trail intersection and a trail marker near the creekbed. Follow the trail and marker to the left.

**6.45** Come to a trail intersection at the end of an open field. Take the trail on the right.

**6.5** The trail crosses a creek and starts climbing.

**6.7** Come to a trail split. Follow the sign and take the trail to the left.

**8.2** The trail intersects with CR 775. Take a left on CR 775.

**8.22** The trail splits from CR 775 to the right. Now on a singletrack trail.

**8.4** The trail merges with another trail. Follow the sign and the trail as it bends to the left.

**8.45** The trail ends at a gravel road and the entrance to the campground. Take a right on the gravel road.

**8.75** Back at the campground. Ride complete.

## **Trail Adoption**

*Cyclists can help maintain this trail by adopting a portion of it. For more information, call or write Hoosier National Forest Headquarters; (812) 275-5987*

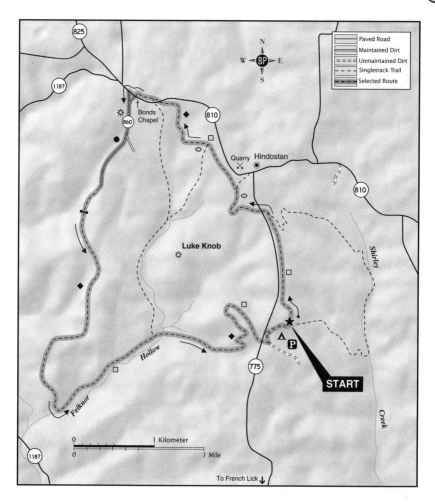

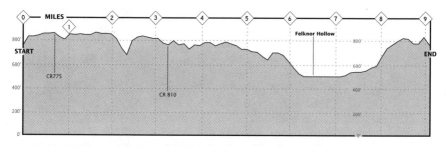

# 25

# Youngs Creek Trail

## Ride Summary

Youngs Creek is a topographer's nightmare. This system is rated difficult because it is the most strenuous trail in Indiana. The majority of the loop is singletrack that is constantly climbing, descending, or winding through the woods. The county road portion of the trail offers a respite, but later harbors a challenging climb. Even the locals seem tougher. Cyclists realize this when they pass the sign that reads, "Trespassers will be violated."

## Ride Specs

**Start:** Parking area off of CR 550 South
**Length:** 10.8 mile-loop
**Approximate Riding Time:** 2½ to 3 hours
**Difficulty Rating:** Difficult
**Trail Surface:** Singletrack, gravel roads and paved roads
**Lay of the Land:** The trail seems to be in constant flux—full of twists, turns, descents, and climbs through wooded ridges and ravines
**Land Status:** National Forest
**Nearest Town:** Paoli
**Other Trail Users:** Equestrians and hikers

## Getting There

**From Bloomington:** Travel south on IN 37 approximately 60 miles to Pine Valley. (In the process, cyclists will pass the "Youngs Creek Campground" sign. Continue past the sign to the more secluded, southernmost parking area.) At Pine Valley at the Marathon Gas Station, turn right at the small Youngs Creek sign, traveling west on County Road 550 south. Go 0.8 miles and turn right into the trailhead parking area. The only sign is a post marked "FR 707." *DeLorme: Indiana Atlas & Gazetteer:* Page 57, E-10

J ust east of the Youngs Creek Trailhead, near the town of Pine Valley, is a historical marker for the Indiana Initial Point Memorial. Established in 1805 by Ebenezer Buckingham Jr., Initial Point marks the intersection of the Second Principal Meridian and the Baseline (the point of origin for all Indiana land surveys). The marker is also a tribute to all the frontiersmen who helped survey the state.

When the point of origin was surveyed, Pine Valley was known as Valley of Hog's Defeat. The origin of this name can be tied to a colorful tale claiming that several irate citizens drove off the feeding herds of hogs that once threatened to destroy their farmland. Over the years, the town thankfully changed its name to Pine Valley.

The Indiana Initial Point Memorial was dedicated to frontier surveyors in 1973, but the stone cutters who crafted the marker apparently left out the stanza that stands as a tribute to the cyclists who survived the Youngs Creek Trail ride.

Youngs Creek is one of the state's most difficult trail systems and is the most appealing for hard-core mountain bikers. The trail itself is a topographer's nightmare because of its constant need to descend, ascend, twist, and turn every 20 yards or so. After a heavy rain, the few flat spots on this loop are covered with muddy quagmires that provide resistance equal to a challenging climb. Even the county roads that make up a small portion of the trail harbor a substantial grade.

The trail begins from the north end of the parking area. In the first 1.5 miles, there are two climbs, both followed by sharp descents (one of which is a white-knuckle switchback descent that leads down to a creekbed).

The rest areas of this system are not limestone ledges like the ones found on other trails in this area. The breaks on this loop come on the gravel roads that pop up at regular intervals along the route. The first rest stop occurs after the initial climbs and descents, but doesn't last long. It quickly leads back to more singletrack, and one short mile later, cyclists will drop down another switchback descent into a creekbed.

During this descent, cyclists will cross over an invisible Indian Treaty Line—one of many treaties that were made as settlers pushed Native Americans west.

Huffing along at Youngs Creek.

Three miles into the ride the trail offers a cul-de-sac stopping place. It is actually a turnaround for campers, but offers a great rest area as well. A short distance from this rest stop, the trail intersects with a gravel road. There should be a sign here warning cyclists of a rooster crossing. This isn't a flock of wild roosters, though. Their home is up the road a bit (marked by the sign: "Trespassers will be violated"). Yikes!

Once the trail leads back into the woods, it turns into mud. This seasonal quagmire provides equal resistance to any of the day's toughest climbs, and a thick forest canopy overhead seems to keep it wet most of the year.

At the five-mile mark, the trail offers yet another thrilling technical descent. This downhill is fairly straight, and cyclists can carry some speed all the way to the creekbed. One mile later, the trail intersects with County Road 550, which leads cyclists back to the parking area.

This is a nice bailout point if supplies are low or if cyclists believe that bonking is eminent. If you choose to continue, this paved road offers only a short break. Once the turn is made on County Road 175, a smaller gear is recommended to make this climb to the trailhead—and the grade doesn't stop here, either.

Finally, after one mile of climbing, the grade tops out and the trail continues along the ridgetop. It's only a short respite, though. After a couple more miles of singletrack, cyclists climb a lengthy hill that tops out at County Road 550 and the parking area.

## Ride Information

**Trail Contact:**
**Tell City Ranger District,** Tell City, IN (812) 547-7051 or *www.fs.fed.us/r9/hoosier*

**Schedule:**
Open daily, year-round

**Fees/Permits:**
$3

**Local Information:**
**French Lick/West Baden Chamber of Commerce,** French Lick, IN (812) 936-2405 or *www.frenchlick.com*

**Local Events/Attractions:**
**Ski Paoli Peaks,** Paoli, IN (812) 723-4696

**Accommodations:**
**Youngs Creek Campground** (primitive) • **French Lick Springs Resort,** French Lick, IN 1-800-457-4042, (812) 936-9300

**Restaurants:**
**The Mineral Springs,** Paoli, IN (812) 723-4648

**Local Bike Shop:**
**Thornes Bedford Bicycle Center,** Bedford, IN (812) 275-4656

**Maps:**
**USGS map:** Valeene, IN • **HNF trail maps** available at HNF headquarters

Like many of the Hoosier National Forest recreation areas, camping is free and open to anyone. The campground is located north of the trailhead parking area at the northernmost point of the trail. There are primitive sites available, the only amenities being pit toilets, hitching racks, and a picnic shelter.

## **Miles**Directions

**0.0 START** at the north end of the trailhead parking area.

**0.5** Bear left at the trail split, following the trail signs.

**1.3** Ride down a number of switchbacks to Youngs Creek.

**1.5** Cross Youngs Creek. Continue straight.

**1.6** Turn left on the gravel road. Immediately turn right back onto the singletrack trail.

**3.4** Arrive at a turnaround for campers. Ride straight, crossing this "cul-de-sac," and look for the Main Trail sign.

**3.5** Turn left on the gravel road. Watch out for roosters crossing your path!

**3.6** Continue straight. Pass a gravel road heading off to the right. This is private property and home of the roosters.

**3.62** Follow the singletrack gravel split to the right.

**5.5** Cross a creekbed after a technical descent.

**5.9** Turn right on CR 550 South. You can turn left and head back to the parking area from here if you're tired.

**6.4** Turn left on CR 175 West. Don't be deceived by the pavement. CR 175 West has a climb worthy of respect.

**6.6** Keep your eyes peeled for the trailhead marker on the left. Turn left onto a singletrack trail.

**8.1** Take the trail to the right, following the trail sign.

**10.8** Reach CR 550 South after completing a long, tough climb. Turn right, then a quick left into the trailhead parking area. Back at last!

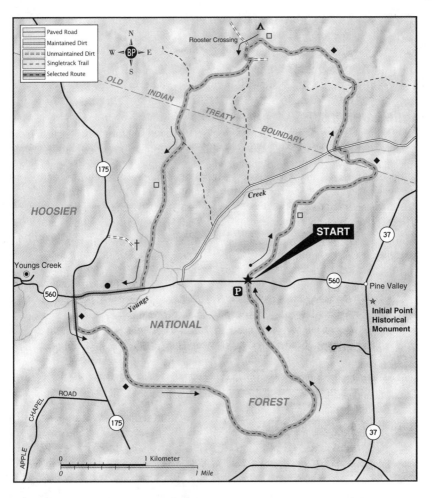

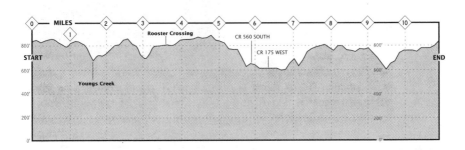

# Lick Creek

## Ride Summary

Lick Creek is Youngs Creek's nearest neighbor. Geographic proximity, though, doesn't guarantee topographic equality. The singletrack and forest roads here are moderate and more forgiving. Of tourist interest, the trail passes "Little Africa"—one of the earliest African-American settlements in Indiana.

## Ride Specs

**Start:** At the east end of the parking lot, the trailhead is marked by a "Stay on Trail" sign
**Length:** 8-mile loop
**Approximate Riding Time:** 1 to 1½ hours
**Difficulty Rating:** Moderate due to a handful of short descents and climbs
**Trail Surface:** Singletrack and Forest Service road
**Lay of the Land:** Trail winds through forested and rolling hills
**Land Status:** National forest
**Nearest Town:** Paoli
**Other Trail Users:** Hikers and equestrians

## Getting There

**From Paoli's Town Square:** Follow IN 37 for 5.3 miles to County Road 450 South, a sign for Marengo Cave marks the intersection. Turn left onto County Road 450 South and follow it for one mile to Lick Creek parking area. Turn left into the parking area. *DeLorme: Indiana Atlas & Gazetteer:* Page 57, E-10

L ick Creek's nearest trail neighbors are the more challenging trails of Youngs Creek. This is worthy of mentioning because it would appear that Lick Creek did not inherit the extremities of its multi-purpose trail kin, proving the maxim that geographic proximity doesn't guarantee topographic equality. What Lick Creek lacks in gear-grinding geography, it makes up for with interesting road names and fascinating history. As the trail meanders past Grease Gravy Road (mmm-mmm, please pass the biscuits), trail users will come to an area known locally as "Little Africa."

Getting ready for the ride.

The area evolved into settlement for freed slaves who moved here from North Carolina sometime between 1815 and 1820. Quakers, looking for a land that was more tolerant as well as less restrictive, brought the liberated slaves to this settlement. Upon their arrival, they settled on Ishmael Roberts' property, a black Revolutionary War veteran. In nearby Chambersburg, the first school for blacks was built in Orange County. Other than the school, the only other building of note was the African Methodist Episcopal Church. There were no stores or town square and the settlement was never incorporated. The residents resided in clapboard-covered log cab-

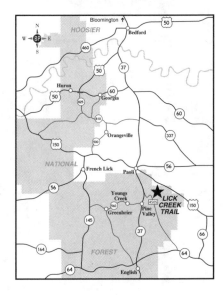

ins, supporting themselves with farming, horse training, wagon making, carpentry, and logging. At the height of the settlement, according to the 1860 census, more than 260 blacks owned approximately 500 acres of farmland and forest. The church is all that remains of the settlement. The forest has slowly reclaimed this property with only the stones of the foundation and cemetery markers remaining. No one knows exactly what happened to the settlement, though history books suggest sickness, flight, and isolation or a combination of these factors eventually taking their toll on the settlement.

In 1970, Paoli Boy Scouts took it upon themselves to delve into the history of the settlement, restore it, and raise awareness about "Little Africa." They cleared the overgrowth, erected white crosses on unmarked graves, constructed a monument, and surrounded the area with a split-rail fence. Upon completion of their project, the troop posted a sign: "Free men of color who came to Indiana early in the 1800s to find freedom settled in this area that is now known as Little Africa. The former slaves were given the opportunity to toil and earn their own living, and their children would have the rights and privileges of all men in this new country. They took their place in the state and nation as soldiers, farmers, and most of all ... free men."

## Ride Information

### ● Trail Contacts:
**Hoosier National Forest Headquarters,** Bedford, IN (812) 275-5987 or *www.fs.fed.us/r9/hoosier*

### ● Schedule:
Open daily, year-round

### ● Fees/Permits:
$3

### ● Local Information:
**French Lick/West Baden Chamber of Commerce,** French Lick, IN (812) 936-2405 or *www.frenchlick.com*

### ● Local Events/Attractions:
**Ski Paoli Peaks,** Paoli, IN (812) 723-4696

### ● Accommodations:
**Youngs Creek Campground,** French Lick, IN (812) 936-9300 or 1-800-457-4042-primitive sites

### ● Restaurants:
**The Mineral Springs,** Paoli, IN (812) 723-4648

### ● Local Bike Shops:
**Thornes Bedford Bicycle Center,** Bedford, IN (812) 275-4656

### ● Maps:
**USGS map:** Valeene, IN • **HNF trail maps** available at HNF office (812) 275-5987

Today, as free men and women, we cannot only absorb some of the lessons learned from the area's history, but enjoy a moderate workout as well. There are some challenging sections of the trail with the first being the spur trail leaving the parking lot. This singletrack jaunt, which leads to the main loop, harbors a speedy descent that later becomes a challenging climb on the return trip, with a few whoop-de-dos thrown in for fun.

The main loop is an equal split of singletrack and doubletrack with creek and gas pipeline crossings. The ride includes an enjoyable descent through a pine forest, with the majority of the ride passing quietly through hardwood forests. Depending on the level of the cyclist, this loop can be used as a warm-up ride for Youngs Creek. It can also serve as a cool down of sorts for those who have tackled Youngs Creek first and are looking to unwind a bit before heading home.

## MilesDirections

**0.0 START** from the trailhead at the east end of the parking area. The "Stay on Trail" sign marks the trailhead.

**1.6** The parking area spur trail connects to main trail loop. Follow the loop to the right.

**1.7** The trail bends to the left and past a faint trail on the right. Follow the arrow and continue on the main trail to the left.

**2.4** The trail crosses a natural gas pipeline clearing.

**2.9** The trail crosses a creek bed.

**4.4** The trail comes to a "T." Follow the trail and the arrow to the left.

**4.7** The trail merges into a grassy forest road. Follow the arrow and trail to the left.

**5.5** Past a deer pond on the left.

**5.5** The trail crosses a natural gas pipeline clearing.

**6.0** The Forest Service road/trail comes to a singletrack trail to the left. Follow the Lick Creek Loop to the left. The Forest Service road leads to a dead end at Grease Gravy Road.

**6.5** Come to the parking area spur trail. Turn right and return to parking area or take another loop.

**8.0** Ride ends at parking area.

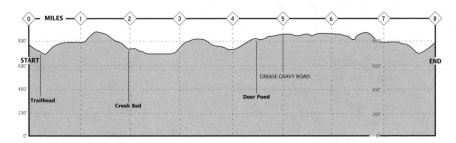

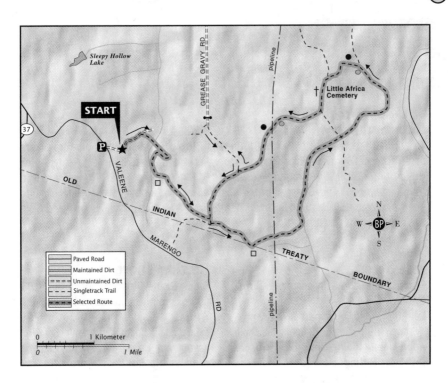

Paved Road
Maintained Dirt
Unmaintained Dirt
Singletrack Trail
Selected Route

0   1 Kilometer
0   1 Mile

START

Sleepy Hollow Lake

GREASE GRAVY RD.

Pipeline

Little Africa Cemetery

OLD

INDIAN

MARENGO

RD

TREATY

BOUNDARY

VALEENE

pipeline

37

N
W — BP — E
S

**Birdseye Trail**

## Ride Summary

To paraphrase the nearby town's founder, "Birdseye Trail suits mountain bikers to a T-y-tee." Birdseye is a light-hearted blend of forest roads and singletrack which loops around a small lake, across Mitchell Creek, and through the surrounding woods. The easy grade of this trail allows ample time to spot wildlife such as grouse, wild turkeys, and pileated woodpeckers. Cyclists beware: ATVs are common on this trail.

## Ride Specs

**Start:** Gated forest road off of Birdseye Loop
**Length:** 6-mile loop, part of a 10-mile system
**Approximate Riding Time:** 1 to 1½ hours
**Difficulty Rating:** Easy to moderate
**Trail Surface:** Easy-grade forest roads and singletrack
**Lay of the Land:** Forest roads and singletrack wind past a small lake, through the woods, and over Mitchell Creek
**Land Status:** National forest
**Nearest Town:** Birdseye
**Other Trail Users:** ATVs, hikers, and equestrians

## Getting There

**From Evansville:** Go north on I-164 approximately 12 miles to I-64. Take I-64 east 43 miles to IN 145 (Exit 72). Take IN 145 north for six miles to Birdseye Loop Road. Turn right, heading east on the dirt road. Turn right into the parking area after one mile. The parking area is little more than a widened fire road with a gate marking the trailhead. **DeLorme: Indiana Atlas & Gazetteer: Page 57, H-8**

Not to be confused with the successful frozen vegetable brand, the Birdseye Trail is sandwiched between Ferdinand State Forest to the south and the town of Birdseye to the north.

It seems Birdseye was named after local clergyman, state legislator, and postmaster Reverend Benjamin Talbott Goodman,

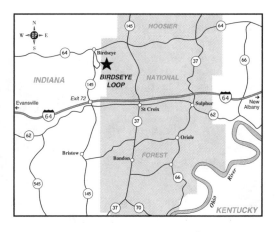

whose nickname was "Bird." In 1856, the residents of the crossroads desired a post office. After surveying the proposed location, Goodman supposedly proclaimed, "It suits Bird's eye to a T-y-tee," which is about as believable as any Hoosier tale I've heard.

With a booming lumber industry, as well as a 1903 newspaper headline proclaiming, "Birdseye May Become Oil Center of the U.S.," the town became a bustling center. Drillers rushed in, leased the land, and constructed their wells. This early petroleum production was very intense and conservation policies were nonexistent. By and by, the wells dried up, the boom was over, and Birdseye bustled no more. Today, near that same intersection where Goodman took in his bird's-eye view, lies an antique shop, a city park, a few abandoned brick buildings, and Birdseye's historic post office.

Through all of the town's ups and downs, Birdseye plays host to yet another Hoosier National Forest off-the-beaten-path trail system. With a parking area that's nothing more than a notch off the county road, cyclists should see few other trail users during their ride.

This loop consists predominantly of wide paths and a few climbs blessed with forgiving grades. This combination makes the ride enjoyable and somewhat suitable for introducing a novice to a backwoods bicycle ride.

A word of caution: motorized travel along this trail is prohibited, though locals use this area to go mudding with ATVs, motorcycles, and, judging by the large paths, four-wheel-drive trucks. Yielding to all motorized vehicles is highly recommended.

Away from the drone of revving engines, a rhythmic knocking can be heard from a distant tree. The source is a head-banging raptor known as a pileated woodpecker. These birds are common in southern Indiana and are easy to spot. With a carrot-top head and black body, these large birds can be seen scampering up and down trees tapping out their nests or looking for food.

Does this horse have dual-suspension?

Since this ride is less demanding than others, more time can be spent looking for wildlife such as deer, raccoons, turkey vultures, and red-tailed hawks. The beginning of the route travels along a fire road and singletrack that leads to the system's only lake. The trail follows the edge of the lake for a short while as it winds along a wooded bank.

Once out of the trees, cyclists will find the first climb. This is also one of the high-traffic areas for four wheelers. From this point, all the way to the Anderson River, the trail travels along a flat fire road. As soon as you cross the river, you'll come upon another section of singletrack.

This is the most challenging section of the loop, which includes the ride's only difficult climb. This section provides a nice change of pace, leading out to the dirt road that will take you back to your vehicle.

As far as camping is concerned, overnight accommodations can be found at Ferdinand State Forest. The state park literature claims that Ferdinand has some of the prettiest campsites in the state. There are 68 campsites with seven primitive sites circling the 42-acre lake. Swimming, fishing, and boating are the main attractions here.

## Ride Information

### ◉ Trail Contact:
**Tell City Ranger District**, Tell City, IN (812) 547-7051

### ◉ Schedule:
Open daily, year-round

### ◉ Fees/Permits:
$3

### ◉ Local Information:
www.patoka-lake-net.com

### ◉ Local Events/Attractions:
Patoka Reservoir

### ◉ Accommodations:
**Camping—Ferdinand State Forest,** Ferdinand, IN (812) 367-1524
**White Oaks Cabins,** Taswell, IN (812) 338-3120

### ◉ Restaurants:
**Carl's Pizzeria & Bar,** Taswell, IN (812) 338-2870

### ◉ Other Resources:
**Indiana Wildlife Viewing Guide,** Seng/Case

### ◉ Local Bike Shop:
**Bicycle World,** Evansville, IN (812) 473-2453

### ◉ Maps:
**USGS map:** Birdseye, IN • **HNF trail maps** available from HNF office

## **Miles**Directions

**0.0 START** from the parking area beside the dirt road. Head south from the parking area to the Birdseye Trail.

**0.1** The trail crosses a creek.

**0.4** Come to a trail intersection. Follow the trail and arrow to the right.

**0.5** The trail crosses over the small lake's dam. In late summer, waves of grasshoppers dive for cover from your wheels as you pass.

**0.51** The trail bends to the right and heads back into the woods.

**1.5** Begin the first climb on the trail.

**1.7** The trail splits. Take the right split.

**2.2** Cross a small creek.

**2.4** Arrive at a trail intersection. Take the left trail. Cross a creek.

**2.5** Begin the second notable climb of the trail.

**3.0** Arrive at a trail intersection. Continue straight.

**3.2** Pass a gate and a trail on the right. Continue straight.

**3.7** Cross Mitchel Creek. Turn left on a dirt road. Following the dirt road to the right will take you to the longer loop to the north.

**5.2** Cross a bridge over the Anderson River. Turn left off the dirt road onto a singletrack trail.

**5.3** Begin the third notable climb of the trail.

**5.4** Reach the summit of the climb, cross an open field, then head back into the woods.

**5.6** Birdseye Trail dumps out into an open field and bends to the right. The trail then follows the right perimeter of the field.

**5.9** The singletrack intersects with a gravel road. Turn left on the gravel road.

**6.1** Return to the trailhead parking area. Ride complete. Hopefully this ride suited you to a "T-y-tee!"

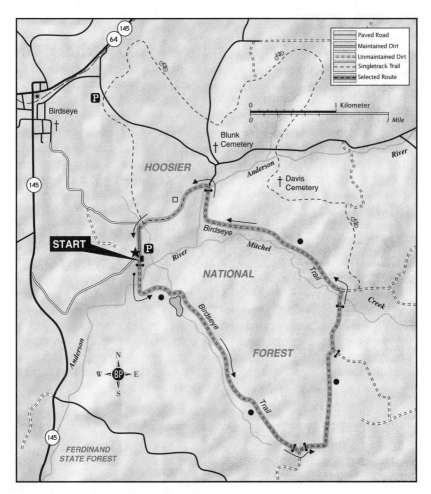

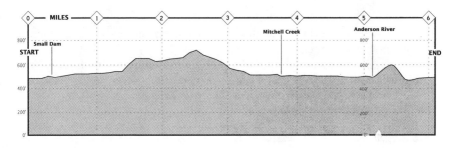

# Oriole Trail

## Ride Summary

Starting at Jeffries Cemetery should not be read as an omen. Oriole Trail is graced with easy grade forest roads, singletrack, and an exciting gravel-road descent. There are some climbs, but few threatening obstacles warrant reserving a grave plot. This unattended trail system sees little traffic and is a great getaway for simple gear spinning and fat-tire fun.

## Ride Specs

**Start:** Forest road gate next to Jeffries Cemetery
**Length:** 6.2-mile loop, part of a 10-mile system
**Approximate Riding Time:** 1 to 1½ hours
**Difficulty Rating:** Easy to moderate
**Trail Surface:** Forest roads, singletrack, and gravel roads
**Lay of the Land:** The variety of paths leads cyclists through woods, creeks, and pasture. The gravel-road descent is a definite a highlight
**Land Status:** National forest
**Nearest Town:** Sulphur
**Other Trail Users:** Hikers, hunters, and equestrians

## Getting There

**From Evansville:** Go north on I-164 approximately 12 miles to I-64. Take I-64 east 57 miles to IN 37/IN 66 west (Exit 86). Go south on IN 66 west four miles to Jeffries Cemetery. Look for a small Hoosier National Forest sign on the right side of the road. Turn left into the parking area next to Jeffries Cemetery. *DelLorme: Indiana Atlas & Gazetteer:* Page 63, B-9

You can get your kicks on Indiana's Route 66. The singer wasn't talking about the anonymous Hoosier route; nonetheless, that didn't stop many turn-of-the-century folks from getting their kicks out here!

During the Civil War, would-be oil drillers struck mineral water instead of black crude near the town of Sulphur Springs. Instead of being set back, the drillers made lemonade from lemons. They switched hats, became developers, and opened the White Sulphur resort, bottling and selling their newly discovered powerful placebo. Vacationers and clients

consumed the ill-tasting waters, but boasted of its medicinal powers; they kept the three-story resort in business for many years.

Records don't show when the hotel went belly-up, but it's possible at least one of the founders is buried in Jeffries Cemetery. Since you are parking at the foot of many, if not all, of the Jeffries who made this area their home, it is customary to climb the steps of the cemetery and pay your respects to the family. The plot of R.B. Jeffries, who died in 1872, looks to be the oldest stone.

With homage and tourism plugs out of the way, pull your bike off the rack and begin the ride. With the small parking lot and lack of trailhead signs, solitary cyclists can enjoy this somewhat anonymous trail.

Riding this quiet route will bring you close to many white-tailed deer. Although it may be hard to believe, white-tailed deer were once eliminated from Indiana. They were reintroduced in the 1940s, and with careful management they now flourish and can be found in every county in the state.

Hunting is permitted here, as in many other Hoosier National Forest recreation areas. Hunters will often set up deer camps in the parking areas. With hunters dressed in camouflaged gear and cyclists clad in Lycra, the gap between the groups can seem fairly wide. (*See Sidebar on page 206*).

Oriole Trail is made up predominantly of forest roads, and features an occasional climb. Most descents are on a fairly easy grade, with the most memorable ones along the gravel road. The beginning of the trail is adequately maintained, but at the first turn, cyclists will find themselves riding through knee-high grass. Following the tire tracks on the road is like riding parallel singletrack.

During the late summer months, spiders like to spin their webs across this somewhat abandoned section of trail. Rolling along on an early morning ride with cobwebs covering your face will either cause uncontrollable convulsions or banishment of your arachnophobia!

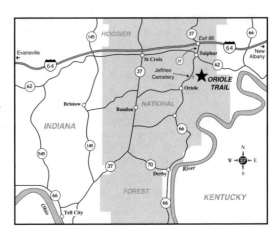

Two miles into the ride and out of the webs, the fire road intersects with a gravel road. Here lies your fastest descent of the day. Be careful, though, to ride this one at your own pace. The loose gravel is challenging and can be a bit intimidating. After the downhill, the trail follows the gravel road for the next 1.5 miles before turning back onto a forest road.

The forest road winds north and northwest, climbs slightly near the gate, and returns to Jeffries Cemetery.

Assuming that your group has complete use of their faculties, why not check out nearby Marengo Cave. This U.S. National Landmark was originally discovered by a couple of kids in 1883. I wasn't there, but I think the conversation went something like this: First child: "What's this depression in the ground over here? Wow! I think it looks like a caaaaaaaavvvvvve!"

Second child (and incidentally the one credited with finding the cave): "I'd better run and get help. But only after I've registered the cave as a national landmark."

## Ride Information

### ● Trail Contact:
**Tell City Ranger District,** Tell City, IN (812) 547-7051

### ◔ Schedule:
Open daily, year-round

### ⑤ Fees/Permits:
$3

### ❓ Local Information:
**Corydon Visitors Center** (812) 738-4890

### ♀ Local Events/Attractions:
**Marengo Cave,** Marengo, IN (812) 365-2705 or www.cavern.com/marengocave
**Squire Boone Caverns,** Corydon, IN (812) 732-4382 or www.squire-boonecaverns.com • **Wyandotte Caves,** Leavenworth, IN (812) 738-2782 or www.explore-si.com/Wyandotte.html

### ⊜ Accommodations:
**Old Capitol Inn,** Corydon, IN (812) 738-4192 • **Budget Inn,** Corydon, IN (812) 738-1500

### ⑪ Restaurants:
**Jocks Lunch,** Corydon, IN (812) 738-3250 • **Magdalena's Restaurant,** Corydon, IN (812) 738-8075

### ⑯ Local Bike Shop:
**Bicycle World,** Evansville, IN (812) 473-2453

### Ⓝ Maps:
**USGS map:** Beechwood, IN • **HNF maps** available at HNF office

All smiles on the Oriole Trail.

## **Miles**Directions

**0.0 START** at Jeffries Cemetery. The trail starts from the gate at the southwest corner of the parking area.

**0.2** The trail splits. Take the right split.

**1.2** The trail travels along the rocky creekbed.

**1.55** Cross Mill Creek. The trail does a 180-degree turn and heads back on itself.

**1.56** The trail does another 180-degree turn and begins to ascend. These switchbacks aren't marked on the map.

**1.85** The trail crosses the creek.

**2.4** Roll past a gate and turn left on the gravel road. Now on a fast descent. Beware of the loose gravel.

**2.8** Gravel road bends to the left.

**3.1** Cross Mill Creek. The road bends slightly to the left and begins to ascend.

**3.7** The gravel road bends to the right.

**3.95** The gravel road bends to the left. There is a logging road to the right, but stay on the gravel road to the left.

**4.0** Turn left on the logging road past the gate.

**4.2** The trail splits with arrows pointing both directions. Take the trail to the left.

**4.3** The trail splits. Take the left split.

**5.0** Pass a marked trail on the right. Continue straight on the main trail.

**5.9** Pass through an open gate.

**6.2** Return to the parking area and Jeffries Cemetery.

## **Hunters vs. Mountain Bikers**

*During deer hunting season, especially during opening weekends when hunters are feeling the most zealous, it's best to follow these precautions:*

1. *Wear an orange hat or orange vest. If you can't stretch a hat over your helmet, opt for the hat.*
2. *Avoid riding early in the morning. Allow hunters to have their prime time. Ride late in the morning and early in the afternoon.*
3. *Make noise when you ride. Don't shuffle quietly behind the bushes. You don't want to be mistaken for game. Just ask Greg LeMond about this one. He still has the shotgun pellets lodged in his body.*

### *Hunting seasons are:*

- *Early archery season: early October to late November*
- *Shotgun season: mid-November to late November*
- *Muzzleloader season: Early to mid-December*
- *Late archery season: Early December to early January*

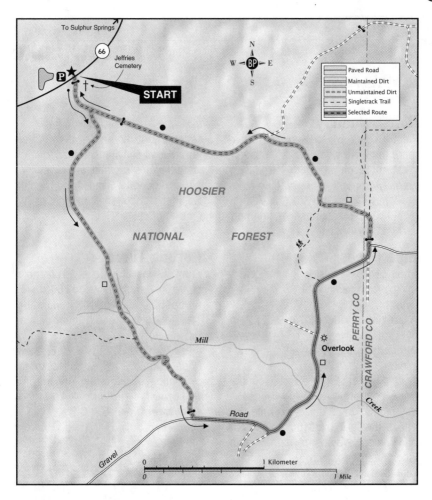

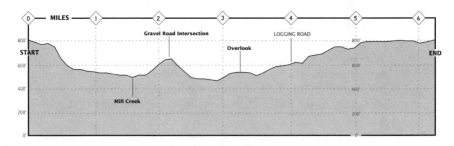

207

# Tipsaw Lake

## Ride Summary

Tipsaw Lake, one of Hoosier National Forest's newest recreation areas, offers more than five miles of predominantly singletrack trail circling the lake. This is a great route on which to introduce novices to Indiana's National Forest. The grades are relatively easy, there are a couple of moderate climbs, and the lake stays in view much of the ride. After the ride, go for a swim, angle for fish, or simply relax at your campsite—then ride some more, of course.

## Ride Specs

**Start:** The east side of the swimming/picnic parking lot
**Length:** 5.2-mile loop
**Approximate Riding Time:** 45 minutes to 1 hour
**Difficulty Rating:** Easy with moderate climbs
**Trail Surface:** Singletrack, doubletrack, and forest road
**Lay of the Land:** The easy-grade trail edges the lake, cuts through woods and fields, traverses the dam, and finishes near the beach
**Land Status:** National forest
**Nearest Town:** Bandon
**Other Trail Users:** Hikers, equestrians, and anglers

## Getting There

**From Evansville:** Take I-164 north approximately 12 miles to I-64. Take I-64 east 51 miles to IN 37 south (Exit 79). Take IN 37 south approximately 6.5 miles to Tipsaw Lake Recreation Area. Turn right on the Park Entrance Road and drive three miles to the swimming/picnic area parking lot. **_DeLorme: Indiana Atlas & Gazetteer:_** Page 63, C-8

T
ipsaw Lake is the newest recreation area in Hoosier National Forest. The lake draws its water from Sulphur Fork Creek, Massey Branch, Snake Branch, and other smaller tributaries, and is surrounded by one of the best introductory mountain bike trail systems in the national forest. This five-mile loop gives novices a taste of rugged singletrack, as well as some moderate climbs. At the end of the ride, cyclists can reward themselves with a cool dip in the lake.

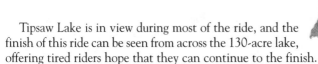

Tipsaw Lake is in view during most of the ride, and the finish of this ride can be seen from across the 130-acre lake, offering tired riders hope that they can continue to the finish.

The trail begins as a paved path heading away from the picnic area. It changes to gravel and cuts across the boat-launch parking lot before leading to the first section of singletrack. The first part of the trail switches between woods and grassy fields before circling around the east end of the lake.

Once around this section of the lake, the trail cuts through a couple of open fields before returning to the wooded singletrack. From this point, the lake stays in view for the majority of the ride.

As the trail merges with a dirt road, you will come across the first of three spots that look as if they were designed specifically to offer a respite to leg-weary cyclists and hikers. At the three-mile mark, come to a dirt-road turnaround and what resembles a mini limestone Stonehenge. This group of stone benches offers a place to stretch out or lean your bike as you skip rocks across the lake.

For cemetery buffs interested in seeing Lanman Cemetery, the second stop comes just after the first. Down the road a short distance past Stonehenge there is a small path off to the left that leads to the cemetery.

The third rest area affords the best view along this ride. This break comes four miles into the ride as the trail rolls over the dam. During the summer, knee-high grass sways in the breeze and the full view of the lake and surrounding wooded hills is quite dramatic. Take time for a little lizard spotting—blue-tailed skinks and other small lizards like to run through the grass here.

After rolling across the open area near the dam, prepare to ride the more challenging portion of the trail. The singletrack twists around the lake and leads to a few challenging climbs. For beginners, just remember that the final leg of the trail and the beach are near.

After the ride, activities at the swimming beach will easily fill the remainder of the day.

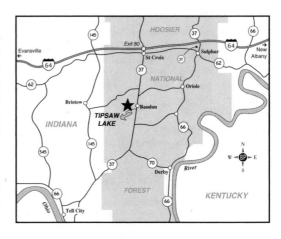

There is a boat ramp that permits electric motors, and panfishing here is rated as excellent. The beach is clean for swimming, but there is no lifeguard on duty.

As far as camping is considered, Tipsaw offers 44 sites to weary travelers. The amenities include water, flush toilets, showers, and electricity on roughly half the sites. Cost: $13 for electric campsites; $9 for non-electric. Primrose and Goldenrod are group campsites that can be rented for $25 per night. The five-star campsite is in the Catbriar Loop, and it can be rented for $45 per night. It has electrical hookups, lights, and a shelter.

Fifteen picnic sites, two shelters, a modern changing area, and horseshoe pits line the north shore of the lake. If you lose track of time during a sunny day, look to the sundial near the bathhouse to see how late you really are.

# Ride Information

## Trail Contact:
**Tell City Ranger District,** Tell City, IN (812) 547-7051

## Schedule:
Open daily, year-round

## Fees/Permits:
$3

## Local Information:
**Perry County Convention and Visitors Bureau** website; *www.perrycountyindiana.org*

## Accommodations:
**Tipsaw Campground,** 44 sites total; nonelectric $9, electric $13/night • **Ohio River Cabins,** Derby, IN (812) 836-2289 or *www.ohiorivercabins.com*

## Restaurants:
**Patio Steakhouse,** Tell City, IN (812) 547-4949 • **Good Time Charlies,** Leopold, IN (812) 843-5548

## Local Bike Shop:
**Bicycle World,** Evansville, IN (812) 473-2453

## Maps:
**USGS maps:** Bristow, IN; Gatchel, IN • **HNF trail maps** available at HNF office

## **Miles**Directions

**0.0 START** at the swimming/picnic area parking lot. Follow the paved path from the east end of the parking lot toward the boat ramp parking area. Roll past a shelter as the path turns to gravel.

**0.1** The gravel path crosses into the boat ramp parking area. Continue straight.

**0.15** Turn left out of the parking lot, then a quick right at the trailhead following the singletrack Hike/Bike Trail east.

**0.2** Arrive at a trail intersection. Continue straight.

**0.6** Cross a creek. Continue straight.

**1.0** Arrive at a trail intersection. (This is another trailhead, which leads to entrance road.) Bear right around the gate.

**1.1** Bear hard right. Now at the east end of the loop.

**1.25** Hike/Bike Trail crosses an open field, traveling straight along the right perimeter of the field.

**2.2** The lake comes back into view.

**3.1** Pass the mini Stonehenge on a forest road turnaround. Now at the shallow end of the lake. The rocks are a great place for a break. The turnaround leads to a dirt road. Turn right on the dirt road.

**3.3** Arrive at an intersection. Turn right on the dirt road.

**3.4** Come to a trailhead. Follow the signs and take the Hike/Bike Trail to the right. Pass a gate and cross a bridge. Now traveling on a grass-covered fire road.

**3.6** Tipsaw Lake comes back into view.

**3.85** Cross a creek and look for a trail marker to the right.

**4.1** Come to a short, steep rise up to Tipsaw Lake dam. Wonderful view of Tipsaw Lake. Lizards are found here during the summertime.

**4.5** The open grassy Hike/Bike Trail narrows to a singletrack and leads back into the woods.

**4.8** Cross a shallow creek and begin a moderate climb.

**5.1** Hike/Bike Trail splits. Take the right split. (This is a slight deviation from official HNF trail.)

**5.2** The ride ends at the gate and parking lot. Options include returning to your vehicle or taking a cool dip in the lake!

Hoping to catch big one at Tipsaw Lake.

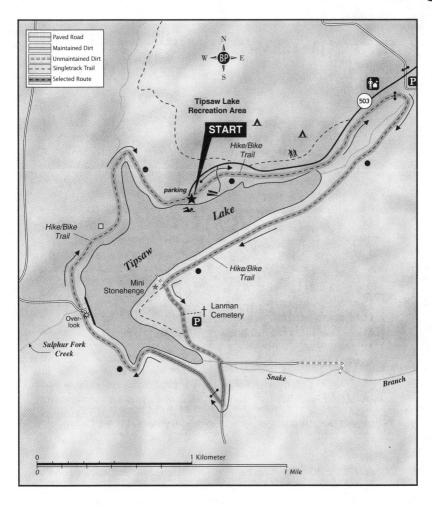

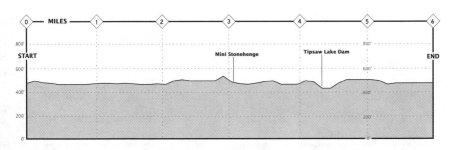

# Mountain Biking With Your Dog

Many people love to bring their canine companion along on mountain bike trails. Our furry friends make great trail partners because they're always good company and they never complain. If you take your dog mountain biking with you, or you're considering it, remember that there are a number of important items to keep in mind before hitting the trails.

## Getting in Shape

It would be no better for your dog than it would you to tackle running a marathon without first getting into good physical condition. And if your pet has been a foot warmer much of his life, you will need to train him into reasonable shape before taking him along on those long weekend bike rides.

You can start your dog's training regimen by running or walking him around the neighborhood or, better yet, a local park. Frisbees and balls are also great tools to help get your dog physically fit for those upcoming mountain bike rides. Always remember that on a trail your dog probably runs twice as far as you ride. Build your dog's exercise regimen based on the mileage you plan to ride each time you head out. If you're going on a five-mile trail, assume your dog needs to be in shape for a 10-mile trail. Gradually build up your dog's stamina over a two to three month period before committing him to arduous afternoons of trying to keep up with you as you pedal along on your bike.

## Training

Teaching your dog simple commands of obedience may help keep both you and your dog out of a heap of trouble while out there on public trails. The most important lesson is to train your dog to come when called. This will ensure he doesn't stray too far from the trail and possibly get lost. It may also protect him from troublesome situations, such as other trail users or perhaps coming in contact with local wildlife. Also teach your dog the "get behind" command. This comes in especially handy when you're on a singletrack trail and you run into other bikers. Teaching your dog to stay behind you and your bike and to follow your lead until the trail is clear can be a valuable and important lesson. Remember also to always carry a long leash with you in case, after all your prior training, you still have to tie your dog up to a tree at a campsite or succumb to local leash laws on crowded trails.

There are a number of good dog training books on the market that should help train you and your dog how to stay out of trouble with other trail users. Also, look to your local SPCA or kennel club for qualified dog trainers in the area.

## Nutrition

Nutrition is important for all dogs. Never exercise a dog right after eating for the same reasons people shouldn't exercise right after eating. Feed your pet a high quality diet such as Hills Science Diet™ or Iams™. These products have higher quality ingredients and are more nutritionally balanced than generic grocery store dog foods. They may be more expensive than some generic brands, but your dog also doesn't need to eat as much of it to get the same nutrition and calories. If you insist on feeding your dog a grocery store diet, stick with the Purina™ brand, as it is still better for your dog than most others in this class.

## Trail Tips

Try to pick your riding trails near lakes or streams. The biggest threat to your dog when biking is the heat, and water is essential to keep him cool. If the trail doesn't have water nearby then you need to bring as much liquid for him as you would drink yourself. A small lightweight plastic bowl can be used to give your dog water, or you can purchase a collapsible water bowl made from waterproof nylon (*Call Ruff Wear*™ ; *(541) 388-1821*). Also, you can use a waterbottle to squirt water into your dog's mouth.

- Try not to take your dog riding with you on a really hot day—hotter than 80 degrees. To avoid these temperatures, take your dog riding in the early morning or evening when the air is cooler and safer for your pet.

- Watch for signs of heat stroke. Dogs with heat stroke will: pant excessively, lie down and refuse to get up, become lethargic and disoriented. If your dog shows any of these signs, immediately hose him down with cool water and let him rest. If you're on the trail and nowhere near a hose, find a cool stream and lay your dog in the water to help bring his body temperature back to normal.

- Avoid the common foot pad injuries. Don't run your dog on hot pavement or along long stretches of gravel road. Always bring a first aid kit that includes disinfectant, cotton wrap, and stretchy foot bandage tape so you can treat and wrap your dog's paw if it becomes injured. You might also want to look into purchasing dog booties, useful for protecting your dog's pads and feet during long runs outdoors.

- Be sure to keep your dog's nails trimmed. If your dog's nails are too long, they might catch on an object along the trail and lead to soft tissue or joint injuries.

- Don't take your dog on crowded trails and always carry a leash with you. Remember, just because you love your dog doesn't mean other people will.

# Mogan Ridge MTB Trails

## Ride Summary

Mogan Ridge is a moderate trail system with a blend of singletrack and forest road. This South-America-shaped trail descends toward IN 70, then basically climbs its way back to the trailhead. The trail is sparsely used. So many encounters will be with wildlife instead of hikers or cyclists. Cyclists beware: hunting is permitted on this property. So be careful, particularly during deer season. *(See Sidebar on page 206.)*

## Ride Specs

**Start:** Trailhead at the radio tower parking area
**Length:** 6.3-mile loop of an 11-mile system
**Approximate Riding Time:** 1 hour
**Difficulty Rating:** Moderate
**Trail Surface:** Forest roads and singletrack
**Lay of the Land:** Overgrown forest roads descends toward IN 70. Once at the bottom, the trail has some challenging singletrack and gravel-road climbs before returning to the trailhead
**Land Status:** National forest
**Nearest Town:** Leopold
**Other Trail Users:** Hikers, hunters, and equestrians

## Getting There

**From Evansville:** Go north on I-164 approximately 12 miles to I-64. Travel east on I-64 51 miles to IN 37 south (Exit 79). Go south on IN 37 approximately 18 miles to IN 70. Go east on IN 70 no more than 0.1 miles to Old IN 37. Travel north on Old IN 37 1.1 miles to the Mogan Ridge sign on the right side of the road. Turn right, traveling east on an unmarked gravel road for 0.4 miles to the radio tower parking area on the left. Look for the radio tower. *DeLorme: Indiana Atlas & Gazetteer:* Page 63, D-8

As you drive along the road that leads to Mogan Ridge, you might be greeted by an American kestrel. Commonly called sparrow hawks for their sparrow size and hawk features, kestrels can be spotted hovering at the road's edge above the high grass.

With greetings and salutations out of the way, it's time to take a look at the map. One can't help but notice that a portion of the Mogan Ridge route is shaped like South America. In tribute to jungles and rugged lands of our continental neighbor, the land of Mogan Ridge is also rugged and unkept. The benefit of such a route is less usage and a very quiet ride.

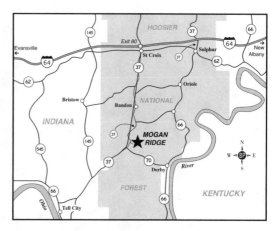

The majority of this trail is doubletrack, forest, and gravel roads. There is some singletrack on the backside of the trail, but it acts more as a connector between two forest road sections. Even though you are riding on forest roads, the lack of maintenance keeps even the wider areas fairly rugged.

The wild nature of this path can be traced to the fact that the trail was just recently opened for recreational use. In years past, this land was managed solely for timber, wild turkey, and other wildlife. Many of the trail markers are faded, but forest rangers are in the process of updating them.

For the most part, the first part of the loop is easy going, without any notable climbs or descents. During the summer, the grass here is uncut and tickles your knees. As you approach the western portion of the loop, stay alert as there is a section that is not well marked, and getting lost is never much fun.

At 1.2 miles you'll come to an open field where the trail fades (the route is more distinct now that more cyclists have ridden the trail). But if you do lose the trail, follow the fenceline on the right until you come to an opening at a tree marked with a blue diamond sign.

After this marker, the path becomes a grass-covered doubletrack trail. This route slowly descends to the southernmost part of the loop, and the closest point you will be to civilization.

As you round Cape Horn (the southernmost section of the loop), you will see IN 70. Remember this point if you have a flat and need a ride back to your car. Once around the horn, you will be approaching the loop's most challenging section. The first part, a forest road, follows the eastern portion of this loop (what could be considered the east coast of South America). The road climbs slightly, taking you from Argentina all the way to the coast of Brazil (get out your atlases folks), where the loop's most challenging section awaits.

Here you will find climbs that warrant this ride's moderate classification. There are a couple of tricky, sparsely marked sections here, but follow the directions and look for the faint blue diamonds on the tree

trunks. These markers will help confirm that you are heading in the right direction.

As you circle around the northern section of the loop, the blue trail passes two trails that lead to the five-mile eastern section of this trail system. Here the trail also dumps out to a gravel road. This road harbors a swift descent then up another climb. After the rise, the road finally returns back to where you left your vehicle.

Away from the trail to the east, two burial grounds exist. Talley and Phelps Cemeteries can be accessed off IN 70. The road is hard to find, but if you have the time, take the second U.S. Forest service road to the east of IN 37. Follow the service road north and you will find the parking area near Talley Cemetery.

Also close to Mogan Ridge is the town of Tell City. Named after the famed apple-shooting archer William Tell, the town was founded by German and Swiss emigrants. Here is where you will find the closest ranger office, where you can stop by and purchase some maps or pick up some of their free literature.

Also in town is the Tell City Pretzel Company. Following Casper Goor's original recipe (one of the town's founders), these pretzels are hand twisted, glazed, salted, baked, and made available to the public for a great post-ride snack that's also low in fat!

## Ride Information

**⬤ Trail Contact:**
Tell City Ranger District, Tell City, IN (812)547-7051

**⬤ Schedule:**
Open daily, year-round

**⬤ Fees/Permits:**
$3

**⬤ Local Information:**
Perry County Convention and Visitors Bureau website; www.perrycountyindiana.org

**⬤ Local Events/Attractions:**
Tell City Pretzel Company

**⬤ Accommodations:**
Primitive camping along Mogan Ridge Trail • Tipsaw Campground, 44 campsites total; nonelectric $9,

electric $13/night • Ohio River Cabins, Derby, IN (812) 836-2289 or www.ohiorivercabins.com

**⬤ Restaurants:**
Patio Steakhouse, Tell City, IN (812) 547-4949 • Good Time Charlies, Leopold, IN (812) 843-5548

**⬤ Other Resources:**
Indiana Wildlife Viewing Guide, Seng/Case

**⬤ Local Bike Shop:**
Bicycle World, Evansville, IN (812) 473-2453

**⬤ Maps:**
USGS map: Derby, IN • HNF trail maps available at HNF office

## **Miles**Directions

**0.0 START** from the radio tower parking area. Turn left out of the parking area to the gravel road. (Cyclists can follow the new singletrack path, which connects to the gravel road just past the gate.)

**0.1** Roll past a gate.

**0.2** Pass a faint trail on the right that merges into the main gravel trail. Continue straight on the gravel road.

**0.3** Arrive at a trail intersection. Turn right and roll past a gate.

**0.6** Pass a trail that splits off to the right. Continue straight on the main trail.

**0.8** The trail becomes faint. Follow the blue signs, taking the right split.

**1.35** The trail splits. Take the right split. There's a slight gap between trail markers here.

**2.7** IN 70 is now in view. Take the forest road to the left.

**3.8** The trail changes to singletrack.

**4.5** The trail dumps out onto a gravel road. Turn left onto the gravel road.

**5.0** A marked trail veers off to the left. Stay on the gravel road. Taking the road to the right leads to the eastern loops of Mogan Ridge.

**5.5** Pass a logging road on the right. Stay on the gravel road. Now climbing one of the tougher climbs of the trail.

**6.0** Pass the gate that marked the beginning of the loop. Continue straight on the gravel road.

**6.3** Complete the loop and arrive back at the parking area. Time to grab some pretzels in Tell City!

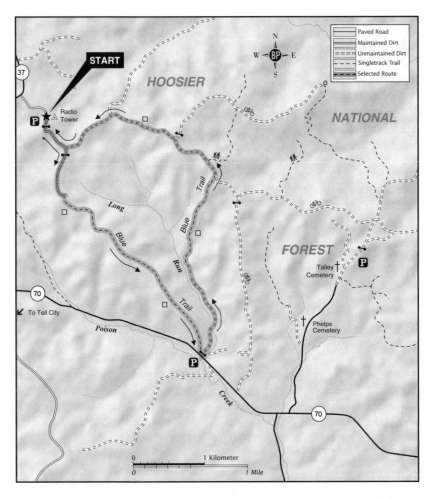

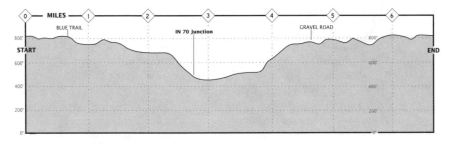

# German Ridge Recreation Area

## Ride Summary

German Ridge holds 23 miles of trails ranging from easy to difficult. Yet, surprisingly, few mountain bikers take advantage of these trails. Take it from me, Hoosier National Forest's southernmost trail system is worth the drive. A weekend could easily be filled exploring the challenging blend of singletrack, doubletrack, and forest roads.

## Ride Specs

**Start:** Bulletin board in the day-use parking area

**Length:** 12.3-mile loop; part of a 23-mile system

**Approximate Riding Time:** 2 to 3 hours

**Difficulty Rating:** Moderate to difficult

**Trail Surface:** Singletrack, doubletrack, and forest and paved roads

**Lay of the Land:** Trail begins as gravel-covered doubletrack. From there it switches to a variety of terrain leading to many challenging descents and climbs.

**Land Status:** National Forest

**Nearest Town:** Rome

**Other Trail Users:** Hikers and equestrians

## Getting There

**From Evansville:** Take I-164 north approximately 12 miles to I-64. Take I-64 east 51 miles to IN 37 south (Exit 79). Take IN 37 south approximately 18 miles to IN 70. Go east on IN 70 approximately 6.2 miles to IN 66. Turn right on IN 66, following signs to German Ridge Recreation Area. Travel 11.6 miles and turn right on German Ridge Road. Drive 0.8 miles and turn left at the Hoosier National Forest sign on the Park Entrance Road. Bear left into the campground area. At 0.5 miles turn right into the day-use parking area. **DeLorme: Indiana Atlas & Gazetteer:** Page 63, F-8

German Ridge has the distinction of being the first recreation area in Hoosier National Forest. By using the sizable work force of the Civilian Conservation Corps, the U.S. Forest Service was able to develop the property during the years 1939-1940. On May 17, 1942, German Ridge was dedicated and became the role model for the establishment of other recreation areas in the forest.

Backing up a bit to the Civil War, long before the CCC developed this recreation area, an attempted coup occurred, aimed at taking over this land along the Ohio River. In 1863, Confederate Captain Thomas Hines led his gray-coated troops across the Ohio River to contact south-

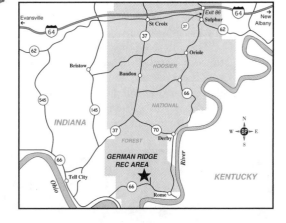

ern sympathizers and their Copperhead organizations. But Hoosiers were not fooled into believing that Hines was leading a Union troop, seeking deserters, as he purported. When his coup was called, Hines' troop was wiped out and he and a few others narrowly escaped back to Kentucky.

An historical marker documenting these events is found east of German Ridge along IN 66. Hines may have been better off looking for a place to ride his mountain bike than trying to start war. He could have enjoyed one of Indiana's "deep south" trail systems and avoided this little skirmish altogether.

For cyclists, this southernmost recreation area can provide a full weekend of riding. German Ridge spans 250 acres and holds 23 miles of rideable trails. For cyclists looking to combine a weekend of trail riding and primitive camping, German Ridge is ideal.

Moo!

The four-acre lake also offers other activities such as swimming and fishing. Additionally, there are some incredible hiking trails (off-limits to mountain bikes) with many outcrops of sandstone worth checking out.

Unlike most Hoosier National Forest recreation areas, there is a fee for camping at German Ridge: $4 per night, $6 per night with horses, and $10 per night with horses on a double site. There are 20 campsites, 10 doubles, and 10 singles. The sites are equipped with vault toilets, hitching racks to tie off the bikes, and a bonfire pit to burn discarded energy bar wrappers (non-toxic only, of course).

The soils along this loop are extremely soft. Rangers encourage equestrians and cyclists to make as little impact on the area as possible, and park literature asks that equestrians and cyclists ride single file and avoid skirting puddles and minor obstacles so no further damage to the area is done. Also, if there are fallen logs or brush on the trail, take the time to remove them from the trail.

As you will see, there are some areas along the trail where these requests have been ignored. The result is a wide, swampy, and rutted track that is unrideable. Hopefully over time the trail will be repaired and remain open.

Overall, the trails are a wonderful balance of singletrack and forest roads. The featured trail loop is one of the more challenging ones around. Away from the campground, climbs and descents become the norm. If the trail becomes too difficult, though, the 23-mile trail system has other routes that are easier to tackle.

Some possible stopping points along the ride are the deer ponds where the grass and banks around the ponds are havens for various wildlife. Blue-tailed skinks can be found in the grass, while many birds use the pond to bathe and drink.

Huge slab of limestone serves as a natural park benches and a place to take in some quiet time. There are also two old burial grounds to explore. German Ridge Cemetery can be found just off Tower Road in the middle of the recreation area. The second is off the northern perimeter of the trail system. Schraner Cemetery sits at the northernmost point of the property and can be accessed via County Road 3.

## Ride Information

**Trail Contact:**
**Tell City Ranger District,** Tell City, IN (812) 547-7051

**Schedule:**
Open daily, year-round

**Fees/Permits:**
$3

**Local Information:**
**Perry County Convention and Visitors Bureau** website;
*www.perrycountyindiana.org*

**Accommodations:**
**German Ridge Campground (primitive)** $4/night, $6/night with horses, $10/night for double sites

**Ohio River Cabins,** Derby, IN
(812) 836-2289
*www.ohiorivercabins.com*

**Restaurants:**
**Patio Steakhouse,** Tell City, IN (812) 547-4949 • **Good Time Charlies,** Leopold, IN (812) 843-5548

**Local Bike Shop:**
**Bicycle World,** Evansville, IN (812) 473-2453

**Maps:**
**USGS map:** Rome, IN • **HNF trail maps** available at HNF office

## **Miles**Directions

**0.0 START** from the day-use parking area next to the bulletin board and follow the multi-use trail into the woods. This trail is marked with horseshoes to the right of the trail.

**0.1** Cross the Park Entrance Road. Continue straight on the gravel multi-use trail.

**0.7** Arrive at a trail intersection. Bear left at the split. Going right leads to the campground.

**1.0** Pass a small trail off to the right. Stay on the main trail.

**1.2** Cross two shallow creeks. There's a pretty steady climb after the creek crossings.

**2.1** A trail splits off to the left. Stay on the main trail.

**3.5** Cross East Deer Creek. Still on gravel doubletrack.

**4.4** Pass a deer pond.

**4.75** Come to a trail intersection. Continue straight. The trail to the right heads toward Tower Road.

**5.5** The gravel ends at the descent and the creek. The trail is now dirt doubletrack.

**6.1** Come to a faded "T." Turn right. The trail to the left is overgrown with weeds.

**6.6** Come to a trail intersection marked with blue and red arrows. Follow the red arrow to the right.

**6.9** Come to a gravel trail intersection. Take a right on the gravel trail. The trail soon turns to dirt.

**7.1** Come to a trail intersection. Follow the arrow and gravel trail to the right. The great descent ends at the creek. Beware of the loose gravel.

**8.1** Ford sandstone creek crossing. Check out the small waterfall next to the trail.

**8.2** Pass a larger waterfall on the right.

**8.3** Just before coming to a gate, follow the arrow and trail to the right.

**8.5** Come to Tower Road intersection. Take a left on the road, then a quick right back on the trail.

### Ticks

*The downside of this unkept, rugged trail, especially in the sections where you are pedaling through the knee-high grass, is that it is prime ground for ticks. A brochure, distributed at the Hoosier National Forest offices, recommends taking these precautions while riding in tick-infested areas:*

- *Avoid tick habitats. (We as mountain bikers know this to be impossible, so we will ignore this tip.)*
- *Dress properly if you must go into a tick habitat. (Shaved legs covered to mid-thigh with Lycra shorts are not the best tick-repelling clothes.)*
- *Check for and remove any ticks on you or others in your company as soon as possible after leaving a tick habitat. (This is the best preventive tip for mountain bikers. But beware that this can resemble a primate social activity. To avoid any resemblance to primates, refrain from eating the ticks that you pull from your group members.)*
- *Check pets for ticks and use tick-control pet products. (Hot match heads are still one of the best removal methods. Alcohol also works)*

*Checking for ticks after a ride through the woods or the weeds is as essential as replacing fluids. One bout with Lyme disease will provide a lasting reminder for this. An ounce of prevention and one coat of tick-repellent spray is helpful to stop the bloodsuckers from latching on to any bare skin.*

*Early signs of Lyme disease include a slowly expanding rash and flu-like symptoms. Left untreated, Lyme disease can cause a form of arthritis resulting in aching joints and swelling dizziness, an irregular heartbeat, or a weakening of facial muscles.*

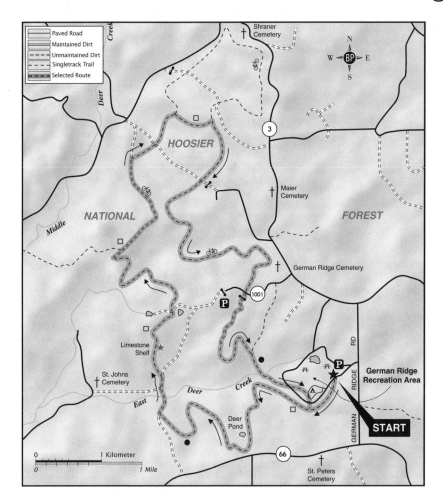

**10.1** Pass a deer pond.

**11.4** Come to a trail intersection. Follow the arrow and the trail to the left.

**11.5** The trail dumps out onto a paved road. Continue straight on the paved road.

**12.2** Ride around gate, pass the entrance to the campground, and continue straight on the paved road.

**12.3** Arrive back at the day-use parking area. Ride complete.

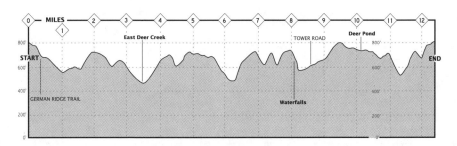

# Appendix

# Bicycle Clubs and Organizations

## National Clubs and Organizations

### American Trails
The only national, nonprofit organization working on behalf of ALL trail interests. Members want to create and protect America's network of interconnected trailways.
POB 200787
Denver, CO 80220
(303) 321-6606, *www.outdoorlink.com/amtrails/*

### International Mountain Bicycling Association (IMBA)
Works to keep public lands accessible to bikers and provides information of trail design and maintenance.
POB 7578
Boulder, CO 80306
(303) 545-9011, *www.greatoutdoors.com/imba/*

### National Off-Road Bicycling Association (NORBA)
National governing body of US mountain bike racing.
One Olympic Plaza
Colorado Springs, CO 80909
(719) 578-4717, *www.usacycling.org/mtb*

### Outdoor Recreation Coalition of America (ORCA)
Oversees and examines issues for outdoor recreation. Boulder, CO.
(303) 444-3353,*www.orca.org, info@orca.org*

### Rails-to-Trails Conservancy
Organized to promote conversion of abandoned rail corridors to trails for public use.
1400 16th Street, NW, Suite 300
Washington, D.C. 20036-2222
*www.railtrails.org*

### League of American Wheelmen
190 West Ostend Street #120
Baltimore, MD 21230-3731
(410) 539-3399

### United States Cycling Federation
Governing body for amateur cycling.
Colorado Springs, CO
(719) 578-4581, *www.usacycling.org*

### USA Cycling
One Olympic Plaza
Colorado Springs, CO 80909
(719) 578-4581, *www.usacycling.org*

## Local Indiana Clubs

### IBC (Indiana Bicycle Coalition)
P.O. Box 20243
Indianapolis, IN 46229
1-800-BIKE-110, (317) 327-8356

### Blazing Saddles Bicycle Club
c/o Rick Lichtenberger
209 W. Jefferson St.
Decatur, IN 46733
(219) 724-2705, *indianajim@juno.com*

### Bloomington Bicycle Club
P.O. Box 463
Bloomington, IN 47402
(812) 332-6028, *jbanders@iquest.net*

### Breakaway Bicycle Club
P.O. Box 6906
Kokomo, IN 46904
(765) 4594414

### Circus City Cyclists
154 N. Grant St.
Peru, IN 46970

### Calumet Crank Club
P.O. Box 2202
Valparaiso, IN 46384
(219) 762-9388, *jwwrigh8@netnitco.net*

### Central Indiana Bicycling Association
P.O. Box 55405
Indianapolis, IN 46205
(317) 327-2453

### Delaware Cycling Club
P.O. Box 763
Muncie, IN 47308
(765) 287-8939

### Driftwood Valley Wheeler
P.O. Box 1552
Columbus, IN 47202

## Evansville Bicycle Club
P.O. Box 15517
Evansville, IN 47716
(812) 853-7320, *darrylb@gateway.net*

## Folks On Spokes Club
P.O. Box 824
Homewood, IL 60430
(708) 730-5179, *www.LincolnNet.net/FOS/*

## Madison Area Bicycle Club
P.O. Box 814
Madison, IN 47250
(812) 265-6313, *jrubio@seidata.com*

## Maple City Bicycling Club
c/o Dave Wolfe
1209 Weller Ave.
LaPorte, IN 46350,Club
(219) 362-4200

## Michiana Bicycle Association
P.O. Box 182
Granger, IN 46530
(219) 674-0088

## National Road Bicycle Club c/o Don Watson
240 Van Buren Blvd.
Terre Haute, IN 47803
(812) 234-1215, *rapidr129@aol.com*

## NIMBA (Northern Indiana Mountain Biking Association) c/o Jim Fulton
P.O. Box 6383
South Bend, IN 46660
(219) 282-1353, *jfulton@csronline.com*

## Patoka Valley Cyclists c/o REM Bicycle Center
804 Main St.
Jasper, IN 47546
(812) 634-1454

## River Valley Bicycle Club
Perry County Parks Courthouse Annex
Cannelton, IN 47520
(812) 547-3453

## Southern Indiana Wheelmen
111 Highway 131
Clarksville, IN 47129
(812) 948-2453

## Spoke and Wheel Bicycle Club
c/o Walter Dick
P.O. Box 597
Anderson, IN 460182597
(765) 641-5556, *bikewalt@netusa1.net*

## Three Rivers Velosport
P.O. Box 11391
Fort Wayne, IN 46857
(219) 482-2845, *velomail@aol.com*

## Wabash River Cycle
Brown Street Levee P
West Lafayette, IN 47905
(765) 743-6261, *smills@purdue.edu*

## Wheel People Bicycle Association
c/o Bob Lee
10644 East 1300
South Galveston, IN 46932
(219) 699-6825, *bettylee@netusa1.net*

## Whitley County 4H Bicycle Club
c/o Eric Blank
P.O. Box 523
Columbia City, IN 467250523
(219) 244-4914

---

*Dear Reader:* It's the very nature of print media that the second the presses run off the last book, all the phone numbers change. If you notice a wrong number or that a club or organization has disappeared or that a new one has put out its shingle, we'd love to know about it. And if you run a club or have a favorite one and we missed it; again, let us know. We plan on doing our part to keep this list up-to-date for future editions, but we could always use the help. You can write us, call us, e-mail us, or heck, just stop by if you're in the neighborhood.

**Outside America**
300 West Main Street, Suite A
Charlottesville, Virginia 22903
(804) 245-6800
editorial@outside-america.com

# Fat Tire Vacations

## [Bicycle Touring Companies]

There are literally dozens of off-road bicycling tour companies offering an incredible variety of guided tours for mountain bikers. On these pay-as-you-pedal, fat-tire vacations, you will have a chance to go places around the globe that only an expert can take you, and your experiences will be so much different than if seen through the window of a tour bus.

From Hut to Hut in the Colorado Rockies or Inn to Inn through Vermont's Green Mountains, there is a tour company for you. Whether you want hardcore singletrack during the day and camping at night, or you want scenic trails followed by a bottle of wine at night and a mint on each pillow, someone out there offers what you're looking for. The tours are well organized and fully supported with expert guides, bike mechanics, and "sag wagons" which carry gear, food, and tired bodies. Prices range from $100-$500 for a weekend to more than $2000 for two-week-long trips to far-off lands such as New Zealand or Ireland. Each of these companies will gladly send you their free literature to whet your appetite with breathtaking photography and titillating stories of each of their tours.

acations

## Selected Touring Companies

**Elk River Touring Center**
Slatyfork, WV
(304) 572-3771

**Vermont Bicycling Touring**
Bristol, VT
1-800-245-3868

**Backroads**
Berkley, CA
1-800-BIKE TRIP

**Timberline Bicycle Tours**
Denver, CO
(303) 759-3804

**Roads Less Traveled**
Longmont, CO
(303) 678-8750

**Blackwater Bikes**
Davis, WV
(304) 259-5286

**Bicycle Adventures**
Olympia, WA
1-800-443-6060

**Trails Unlimited, Inc.**
Nashville, IN
(812) 988-6232

# Repair and
## Mainter

# FIXING A FLAT

## TOOLS YOU WILL NEED

- Two tire irons
- Pump (either a floor pump or a frame pump)
- No screwdrivers!!! (This can puncture the tube)

## REMOVING THE WHEEL

The front wheel is easy. Simply open the quick release mechanism or undo the bolts with the proper sized wrench, then remove the wheel from the bike.

The rear wheel is a little more tricky. Before you loosen the wheel from the frame, shift the chain into the smallest gear on the freewheel (the cluster of gears in the back). Once you've done this, removing and installing the wheel, like the front, is much easier.

## REMOVING THE TIRE

*Step one:* Insert a tire iron under the bead of the tire and pry the tire over the lip of the rim. Be careful not to pinch the tube when you do this.

*Step two:* Hold the first tire iron in place. With the second tire iron, repeat step one, three or four inches down the rim. Alternate tire irons, pulling the bead of the tire over the rim, section by section, until one side of the tire bead is completely off the rim.

*Step three:* Remove the rest of the tire and tube from the rim. This can be done by hand. It's easiest to remove the valve stem last. Once the tire is off the rim, pull the tubeout of the tire.

## CLEAN AND SAFETY CHECK

*Step four:* Using a rag, wipe the inside of the tire to clean out any dirt, sand, glass, thorns, etc. These may cause the tube to puncture. The inside of a tire should feel smooth. Any pricks or bumps could mean that you have found the culprit responsible for your flat tire.

*Step five:* Wipe the rim clean, then check the rim strip, making sure it covers the spoke nipples properly on the inside of the rim. If a spoke is poking through the rim strip, it could cause a puncture.

*Step six:* At this point, you can do one of two things: replace the punctured tube with a new one, or patch the hole. It's easiest to just replace the tube with a new tube when you're out on the trails. Roll up the old tube and take it home to repair later that night in front of the TV. Directions on patching a tube are usually included with the patch kit itself.

## INSTALLING THE TIRE AND TUBE
*(This can be done entirely by hand)*

*Step seven:* Inflate the new or repaired tube with enough air to give it shape, then tuck it back into the tire.

*Step eight:* To put the tire and tube back on the rim, begin by putting the valve in the valve hole. The valve must be straight. Then use your hands to push the beaded edge of the tire onto the rim all the way around so that one side of your tire is on the rim.

*Step nine:* Let most of the air out of the tube to allow room for the rest of the tire.

*Step ten:* Beginning opposite the valve, use your thumbs to push the other side of the tire onto the rim. Be careful not to pinch the tube in between the tire and the rim. The last few inches may be difficult, and you may need the tire iron to pry the tire onto the rim. If so, just be careful not to puncture the tube.

## BEFORE INFLATING COMPLETELY

*Step eleven:* Check to make sure the tire is seated properly and that the tube is not caught between the tire and the rim. Do this by adding about 5 to 10 pounds of air, and watch closely that the tube does not bulge out of the tire.

*Step twelve:* Once you're sure the tire and tube are properly seated, put the wheel back on the bike, then fill the tire with air. It's easier squeezing the wheel through the brake shoes if the tire is still flat.

*Step thirteen:* Now fill the tire with the proper amount of air, and check constantly to make sure the tube doesn't bulge from the rim. If the tube does appear to bulge out, release all the air as quickly as possible, or you could be in for a big bang.

• When installing the rear wheel, place the chain back onto the smallest cog (furthest gear on the right), and pull the derailleur out of the way. Your wheel should slide right on.

# LUBRICATION PREVENTS DETERIORATION

Lubrication is crucial to maintaining your bike. Dry spots will be eliminated. Creaks, squeaks, grinding, and binding will be gone. The chain will run quietly, and the gears will shift smoothly. The brakes will grip quicker, and your bike may last longer with fewer repairs. Need I say more? Well, yes. Without knowing where to put the lubrication, what good is it?

### THINGS YOU WILL NEED
• One can of bicycle lubricant, found at any bike store.
• A clean rag (to wipe excess lubricant away).

### WHAT GETS LUBRICATED
• Front derailleur
• Rear derailleur
• Shift levers
• Front brake
• Rear brake

- Both brake levers
- Chain

## WHERE TO LUBRICATE

To make it easy, simply spray a little lubricant on all the pivot points of your bike. If you're using a squeeze bottle, use just a drop or two. Put a few drops on each point wherever metal moves against metal, for instance, at the center of the brake calipers. Then let the lube sink in.

Once you have applied the lubricant to the derailleurs, shift the gears a few times, working the derailleurs back and forth. This allows the lubricant to work itself into the tiny cracks and spaces it must occupy to do its job. Work the brakes a few times as well.

## LUBING THE CHAIN

Lubricating the chain should be done after the chain has been wiped clean of most road grime. Do this by spinning the pedals counterclockwise while gripping the chain with a clean rag. As you add the lubricant, be sure to get some in between each link. With an aerosol spray, just spray the chain while pedalling backwards (counterclockwise) until the chain is fully lubricated. Let the lubricant soak in for a few seconds before wiping the excess away. Chains will collect dirt much faster if they're loaded with too much lubrication.

# Index

# Index

# Euphoria...
# in many different states.

# Meet the Author

Layne Cameron, a native of Indiana, has been involved with bicycle racing and recreational riding for many years. When he's not contributing articles to *Bicycling*, *Scouting*, the *American Legion Magazine*, *Boys' Life*, *U.S. Kids*, and *Indianapolis Monthly*, Layne can be found conquering new and uncharted Hoosier singletrack, spinning thin tires in his hometown of Indianapolis, or spending time with his family boating on Monroe Lake.

Author